Praise for *Visions of the Divine*

"*Visions of the Divine* pairs sacred art with the structure of the Mass, unveiling the beauty and mystery of the Eucharist. From Rembrandt's *Supper at Emmaus* to Veronese's *Wedding Feast at Cana*, Stephen Auth and his coauthors explore how centuries of masterpieces draw us closer to Christ. Perfect for seekers, believers, and art lovers, this guide offers a fresh lens to encounter the Eucharist and deepen your faith. You will never look at these paintings—or the Mass—in the same way again."

—***Andrew V. Abela, Ph.D.,*** Dean,
Busch School of Business; Author, *Superhabits*

"To read this book is to deepen your faith in ways you never expected. Stephen Auth has somehow made the sacrifice of Christ in the Mass even more moving, personal, and profound."

—***Tim Busch,*** Cofounder, Napa Institute

"In *Visions of the Divine*, Steve Auth explores the historical importance of art in man's understanding of, and relationship with, God. It is an enjoyable and edifying book that will transport readers to places that will not only captivate their imaginations but also help them to appreciate the beauty of the Eucharist more fully."

—***Jason DeSena Trennert,*** Founder, Chairman, and
Chief Investment Strategist, Strategas Securities, LLC

"Steve and Evelyn Auth's encyclopedic *Visions of the Divine* brilliantly unites art, past and present, to accompany readers into the mystery of the liturgy. The Auths highlight an array of artists, from Fra Angelico to Robert Zund, who reveal the facets of divinity throughout the Mass through the lens of human creativity. Framed by Msgr. Landry's insightful catecheses and the Auths' interpretive genius, this book makes a compelling argument for the importance of beauty as a cornice to the sacraments."

—***Elizabeth Lev,*** Art Historian;
Author, *How Catholic Art Saved the Faith*

"What a unique and special way to see the beauty of God's love through human hands that create the most wonderful works of art! Many of the nuances and stories that could be missed by a glance are revealed in *Visions of the Divine*—a profound volume that will inform and delight its readers."

—***Dana Perino,*** Former White House Press Secretary;
Member, Fox News Channel

"Steve and Evelyn Auth have a knack for turning encounters, even street encounters, into conversations for reflecting on the deeper meaning of temporal and eternal life. This book invites the reader to appreciate the beauty of the art contemplated while acknowledging how it touches the human heart's desire for the Beauty that is 'ever ancient, ever new'—in whom our profoundest longings and desires will find their joyful rest."

—***Fr. Shawn Aaron, L.C.,***
Territorial Director, Legionaries of Christ

"Steve and Evelyn have done it again, strengthening our faith in God and crystallizing our understanding of religion through the journey of beauty and art history. I am grateful for this book."

—***Maria Bartiromo,*** Fox News Anchor

VISIONS OF THE DIVINE

Also by Stephen F. Auth
from Sophia Institute Press:

*The Missionary of Wall Street:
From Managing Money
to Saving Souls on the Streets of New York*

*Pilgrimage to the Museum:
Man's Search for God through Art and Time*

VISIONS *of the* DIVINE

An Artistic Journey into the Mystery of the Eucharist

By Stephen F. Auth

with Evelyn Moreno Auth
and Msgr. Roger Landry

Foreword by Timothy Cardinal Dolan

SOPHIA INSTITUTE PRESS
Manchester, New Hampshire

Cover design by Updatefordesign Studio.

Cover image: *The Adoration of the Mystic Lamb*
(Ghent Altarpiece, Wikimedia Commons)

Sophia Institute Press
Box 5284, Manchester, NH 03108
1-800-888-9344
www.SophiaInstitute.com

Sophia Institute Press is a registered trademark of Sophia Institute.

paperback ISBN 979-8-88911-358-4

ebook ISBN 979-8-88911-359-1

Library of Congress Control Number: 2024952382

2nd printing

For my very special coauthor and soulmate
on our journey to the light, Evelyn

"I am the bread of life; whoever comes to me will never hunger, and whoever believes in me will never thirst."

—John 6:35

Contents

PART III
LITURGY OF THE EUCHARIST

PART IV
CONCLUDING RITES

Foreword

SINCE THE VERY beginning of the Church, artists have tried to capture the greatest of mysteries: how God became man and revealed Himself to humanity — first, in the Incarnation, then in His teachings and miracles, then in His Passion, Death, and Resurrection, and finally, as we encounter Him today, in the Eucharist.

Visions of the Divine is a celebration of the art created over the centuries to enrich and enliven our attempts to commune with the Divine in and through the source and summit of our faith, the Eucharist. It is told in a plain-spoken narrative style that will appeal to all, from schooled theologians and art historians to everyday Catholics looking to better understand the eucharistic mystery, and right through to seekers of the Divine that are still struggling with their faith. The art you will soon experience, along with the rich yet simple reflections on it, speaks to the soul within all of us.

In the pages that follow, you will enjoy a feast for the senses that will uniquely prepare you to enter fully into the Church's greatest prayer, the Mass. Steve and his fellow pilgrims, Msgr. Roger Landry and Steve's wife Evelyn Auth, comb the halls of the world's greatest museums, from the Vatican and the Uffizi Gallery to the Metropolitan Museum of Art and the Prado and many others, along with art collections off the familiar paths such as the Catacombs and the grand Cathedral at Orvieto. Selecting from their most memorable offerings, they have carefully curated them within the structure of the Mass itself, the purpose for which much of the art was originally created. The result is soul-stirring illumination, joy, and deep spiritual reflection.

No matter where you are on your walk of belief — or what your comfort level with art history might be — you will find inspiration here to enter more deeply into prayer, and experience the Most Holy Eucharist in every possible sense: as a sacrifice, as we are absorbed into the eternal, infinite offering of the Son of God on a Cross; as the Real Presence of Christ's Body, Blood, Soul, and Divinity, as together we adore Him, locked in a tabernacle, or in carried procession in the monstrance; finally, as the most intimate of meals, a sacred meal in which we form one community of faith nourished body and soul by our manna, the Bread of Heaven.

It is through the Eucharist that we are most personally united with our Lord and Savior, Jesus Christ. To live in the Eucharist is to live in communion with God Himself, a mystery so deep that even the most devout among us spend a lifetime grasping its true meaning. Steve's book will serve as both a gift and guide for anyone seeking to deepen their understanding and appreciation of this central element of our Faith.

Capturing the good, true, and beautiful through sacred art is not simply a Catholic endeavor; it is a truly human one. If you are unsure of this, visit any of the great museums of the world from which *Visions of the Divine* has been curated. Much of the art in these museums has its origins in the sacred liturgy of the Mass, and mysteriously, these images continue to appeal to the broad swath of humanity that pass through these museums' doors. These artifacts from an earlier time whisper to us of timeless truths, of the transcendent within all of us. They pull us towards the Divine, the beautiful, even when we don't realize they are doing so.

I have known the Auths for years from their missionary work at the Met and on the streets of our fair city. Steve's distinctive voice, keen observatory skills as a Princeton-educated historian, commonsense speaking style from years of street evangelization with everyday New Yorkers, well-honed analytical skills as a Harvard-educated businessman, and passion for souls as a follower of Christ makes him a trustworthy and authoritative guide. His co-authors, his wife Evelyn Auth and friend Msgr. Roger Landry, add their own insights and perspectives — as do contemporary artists and historians the Auths meet along their pilgrimage.

As you listen to these literary exchanges, I invite you, the reader, to enter into the pilgrimage yourself and revel in the Creator of all that is truly beautiful. Discover a world shot through with His glory and presence. And enter into — or return to — worship the one who is Himself the way, the truth, and the life.

Visions of the Divine is not meant to be merely read and set aside. Steve Auth's exploration of the Mass and the Eucharist is a call to action — a summons to more fully participate in the divine life offered to us through the sacraments. My hope is that readers will be inspired to approach each celebration of the Eucharist with renewed wonder and devotion. May we all, like Steve, allow our encounters with Christ in the Blessed Sacrament to transform us into more effective missionaries in our daily lives. In a world often marked by division and despair, the Eucharist stands as a beacon of unity and hope. Through this sacrament, we are united not only with Christ but with one another as members of His Body. Steve Auth's book reminds us of this profound truth and challenges us to live it out more fully. I commend this work to all who seek a deeper understanding of the Mass and the Eucharist. May it bear much fruit in the lives of individual believers and in the life of the Church as a whole.

†Timothy Cardinal Dolan
Archbishop of New York
October 4, 2024
Feast of St. Francis of Assisi

VISIONS OF THE DIVINE

Introduction

How Should I Use This Book?

IF YOU ARE wondering, "How should I use this book?" I thought it might help to tell you how I am using it. That may sound a bit odd, coming from the author. After all, why would the author need to *use* this book? What's the whole point of writing it, if not to tell us something you already know: how to use art to understand the Mass?

The truth is, when I began this project, I didn't know much about the art of the Mass, and in retrospect didn't know much about the Mass either. Sure, I had a rich understanding of art history and had previously visited and studied much (though not all) of the art we will see on the forthcoming pilgrimage. And yes, between my formative years as an altar boy at St. Leo's Grammar School in Irvington, New Jersey, and my later studies and spiritual formation with the many priests in my life that rescued me from the spiritual ashbin of agnosticism, I had a better-than-average understanding of the theology behind the Roman Catholic Mass, reinforced by the thousands of Masses in which I'd participated over the course of my life.

But no, it had never occurred to me that the two — art and the Eucharist — were deeply connected. Not, at least, until God intervened, through a series of incidents described in the prologue. I do believe it was He who set me out on this course.

Also, I need to admit that I tried to get out of it, offering my usual excuses: "I don't have the time, too busy with my day job!" and "I'm not qualified; I'm not a theologian, not an art scholar. Just a broken vessel!" When additional "pings" persisted, I gradually began to concede, then finally caved. That happened shortly after our first deliberate "Art of the Eucharist" pilgrimage to the Louvre Museum in Paris, where I encountered my old friend Rembrandt before an image of *The Supper at Emmaus.* (You can find that encounter described in the prologue too.)

While there, I remembered a phrase I always tell the new street missionaries in New York City as we are about to set out on a cold dark night to find lost souls: "The Lord does not call the equipped. He equips the called."[1]

And so, I set out on the pilgrimage described in the pages which follow. I knew He would equip me to do it.

Pilgrimages require companions, so my first recruit was my wife, Evelyn. A devout Catholic who knows me inside and out, she would be both my thoughtful companion on the travels to come, as well as the soulmate with whom I could daily unpack the day's writing for real-time processing and revision. Recruiting Evelyn was relatively easy, as she's been at my side through thick and thin in the last forty plus years, and her devotion to the Lord is such that when asked, she doesn't argue like I do. She just looks up and says, "Yes."

My next recruit was Msgr. Roger Landry. Given my own lack of theological training, and given the rich theology within and beneath the liturgy of the Mass, I knew we needed someone with formal training in the field. Msgr. Landry, a longtime friend on many a Catholic adventure in New York City, as well as being a respected theologian and Catholic voice, was an obvious choice. Like Evelyn, he proved a relatively easy mark. When I described the pilgrimage and asked him to join it, his affirmative answer was almost as quick and decisive as Evelyn's.

Others, local experts and guides, were recruited as we travelled to various towns and cities; you'll be hearing from them as we proceed on our journey.

With the core team on board, I then "recruited" some of the greatest theologians I could get my hands on. Ok, not exactly recruited. I read their books. First, the great classics: St. Thomas Aquinas's *Summa of the Summa,* John O'Brien's *A History of the Mass and*

Its Ceremonies in the Eastern and Western Church, Joseph Jungmann's massive *The Mass of the Roman Rite*, and Dom Anscar Vonier's *A Key to the Doctrine of the Eucharist*. Then the modern thinkers and teachers within the Church today—Dr. Edward Sri, Dr. Scott Hahn, George Weigel, Cardinal Dolan, Fr. Armand de Malleray, FSSP, Joe Heschmeyer, and of course the *Catechism of the Catholic Church*, the *General Instruction of the Roman Missal*, and the United States Conference of Catholic Bishops' "Order of Mass." The more I read, the more I understood the vastness of the spiritual complexity that lies within and beneath the liturgy of the Mass, and that deeper understanding itself began to help me enrich my own participation in the Eucharist. But let's face it, the theology alone is a bit dry, and hard for the average lay mortal to fully comprehend.

So my next set of "recruits" were the art historians. They were a tougher lot. I already had many of their books on Western art in my personal library, and the rest were easy enough to assemble. Beyond the books were the hundreds of scholarly articles they'd written on most of the art pieces that we would be visiting. What made them "tougher," though, was that many of the authors were either not Catholic or, if they were, deliberately distanced themselves from the Faith. Their descriptions and texts, while rich in history and detail, were written largely from a cold, archeological perspective. Virtually to a person, with the exception of my good friend and Catholic art historian Liz Lev, their apparent interest or even awareness of the art's connection to the Mass liturgy was entirely absent. Nevertheless, perhaps somewhat mischievously and ironically, I recruited them. Their knowledge of the "science" behind some of the specific art pieces we had in mind was actually quite helpful. After all, God created that, too.

It wasn't until the next step, though, that the richness of the Mass finally began to come alive for me. That step was the art itself, and putting it back where it came from—the Mass. Indeed, until I embarked on this project, or perhaps better said, until this project embarked with me on board, I didn't really "get it." Regrettably, my formal training in art history in college had left me virtually unaware of just how closely tied to the Mass most Catholic art had once been. Then, as our pilgrimage proceeded, we came to realize that the great religious art of Western culture not only described God and beauty in a profound way but also had been created with the express or at least the implicit intent of helping the laity enrich their own participation in the eucharistic liturgy. As the pieces of the puzzle began to come together, we used the outline of the Mass to assemble them into a coherent whole.

Ever so slowly, two of the great streams of Western thought and tradition, theology and art, which had been torn asunder after the Reformation, and later the French Revolution, came back together. Piece by piece, a fuller picture of the Mass began to emerge. As when we slowly solve a jigsaw puzzle, our own excitement and anticipation grew as we journeyed on. Each reflection became a new milestone, a deeper insight. Evening after evening, I could not put it down. And even then, when my pen stopped working, Evelyn and I would embark on long walks to process and revise.

In short, the Mass came alive.

No doubt you will find your own path through *Visions*, as there are many. But there are three in particular that I've found and I now use for my own enrichment. I thought you might want to hear about them before you get started.

The first path is quite literal, simply following the structure as presented. The backbone of the structure is the Mass, and as we studied and reflected, we came to realize that it presents a narrative and suspense in itself that is both thrilling and, yes, divine. It's a real "page turner," as they say in the book business. So just sit back — well, maybe, sit up — and enjoy it!

On another dimension, *Visions* helps me at key moments of the Mass where I struggle to stay focused. Now when that happens, I conjure up one of the great works of art we discovered to help unlock the mystery of that prayer within the Mass, and that seems to help me better lock in. Whether it's a Gospel reading or homily that I'm not quite getting, or one of the five Eucharistic Prayers that the priest is reciting, or the moment I receive Holy Communion, or even that moment at the end when the deacon says, "The Mass is ended. Go in peace," the art of the Mass helps me to focus my mind and enter the mystery more deeply. For this purpose, we created an index at the back of *Visions,* called "appendix A," organized by the order of the Mass itself. That way, if you find yourself struggling with one aspect or section of the Mass, use appendix A to find the *Visions'* reflection on that prayer or section, spend some time with the art pictured there, and either read our reflection on it or develop your own. It will help. It's helped me.

The third way I have been using *Visions* is for visiting different cities in the United States and in Europe. Through the course of developing the work that follows, Evelyn and I visited nearly twenty cities and towns around the Western world searching for the art of the Mass. And after our first pass at the most famous museums of the world, we found ourselves needing in some cases to make a second, or even third, trip. By then, we already had the rudimentary outline of appendix B, which lists the art of the Mass organized by city. So the next time you find yourself in one of these towns, or perhaps even set out on your own pilgrimage to a particular location, you can use "B" to discover which art pieces in that town might help you to better understand the Mass.

The table of contents of *Visions*—the narrative structure borrowed from the Mass itself—should give you a good start on understanding the pilgrimage on which you are about to embark. In the first chapter, we use several paintings and sculptures to explore the struggles we all face in the world outside the Mass, the false prophets of today's culture that can lure us away from God, and the reminders that He is out there, seeking us. In chapter two, we enter into the introductory rites of the Mass, and find artistic masterpieces that inspire us as we join with the community of faith before the altar. In chapters three through eight, we travel to art that helps us to better comprehend the many messages we receive over the course of the liturgical season in the Liturgy of the Word. The following four chapters enter into the Liturgy of the Eucharist itself and present some of the finest images created by Catholic artists over the centuries to help the faithful understand the eucharistic mystery. The concluding chapters thirteen and fourteen are intended to provide you with inspiring images as you leave the Mass and reenter the challenges of the everyday world, grappling (like we all do) to find God there.

One last note. Reading *Visions* is like embarking on any pilgrimage journey. To profit fully from it, you will need to open your heart, and pray to God. So pray a little before you proceed. He's listening. And the art of the Mass is waiting for you.

Prologue

The Meal

The Supper at Emmaus, Rembrandt, 1648, Louvre Museum, Paris, France

Paris, June 2023. Since my student days at Princeton, when I slid unconsciously from the Catholic Faith of my childhood towards the "indifferent agnosticism" of my young adulthood, *The Supper at*

Emmaus by Rembrandt van Rijn (hereafter "Rembrandt") has exuded a mysterious tug at my heart that I could never quite explain. This version, Rembrandt's second attempt, was painted when he was in his forties and is ensconced at the Louvre. It has become a regular stop whenever I am in town.

In this image, Rembrandt depicts the newly resurrected Christ with His two discouraged disciples, Cleopas and an unnamed companion. The Lord has met them on their way "out of Dodge," three days after His gruesome torture and death on Calvary. The owner of the inn is serving the evening meal to the trio.

Unlike most triumphant, heroic Resurrection images of the resurrected Jesus, Rembrandt's is subdued, muted, humble — even a little small. The only light in the scene seems to be emanating from the Lord Himself: a gentle light, softly caressing the faces of His two friends. They had beaten a quick path out of town before they got into any more trouble after Jesus — their Lord, their Master, their best friend — had been brutally executed by the authorities. Intending to go back to their old jobs, they met a stranger along the way who helped them understand how the events of the last few days somehow fit into God's grand plan of salvation. And here, as He breaks the bread, it seems to occur to them that the quiet, humble, yet confident man before them is Jesus Himself. Rembrandt depicts this realization not in the shocked, dramatic fashion of other earlier renditions of Emmaus by various artistic forebears, or even by the great artist himself in his earlier version over two decades past; but rather in a very quiet, "slowly dawning on them" way. A very human way. Gradually, they seem to see a supernatural light forming around Jesus' head. (Incidentally, it would have been unusual for the Protestant Rembrandt to paint Him this way; Protestants at this time avoided referencing the very Catholic 'halo' in their art.)

Cleopas, whose face we can see in full profile, is unconsciously clenching his left hand, trying to suppress his emerging joy, seemingly telling himself, "It's too good to be true." His friend, the second disciple whose face we can't fully see, has shifted his right hand in front of his lips, to suppress an anxious gasp. This restrained drama, centered around the soft and almost withdrawn image of Jesus, leaves me with a serene, peaceful joy. And absent the stage-lighting of earlier versions, I am left experiencing among the three central figures a quiet intimacy and love that has always touched me deep down in my soul. Even when I didn't realize I had one.

But now my soul and I and God are back together again, and I'm here in Paris with my wife and lifelong partner Evelyn for a very specific purpose.

Guadalajara, Mexico, 2008. The first time I received the Eucharist and truly felt the presence of Jesus as I did so was on Easter Sunday morning, in Guadalajara, Mexico. I was blind. Well, not fully blind. Blind in one eye. I was at the dawn Mass, with two fellow missionaries, who from there were to rush me to the airport for a flight back to New York for emergency surgery on that eye of mine.

What I was doing on a mission to Mexico in 2008 is a story for another time. The short answer is, I wasn't doing a lot. The Lord was, though, through me and the others with me. He had found me in a spiritual wasteland several years earlier and had knocked me off my high horse with a near-fatal heart failure. That had led to a painful yet joyous Confession and re-commitment to make God the focus of my life, rather than who it had been (me). That "death-bed Confession" was the beginning of the journey to the light that brought me to Guadalajara and continues to this day. The previous day we had just completed an ambitious Holy Week mission in a large village about three hours outside the city. The village was quite poor; but the villagers were committed Catholics, with faith stronger than that of some missionaries, including me. Yet somehow our presence as New York-based Catholics in that remote village comforted them, and our talks and discussions seemed to inspire. And so, we'd committed to visiting every home in the dusty, sprawling town through the course of Holy Week, a goal the previous year's missionaries had not managed. So as a group, we wanted to be there for every last one of them. That could have changed mid-week, when my left eye went dark.

Total blackness—like a curtain had fallen. No light. At that moment, I knew if I said something, the mission would have ended prematurely for the whole team I was leading; they'd have to get me back to Guadalajara in a hurry. So I prayed before the Lord during Adoration in the chapel that night, and before long, I had my answer.

"Stick with the mission. This is your cup."

"Well, that's it then," I thought to myself. "I suppose the Lord will either fix this eye later, or perhaps I'll lose the other one next and receive a deeper source of vision. Either way, I'm good. I'm where I need to be for now."

The rest of the week remains to this day one of the most joyful weeks of my life. I was completely at peace; I knew He had my back. By late Saturday afternoon, we made it to the last house in the village. I have a picture of us there, with me kneeling at the center of the group, beaming. Not a care in the world! I keep that picture in my dressing room at home, so I can reflect briefly on it every morning before heading out into the world. That's what "being in the zone" for Jesus looks like.

By the following morning, Easter Sunday, I'd already been to a very modern eye clinic in Guadalajara, and my blindness had been diagnosed. Detached retina. Prognosis good, provided the doctors in New York could operate on it within 48 hours. So now I was on an early-morning flight to New York.

Kneeling there in the Holy Mass at dawn on Easter morning, I reflected on the Gospel's scene outside the tomb between Jesus and Mary Magdalen. She, too, was "in the zone." Later, as I received Jesus on my tongue in Communion, literally half-blind, for the first time in my life, I could see Him. Taste Him. Feel His warmth and love within me. I knew He was there, with me, in the Eucharist.

Little did I know then that the Lord had a plan for that blinded eye, the eye He'd restore, then use to help me see the art that would become a journey to the mysteries of the Eucharist itself. But that journey had barely begun.

New York, Autumn 2022. We are in the city for meetings and, as I usually do, I'm out on the Upper East Side for my early morning jog. Processing. *The Pilgrimage to the Museum* has been an unexpected success, and already the wheels are turning. What's next, Lord? Probably due to my lifelong interest in food, and particularly to my many, special shared meals with friends and family, I'd been feeling a tug to write about just that: how a shared meal can be such a wonderful way to deepen friendships, build new ones, and yes, to share the Faith.

As the sun was coming up over Queens, it occurred to me that Jesus Himself frequently shared meals with friends in His ministry, as recorded in the Gospel stories: the meal at Peter's house after He first met Jesus; Matthew the tax collector; Zacchaeus; Martha and Mary; Lazarus; Mary Magdalen; the house of Simon the Pharisee.

The Last Supper.

The Supper at Emmaus.

Then my thoughts drifted off to the markets and the burst of light was stored away in the deep recesses of my mind.

May 2023, somewhere on Interstate 75, Florida. Evelyn and I are driving north from Florida for the summer. Well, Evelyn is driving, I'm on the phone. Once my meetings have ended, I check in with Mary, my trusted assistant. "Mary, what's up? What talks have you got set up along the way this time?" Mary keeps track of incomings for all matters, from client meetings right through to talks for spiritual retreats. Then she schedules them to coincide with my travel calendar, sort of. So I know she must have a few things cooking.

"Well, there's X in Raleigh and there's Y in D.C. No, wait, Y and Z in D.C. And then, of course, there's that talk you agreed to do at the "Catholics at the Shore" conference in Avalon. I figure you can make Avalon by Thursday evening! Talk's at 7:00 Thursday."

"Ok, great. What's the talk on?"

"Art and the Eucharist."

"Mary, I don't have a talk planned on 'Art and the Eucharist.'"

"Well, you're going to need one. By this Thursday."

The good news at this point is that I have Evelyn effectively cornered for three days, as she's driving and I'm talking. Evelyn, diminutive in stature and larger than life in spirit, has been my partner and soul mate in all things since our marriage nearly forty years ago. A devout Catholic, she has a deep love for the Lord and seeks Him in all things. She consumes religious literature for breakfast. And she's impossible to intimidate. Believe me, I've tried.

So, faced with the task of assembling a new talk on a topic of great weight, I turned instinctively to the driver, my wife. Over the ensuing lengthy drive north, she and I put together that first talk on "Art and the Eucharist." As the hours passed, we gradually discovered something that perhaps should have been obvious to someone with an art history background, but wasn't: art and the Eucharist are linked in a very beautiful, very profound way.

Some of the connection is straightforward, because artists often created images to help teach the Faith and, particularly, about the celebration of the Eucharist that Catholics call the Mass. Some of the bond is transcendental and emotive, in a way that's not easily described, analyzed, or understood. And some of it is just plain intimate, the kind of close association that my friend Rembrandt was onto in his second depiction of Emmaus.

That initial talk was just the beginning of a long pilgrim's journey. Especially since the sixteenth century Reformation and "The Age of Enlightenment" that followed, artwork on the Mass has been uprooted by wars and floods, art scholars and collectors, theologians and politicians, and financial calamities of every kind. So to see the art of the Mass, you've got to search. There's no handbook for this kind of thing. Some of the art is still where it was created, for and in churches around Europe. Still more has been dispersed across museums around the world.

So, pack your bags. Let's get going! We're going to have a meal together, a very special meal, the meal of a lifetime: the Eucharist. And we're going to forge a path to it that is lined with some of the most beautiful art in the world.

Oh, and about Emmaus. Don't worry, we'll get there.

PART I

PREPARATIONS

"And it happened that while they were conversing and debating, Jesus himself drew near and walked with them."

— Luke 24:15

– 1 –

Coming In Out of the Cold

Catholics attend Mass for a variety of reasons. For some, it's a weekly obligation of the Faith. Others feel a sense of community as they attend Mass with their fellow believers. Some go for the singing, and others to hear the Word of God and its explanation in the homily. Others attend for the chance to commune with Jesus in the Eucharist. We'll unlock all of these very good reasons in our journey through the Mass, for sure. But before we embark, let's consider another reason nearly all of us go, whether we realize it or not: We need to. In a culture increasingly devoid of faith, the Mass is our cure, our nourishment, our lifeline to the Divine.

It's our chance to come in out of the cold.

It's Cold and Lonely Out Here

Petrie Court, The Metropolitan Museum of Art, New York. Jean Antoine Houdon's image of a mostly naked young woman freezing to death haunts the Petrie Court at the Metropolitan Museum. It inevitably draws a

Winter, Jean Antoine Houdon, 1787, The Metropolitan Museum of Art, New York

small crowd as people pass through the gallery to the Modern Art section. It certainly haunts me.

During the last years of the *Ancien Régime*, just two years before the French Revolution, a young sculptor, heavily influenced by late Baroque Italian sculptors such as Bernini, was making a living creating sculptured portraits of France's nobility. He even occasionally dabbled in American glitterati, including America's first, newly elected president, George Washington. The artist's name was Jean Antoine Houdon, and in 1787 he created an image of loneliness and despair that was in stark contrast to the refined high society in which he worked and played.

The sculpture was shocking enough, but the name he gave the work, *Winter*, puzzled most. Until the moment of *Winter*'s unveiling, the iconic image most often chosen by artists to represent the fourth season, the season before death, had always been an old man. In Houdon's rendition, those expecting to see a dying octogenarian were in for quite a shock: Houdon's model for *Winter* was a young woman, naked except for the pitiful shawl she's used to cover her shoulders. Unprotected from the elements, the young woman's gaze is fixed downward, toward the earth. She squeezes her legs together for warmth, and her left hand grabs tight to her right arm, as a great shiver trembles through her body. She is alone.

And, as implied by the work's title, she is about to die.

The nobility of France might have paused for a moment from their festivities to consider Houdon's revolutionary image of this young woman, alone in the cold, dying of hunger. It's not clear that they did; rather, the Queen's perhaps apocryphal response, "Let them eat cake,"[2] resonates through the ages as one of the most tone-deaf political counterpoints of all time. Within five years, many of them were dead themselves, killed in the Reign of Terror that quickly followed the Revolution. That cataclysm inflicted enormous damage on the Faith in France, destroying many of the churches and the art within them and launching a shift towards secularism that continues to this day. To be sure, the Faith still lives there, but, like most of the developed western world, remains under attack from all sides as cultures slip into moral relativism, where causes of all kinds become "religious" ones and common beliefs in the transcendent no longer seem to apply. The ties that once united us seem to have disappeared.

In "winter," we are all, each of us, alone. Hungry. Barren of hope. Bereft of love. And about to die.

Fortunately, the Lord left us a path out of winter. A path to a place that is beautiful and warm, that is full of fellowship and hope, within a community of believers. A place of Love, of the kind of Love that seems unknown to the people of winter.

It's the path to Emmaus. The Mass.

Most of us are well fed and don't identify with the young woman shivering in the cold of winter. But how different are we? How many times have I hurried off to Sunday Mass a bit begrudgingly, with a busy schedule of more "important stuff" on my agenda: the kids' soccer game, a round of golf, Sunday NFL?

In the hurly-burly of daily life, is it possible that I'm confusing the seasons? Is my spiritual life closer to winter than to spring?

When we're tempted to think about skipping Mass and rushing to an important Sunday brunch instead, let's conjure up this image of *Winter* in our mind. In the world of winter in which we often find ourselves, Mass offers the prospect of a hot meal and fellowship, hope, love.

Who's coming?

Fun, for a Passing Moment

Museo del Prado, Madrid. Gulp! When Evelyn and I first visited *The Garden of Earthly Delights,* we, like most others, were pulled toward it. Standing more than twelve feet long and almost six feet high, its glittering colors and complicated composition exert a magnetic tug on visitors. Most canvases of this size are created using larger-than-life images that can be seen and comprehended from a distance. But in this painting, Hieronymus Bosch turned that formula inside out. Instead of large, comprehensible figures within the giant composition, he chose instead to create a superficial effect of beauty and radiance with hundreds of miniature figures.

The Garden of Earthly Delights, Hieronymus Bosch, ca. 1495, Museo del Prado, Madrid, Spain

To understand it, you must move closer. Only then can you begin to figure out what is going on, what is stirring beneath the shimmering surface. And it's not good.

On the left panel, Bosch seems to be imagining the Garden of Eden. (For a detailed closeup of the left panel, see p. 76.) In this idyllic scene, God, in the person of Jesus,[3] performs the first marriage ceremony, uniting the newly created Eve with Adam. Adam looks innocently at his new bride. All around them, the well-ordered garden is teeming with life, grazing and resting within the garden's bountiful foliage. Even here, though, buried deeply beneath the surface, Bosch hints at the coming rebellion: the cat, possibly a reference to Eve, in the lower left with a dead mouse in its jaws, along with another feline, a lion, in the upper right, who's just killed an innocent antelope.[4] But aside from these small subtle hints, the world of light and love that the Lord created for us seems very much intact.[5]

In the middle panel, we see a more populated version of the same garden, later in time — even the horizons match. Now, though, God is not in the picture. Instead of the monogamous, sacred union He created between Adam and Eve, we see God's creations cavorting almost randomly with each other. No one seems to have a concern in the world other than for their next pleasant hookup, enormous flask of wine, or oversized piece of fruit. It is a highly sensualized world of shallow relationships and temporary pleasures.[6] Despite the pleasures, there isn't much joy. And most tragically, the cavorters have been so desensitized by this world of temporary distractions that they don't even realize they are not in Eden. They believe they are still in Paradise, but it's a "false paradise," a paradise with a small "p."[7]

The panel on the right follows the evolution of the middle panel's corrupted Garden of Eden to its inevitable, horrific conclusion. The place we'd rather not go to and, in today's culture, prefer not to mention. You know where. By now the lost souls of the Earthly Delights have realized, too late, they are not in Eden any longer.

As Evelyn and I contemplate this image — the beauty on the surface, and the ugliness within — we are struck by the modern relevance of Bosch's masterpiece. Although it was created around 1495, the image still reflects the world we sometimes live in. "Fun," for a passing moment. "Love," but the kind that is shallow, gone the next morning, leaving us unsatisfied and empty. "Happy," but not joyful.

To what extent am I confusing paradise with Paradise? Allowing myself to be so caught up in the world around me that I'm losing touch with the world within me? And the World above me?

Another good reason to go to Mass. Paradise on earth, with a capital "P." The real deal.

And False Prophets Abound

"Beware of false prophets, who come to you in sheep's clothing, but underneath are ravenous wolves."

— Matt. 7:15

The Preaching of the Antichrist, Luca Signorelli, 1499–1504, San Brizio Chapel (Orvieto Cathedral), Orvieto, Italy

Orvieto Cathedral, Orvieto. I'd read about Signorelli's famous fresco cycle at Orvieto many years earlier. Even so, I was not fully prepared for the scale and complexity of his masterpiece. Evelyn and I had travelled a few hours from Rome to find it. Painted forty years before Michelangelo's more famous *Last Judgment* in the Sistine Chapel, Signorelli's story of the end of time is simultaneously terrorizing and hopeful. Like Bosch's *Garden of Earthly Delights,* painted at roughly the same time but nearly 1,000 miles apart, it also presents an attractive image on the surface that grows scarier as you dive deeper. The entire San Brizio Chapel, all four walls and vaults, are covered with elements of the "end of times." We're here to see one of them.

Unlike most of the art we view nowadays, *The Preaching of the Antichrist* is still displayed in the original setting for which it was created: a side chapel of the Cathedral at Orvieto. We're in a church, not a museum. And there are no helpful signs hung beneath the frescoes, telling us what we're looking at. We have to figure that out for ourselves.

As we approach, we see what looks like a Renaissance-style image of Christ preaching in a village square. Yet as we zoom in, we see that things are not quite right. First of all, the man we thought was Christ, on closer inspection, is not Jesus at all; he's far less handsome, more brutish. The colors of his robes are off-putting and don't seem to match. What could be horns seem to be popping up out of his head. And instead of God speaking in his ear, we see it's Satan who is inspiring him. The stack of "gifts" that have been brought to him by the crowd morph into what look like a pile of old lamps, no longer useful for providing light. The crowd is arguing among themselves, as what we are realizing is the "Antichrist" sows discord and disruption, not unity and peace. On the left of the painting, a large brutish man is beating an unarmed person, and in the foreground a young woman seems to be selling herself to an older man. The building in the backdrop is unsettlingly distorted, not at all designed in the perfect, ideal proportions of the Renaissance. Around it, a dozen or so mysterious and threatening figures are moving about, clothed in black, bent on adding to the chaos. The two groupings in the background, nearest the building, repeat the image of the Antichrist in the foreground. Each is sowing more discord and disruption, in one case overseeing an execution, in another trying to perform a false miracle. Is this the same false prophet in the front, or another? On the upper left side, we see an image of an archangel, who most believe is Gabriel, throwing a fallen angel, perhaps the Antichrist himself, out of Heaven, hurling him into the chaos below.

As my eyes swirl around the wall, I finally spot the group in the dead center: monks, huddled together, praying. Of the seven figure groupings in the composition, theirs is the only one where everyone appears to be on the same page. And it's the only one not looking at the Antichrist. They are looking at their Bibles. Hmmm.

Scholars have long debated the symbols and meaning in Signorelli's fresco. All fascinating, though most are distractions from the key point. In the world around us, whether it be fifteenth-century Tuscany or twenty-first-century New York, there are plenty of distractions and "false prophets" promising us a route to happiness. And most of these, unfortunately, lead us to chaos and despair instead. Dead ends.

I'm about to move on, thanking God that I'm not misinformed enough to fall prey to the Antichrist. That's when the guide we've hired slips a little Signorelli trivia into her talk. The artist populated the crowd in front of the Antichrist with several well-known, upstanding citizens of the day! Dante, for instance, is the man standing proudly to the Antichrist's left, with a pink cloak and red turban. Is Dante listening to this guy? For goodness' sake, Dante is the one who wrote *The Inferno*! And over on the lower left of the fresco, those two well-dressed fellas looking onto the scene, contemplating it—those are Fra Angelico, the famous Florentine monk and fresco painter of San Marco (don't worry, we'll be visiting there soon), and Signorelli himself!

We're all subject at one point or another to being lured by false prophets. What makes them so attractive is that on the surface they sound true, and certainly "easier" to follow at times than the true Christ. But when have we ever listened to one of these guys and ended up feeling peaceful about it?

And when have we listened to Christ, done what He asked, and been unhappy with the outcome?

The antidote to the Antichrist is waiting for us at Mass: the Christ of God.

And whether we're lost in a fake Garden or find ourselves on a wrong highway following a bad map, there's hope. Someone is out there searching for us.

The Good Shepherd Is Searching for Us, to Bring Us Home

"I am the good shepherd. A good shepherd lays down his life for the sheep."
—John 10:11

Vatican Museums, Rome. We are here in the Vatican Museums on a spiritual tour with a good friend of ours from Rome and one of its many colorful local art guides. A devout disciple of the Lord, in love with His Church, and a staunch defender of the Faith, "Sr. Francesca"[8] also knows the religious art of the Vatican Museums with a depth of understanding that only comes with time, overlaid with a solid theological grounding. She romps around the vast collections as if in her own backyard. My guess is she could walk the museums blindfolded.

The Good Shepherd, Catacombs of Domitilla, ca. 300 A.D., Museo Pio Cristiano (Vatican Museums), Rome, Italy

Sister is anxious to get us to the Sistine Chapel at the appointed time, but, as we're heading out of the Pio Cristiano, I ask her if we could spend a few extra minutes with the *Good Shepherd*. She assumes correctly that we've seen this image many times before, so I explain how we think it fits into our plans for *Visions* and what an important vision of God it presents. So here we are.

Let's clear the air on something right off the bat. Secular scholars have not declared unequivocally that the image we stand before was intended to portray Christ as the Good Shepherd. For sure, Roman sculpting tradition included statues of a shepherd as the Greek god Hermes, and occasionally Orpheus[9]; it's possible this statue is just another one of those. On the other hand, by the third century AD, millions of early Christians had already adopted the image of a young shepherd as one of their favorite symbols of Christ. Their refusal to acknowledge the Roman Emperor as a god made them a target of the Roman authorities. In this environment, public references to their faith would almost certainly land them in jail, or worse, the Colosseum. Practicing their faith within this hostile environment, Christians learned to communicate in secret symbols that their pagan persecutors would not recognize.

A fish stood first for the Christ, because the letters of the word for fish in Greek (*ichthus*) were used as an acrostic code for "Jesus Christ, Son of God, Savior." The sign of the fish also stood more generally for followers of Christ, who came to be called Christians, who Jesus had commissioned to be "fishers of men."[10] The Greek letters *chi* and *rho* also stood for "Christ," since they are the first two letters (the ch and the r) of the title Christ. The peacock, which was thought not to decompose after death, symbolized Christ's Resurrection. Wine and bread stood for the Sacrament of the Eucharist; a lamb, "the Lamb of God"; and, often seen on the walls of the catacombs, a shepherd, for Jesus, the Good Shepherd. So, while the statue before us would have likely seemed normal enough to the Roman authorities, there were clues within it that the Christians would have instantly understood were pointing to their "Good Shepherd."[11]

In fact, the entire statue is a symbol of love.

Jesus calls Himself the Good Shepherd in the Gospel of St. John, where He tells us that "I am the good shepherd, and I know mine and mine know me.... A good shepherd lays down his life for the sheep" (John 10:14,11).

The Parable of the Lost Sheep in the Gospel of Luke has been central to Christian consciousness from the days of Christ. It's a story that Jesus told His disciples to explain His remarkable and mysterious mission.

The Good Shepherd has come to find us. Not collectively, but individually. Here's how Jesus put it:

> *"What man among you having a hundred sheep and losing one of them would not leave the ninety-nine in the desert and go after the lost one until he finds it? And when he does find it, he sets it on his shoulders with great joy and, upon his arrival home, he calls together his friends and neighbors and says to them, 'Rejoice with me because I have found my lost sheep.'"*
>
> *—Luke 15:4–6*

The longer we stand before *The Good Shepherd*, the more the little aspects of His deep love for us — for me — stand out.

According to the parable, the shepherd has lost one sheep from his flock. The creature has gone astray, lured by the scent of greener grass, or by the voice of a false shepherd, or maybe by a garden of earthly delights. Most rational shepherds, we'd guess, would leave it at that. "Well, he didn't listen to me! What can I do? I've got the rest of the flock to care for! I can't be everywhere at once!" But not the Good Shepherd.

The Good Shepherd drops everything and embarks on an all-out search for the one lost sheep: He searches for me, and ultimately finds me, out in some thicket of my own making. The Good Shepherd gently disentangles me. But I'm weak and exhausted from my adventure. He lifts me on His big, broad shoulders and lovingly carries me home. As He does, His beautiful curly hair intermingles with my own smelly coat; for a moment, we become one. No one else is around; it's just Him and me. I look back gratefully at His soft, gentle face, and He gazes lovingly on mine.

He's carrying me home to the Feast.

On one condition — I have to let Him — let Him love me.

Which brings us to Mary Magdalen.

Let Him Love Us

"LORD, you have probed me, you know me:
you know when I sit and stand;
you understand my thoughts from afar....
If I say, 'Surely darkness shall hide me,
and night shall be my light' —
Darkness is not dark for you,
and night shines as the day.
Darkness and light are but one."

— Ps. 139:1–2,11–12

SoHo, March 2014. The missionaries[12] are in SoHo this year, and our theme is "Let Him Love Us." Our goal is to bring as many souls back to the Church, to the Easter Mass, as we can. And ahead of that, to bring them to the Sacrament of Reconciliation, what we sometimes call "the lost Sacrament." What we've experienced on the streets is that, while bringing people to the Mass alone can bring great joy and comfort to them, many of the graces of the Eucharist are lost on them when they are harboring in their hearts a time when they've turned from the Lord in a serious way and haven't had a chance to seek His forgiveness — to receive His mercy. And yes, to let Him love us.

There's plenty of theology and even canon law about why it's a bad idea — even sacrilegious — to receive Communion when not in a "state of grace," or not in full union with God. And while many parishes today, correctly, still preach about the need to confess any serious sin before receiving Eucharist, Confession is not always readily available to the faithful. So there is a gap between the Faith professed and faith practiced.

But let's look past the rules and requirements for a moment. Consider a time when you went to Mass and received Communion shortly after a good Confession. Remember the love and joy you felt for the Lord at that moment?

If you haven't been to confession in a while, and you're unconvinced you need to, let's consider *The Repentant Magdalen*. But to do so we'll have to hop the Amtrak to Washington, D.C.

The Repentant Magdalen, Georges de La Tour, 1635–1640, National Gallery of Art, Washington, D.C.

National Gallery of Art, Washington, D.C. Evelyn and I have arrived at the National Gallery with a lengthy list of works to see. The National Gallery's encyclopedic collection of western art holds a long list of must-see masterpieces. We are particularly looking for one of them that has a close relationship to the mysterious *Penitent Magdalen* that hangs in our own Metropolitan Museum in New York: Georges de La Tour's *The Repentant Magdalen* was painted probably a few years before *The Penitent Magdalen*. It captures Mary at a slightly earlier moment than the Met's painting—the moment she has just returned from her first meeting with Christ. She's contemplating what He's told her.

A Closer Look

La Tour's later Magdalen, painted in 1640, hangs at the Metropolitan Museum and differs in two key ways from the National Gallery

The Penitent Magdalen, Georges de La Tour, 1640, The Metropolitan Museum of Art, New York

of Art's version. First, it shows the jewelry, which Mary now disdains, cast aside on the dresser but still within arm's reach. Second, it positions the light of Christ, the candle, more prominently. It is that light that will lead Mary to Heaven.

Mary is alone. She is dressed provocatively as a prostitute, as she would have commonly been thought of in La Tour's day, with a red skirt, open white blouse, and unkempt hair, as though she has just returned home from plying her trade.[13]

The painting's title tells us that she's also just returned from her first meeting with Jesus. The Good Shepherd has found her lost in the streets; He's forgiven her, but also asked her to "sin no more." So now she's thinking about that. Her left hand strokes a skull, an image of mortality, even of her eventual death. Her right hand supports her head, bowed in contemplation of a life led poorly to this point. Her room, once a garden of earthly delights, has turned dark, now revealed for what it is: a false garden, a garden leading to death and worse. Seeking comfort, she looks to the mirror. Now, instead of seeing her face, she sees the skull of death. The skull itself seems to be the source of the darkness around her.

Then, within the darkness, a light. The candle before her, shining beyond the skull of death which only partially obscures it. It's the light of Christ. His grace, penetrating the darkness. It's the light that is showing the path home. And now, she turns her gaze, her mind, and her body fully towards the light. Away from death.

She's had her confession. She's reconciled with the Lord. She's been transformed. She's ready to let Him love her. She's ready for Mass.

Am I as ready as Mary Magdalen is? Is there any mistake or sin on my mind that is getting between me and God right now that will weigh on me as I try to enter communion with Him in the Mass? If so, maybe I should do what Mary did. Maybe I should have a talk with Him, in Confession.

We have an image of the Mass to reflect on next. Or we should say, a prelude to what the Mass will be. We "found" it in Paris, across from the most famous painting in the world. Mary Magdalen will be returning to us from time to time to help us on our journey to the Eucharist. But for now, we're off to Paris for a meal.

The Feast of a Lifetime!

"On the third day there was a wedding in Cana in Galilee, and the mother of Jesus was there."

—John 2:1

The Wedding at Cana, Paolo Veronese, 1562, Louvre Museum, Paris, France

Louvre Museum, Paris, France. We are art hunting at the Louvre and, after an obligatory stop at Leonardo da Vinci's world-famous *Mona Lisa,* we turn around and head across the gallery. As we do, we look up and see a painting that stops me dead in my tracks. How is it that I've never noticed this before? I realize this painting is not just one of the largest oil paintings in the world (a full thirty-two feet long and twenty-two feet high!), but it also happens to have as its subject the same topic as the *Supper at Emmaus*—the Mass!

The Wedding Feast at Cana is a true masterpiece of Veronese's confident, late-Renaissance style. The giant canvas teems with 130 colorful characters, arrayed quite deliberately within the setting of a Renaissance palace. Amidst all the hustle and bustle, it also projects an order and balance that Signorelli's *Antichrist* so consciously avoids. There's a calm within the storm.

Wanting to meditate on this new discovery, Evelyn and I park ourselves in a quiet eddy of the rapidly moving human river cycling through the gallery for the Mona Lisa. Then suddenly, Evelyn perks up.

"Steve, the whole composition centers on Jesus at the center! It seems wherever my eye scans around to one of the sideshows, I keep getting pulled back to Him! And despite all the hubbub, He seems completely poised. Calm. At peace."

Evelyn has a way of zeroing in on small details that have the most profound impacts. Over our more than forty years together, she's helped me to see so much that I would have missed.

"Yes, and what's interesting," she adds, "is that even though the title is 'Wedding at Cana,' the image of Christ at the center table, with His mother and some disciples around Him, seems to almost be quoting Da Vinci's *Last Supper*! He's drawing a parallel there for us!"

Georgia O'Keefe, the twentieth-century American artist, once said, "To see takes time."[14] So we take more time with *The Wedding*. Off to the right, in the foreground, we see the head waiter testing the water just turned into wine by Jesus, who had just worked His first miracle, at His mother's request.

We're both looking feverishly for the bride and groom, who have been displaced at the center of the head table by Jesus and His mother. "There they are, Steve!" Evelyn whispers. "Over on the far-left corner of the canvas, the edge of the table. How sweet of them to make way for the Lord!"

That's when I notice the head cook carving the roast. Could it be lamb? He's on the balustrade above Jesus and is carving the meat right over His head. And a few seconds later, I get the point.

"This painting is not just the Wedding at Cana. It's the Wedding at Cana, the Last Supper (the Supper of the Lamb), and the Supper at Emmaus — all rolled into one! It's the Mass!" I tell her.

"And Steve," Evelyn replies, "It's not an exclusive club! It looks like everyone has been invited, and even some who didn't have a special ticket are climbing over the balustrades to get in!"

"Sweetie, I've just noticed something really interesting," I add. "This gallery guide says that several famous people are in the picture: Titian, Tintoretto, Veronese himself. Heck, even Charles V of Spain and Suleiman the Magnificent are up there!"

"Veronese is making a big point here, Steve! He's communicating that when we celebrate the Mass in our present time, we are not just commemorating a historical event that happened two thousand years ago, or, for Veronese, fifteen hundred years before. He's teaching us that Jesus is with us now. This is what happens at every Mass, in real time. Jesus is present. He's with us."

It looks like one big, magnificent party. And everyone is invited.

A lot better than freezing out in the cold, chasing around after the phantasms of a false paradise and its deceitful prophets.

There's love in there — lots of it. But before we go inside, a brief warning to our readers.

No Pain, No Gain

As much as we'd all like to get to Heaven with as little work as possible, or to get into the feast for free, it's not that simple. There is sacrifice involved. One of the great mysteries of the Faith is that its joys and triumphs somehow coexist with its pains and its trials. Sort of like life itself.

And just as life has both, so does the Mass.

On one level, the Mass is a celebration of communion with God and, through our communion with Him, with each other — a shared meal. On another, it is a re-presentation of Jesus' great sacrifice for all of us on the Cross, "the unbloody reenactment of the Sacrifice of Christ on Calvary."[15] This is the sacrifice that opened Heaven and its joys to all of us. We could not have one without the other. And the Mass itself has plenty of both.

No pain, no gain.

One of the most iconic images in all of art of the sacrifice of the Cross is by Diego Velásquez. To see it, we'll have to go to Spain.

Museo del Prado, Madrid. Evelyn and I are here in Madrid with our very dear Spanish friends, Carlos and Maria Angeles Sanzo.

Christ Crucified, Diego Velásquez, 1632, Museo del Prado, Madrid, Spain

Their faith runs deep and true, and their humor is contagious. We bonded many years ago on the Camino de Santiago and have been drawn to each other since. Carlos refers to Maria simply as *Angeles* ("my angel"). Maria practically grew up in the Prado, so, when she heard we were going there, she and Carlos made a beeline to the museum.

Velasquez' haunting painting of *Christ Crucified* dominates the room. The painting hangs dramatically in its own special gallery, and when we arrive, all eyes are fixed on the image now before us.

Standing a full eight feet high and more than six feet wide, Velasquez' image of Christ on the Cross eliminates the entire context of the scene on Calvary and imagines Christ alone, hanging there in the blackness. Although presumably dead — the recently inflicted spear wound that assured the Romans He had breathed His last is clearly visible — He somehow seems still alive, His bruised but still beautiful body radiating the only light in the scene. As blood drips from His wounds, His head drops down to His chest. He has just taken His last breath. And although nailed to the Cross, He seems to be standing on it calmly, rather than hanging from it, suffocating.

As our little group of pilgrims stand quietly before the image, we realize that, by not painting the landscape context of Calvary, Velásquez has artfully invited us into the scene. Suddenly, we've been transported to the foot of the Cross, alone with Jesus.

For a moment, we think of the image of *Winter* back at the Met. She, too, was alone, in a dark place, dying. But *Christ Crucified* evokes more than loneliness and despair. That muscular, seemingly still-alive body of Christ up there on the Cross, the light emanating from Him, and yes, that halo around His head, tell us something very different. His Spirit is very much alive. Even in this Crucifixion, in the moment of His greatest sacrifice.

The Cross, for all its gore, hasn't killed Him.

"Can't you see, Steve!?" Maria cries. "Christ hasn't been killed by the Cross! Christ has killed the Cross! He's conquered death with His light, with His love. His halo is glowing!"

Evelyn sums it up, as usual, in just a few words, "He is our light in the darkness."

This is the Christian paradox. This is the paradox of the Mass. Sacrifice and triumph. Death and life.

Okay, now we can go inside that church. Through that open door on the right.

"Behold, I stand at the door and knock. If anyone hears my voice and opens the door, I will enter his house and dine with him, and he with me.... After this I had a vision of an open door to heaven."

—*Rev. 3:20; 4:1*[16]

Façade, Orvieto Cathedral, 14th century, Orvieto, Italy

– 2 –

Introductory Rites

Preparing to See God

Enter the Sanctuary

Orvieto, Italy. Over the last forty years, Evelyn and I have had the joy of visiting many of the great cathedrals of Europe. Magnificent in their awe-inspiring beauty, the cathedrals draw in visitors of all faiths from all over the world. Archaeologists and art scholars marvel at these architectural achievements in stone, creating the soaring walls of glass without the benefit of structural steel to hold them together. These edifices, which dominate the skylines of many medieval European cities, were not built simply to demonstrate the skill of their master builders or to celebrate the authority of the Church prelates who served there. They also housed important relics of saints and miracles, which drew pilgrims from far and wide; in the case of Orvieto, the church houses the relic of a eucharistic miracle that helped to re-animate faith in the true Presence of Jesus in the Eucharist.[17]

Like our more modern (and often more modest) present-day churches, the great Medieval, Renaissance, and Baroque cathedrals were built to house the 'holy of holies,' the eucharistic Lord who comes to us in the Mass and afterwards is kept safely within the church's tabernacle until our next visit. Taking decades, even centuries, for their magnificent construction, these cathedrals were built to evoke, no, to celebrate, the very presence of God on earth — Heaven come to earth, so to speak: the Mass.

For sure, in my agnostic years I told myself that I was drawn to these cathedrals by the science it took to build them. And yes, perhaps for their beauty, with a small "b." Now, my purpose is clearer, less disguised: I come for a taste of Heaven.

Mind you, this was the first time either of us had made it to Orvieto. "Off the beaten track. An inconvenient detour," we were told. But on this chilly, rainy day in March, Evelyn and I are here. We know Orvieto was also built with an important, secondary intention alongside the Mass — to teach the people of the Church about the Faith. To "catechize," as modern-day theologians like to state it.

And now that we're here, we're not disappointed. In fact, our eyes are glued to the façade of Orvieto Cathedral, which is suddenly shimmering as a break in the clouds opens a path for the afternoon sun.

We'll be coming back to this façade soon enough. But for now, let's imagine stepping inside for Mass. Let's get out of the cold and the rain.... Through the open door on the right.

The First Things We Always Do

Making the Sign of the Cross with holy water as we enter the inside of a church is not technically part of the Mass; that self-signing will occur later, as the Mass officially begins. Still, all Catholics perform this ritual, sometimes almost mechanically, sometimes with fervor. Through the course of a visit to Mass, Catholics will make the Sign of the Cross, by my count, at least eight times, sometimes more.

What are we doing?

Msgr. Landry pipes in. "We're first invoking the power of the Holy Trinity to assist and protect us. 'In the name of the Father, and of the Son, and of the Holy Spirit.' The three Persons in one God. The Creator of all that exists. In biblical mentality, a name is a sign and summary of the one called upon, and so to pray in the name of the Trinity is to try prayerfully to immerse ourselves in God! And the gesture we make with our hands is not random. We sign ourselves with our secret weapon, the weapon exorcists will tell you is the most powerful, what Satan himself most fears: the Sign of the

Cross, of Christ's redemptive suffering and death for us. His loving obedience to the will of the Father regains for us what our first parents, Adam and Eve, lost through disobedience."

Evelyn and I have enlisted Msgr. Roger Landry for our "Visions Project." A virtual pilgrimage of this scale, exploring a topic of such theological richness and depth as the Eucharist, would need a priest for sure. Msgr. Landry is an old friend from many shared New York apostolic journeys; his gentle spirit and wry humor bely a rich, deep spiritual core built on a rock-solid theological foundation. Msgr. Landry is one of those cheerful priests who is at once serious and full of joy, rigorously theological and able to speak the faith in plain English. And he is in love with the Eucharist.

His role, among other things, is to keep us theologically on track as we unlock the mysteries of the Mass. So I ask him another question: "Why do we use holy water to bless ourselves as we enter the church?"

"Holy water is a way of recalling and re-affirming our Baptism and the baptismal promises we made when we first became Christians. It also opens us to the way God wants to bless us right now and reminds us of our dignity as God's adopted children. Exorcists tell us that devils run from holy water. It tortures them, so to speak."

So today while some, citing health concerns, don't dip their hands in the holy water available as we enter, I always do. I figure I have a greater need to protect myself from the devil than from whatever germs might have landed there from the person ahead of me.

"When we make the Sign of the Cross, we witness to others around us that we are Catholic, that we're believers, and that we're willing to accept our own cross in life, the sufferings that may come from our witness to the Faith," Msgr. Landry adds. "For all of those reasons, this tradition has been passed down to us from the earliest days of the Church."

"Monsignor, what about the direction? Why do Roman Catholics move their hand from their left shoulder to their right, and Eastern Catholics and Orthodox Christians from their right to their left?" Evelyn asks.

"Actually, no one knows for sure. The most common supposition is that in the East they 'mirrored' the direction of the blessing of the priest and therefore went left when he went right and in the west they copied him and went right to left just like he did. But it's a custom. The important thing is to make a cross as you bless yourself," Father concludes.

St. Paul himself reminds us:

"For Jews demand signs and Greeks look for wisdom,
but we proclaim Christ crucified, a stumbling
block to Jews and foolishness to Gentiles."
— 1 Cor. 1:22–23

As I said, we Catholics make the Sign of the Cross several times during our attendance at Mass, so we're going to see some crosses as we go. Or more correctly, we're going to see some *crucifixes* as we go. As Catholics, we almost always show the body of Jesus on the Cross, to remind ourselves of His sacrifice there. And when we do, the "cross" becomes a "crucifix."

To keep things interesting, we've chosen Crucifixion images that emphasize different elements of the mystery of the Cross. We've already seen one, by Velásquez, which mysteriously invited us into the scene on Calvary. Now for our first official "Sign of the Cross," as we enter the church for Mass, let's swing back in time to a Cross created during the height of the Middle Ages. Technically, it's not a painting but an "icon," a symbolic image of the Crucifixion rather than a realistic picture of the event.

Abbey Church of Sainte-Foy, Conques, France, eleventh century. The Abbey Church at Conques goes back in time to the Roman era and at least since the eighth century has housed a community of monks. Having failed to secure the relics of St. Vincent of Saragossa (those went to a rival church abbey in Paris called St. Germain-des-Prés)[18], the abbey obtained the relics of another Roman-era martyr, St. Foye.

The Crucifixion Medallion, Abbey Church at Conques, ca. 1100, The Metropolitan Museum of Art, New York

The arrival of St. Foye's relics put Conques on the map, as the abbey became a heavily frequented pilgrimage stop for pilgrims on the long Camino de Santiago from France to Compostela, Spain, where the bones of St. James the Apostle are kept. With pilgrims came wealth, which the monks used, among other religious pursuits, to create ever more special and valuable illustrated Bibles and other prayer books. The monks of Sainte-Foye were particularly skilled at creating gold-plated enamels, which they used for book covers, and this small crucifix image we have at the Met is believed to have been one of these. The care and love that went into creating this glimmering image, fired multiple times as each color of the enamel was applied, would have required someone with a lot of patience and a very steady hand.

Reflecting on this Cross, I can sometimes imagine myself as an eleventh-century pilgrim making the long difficult trek to Santiago de Compostela. Having climbed the hill to Conques and reached the beautiful new abbey church there, I bless myself as I enter Sainte-Foy. Like many churches then and now, it is built cruciform, that is, in the shape of a cross, and so the church itself is a symbol of the central mystery of our Faith. As we make the Sign of the Cross, we call to mind the image of this glistening medallion.

Painted in a two-dimensional space, the scene here is heavenly, and is meant to transport us there. Jesus is shown symbolically crucified to a beautiful blue Cross. Both He and the Cross are larger than life, as indicated by the smaller images of Mary and John who attend Him. And while the enamel suggests the Lord is attached to the Cross, He almost appears to be standing with it, rather than hanging from it; His body shows no sign of stress. His arms seem to be spread wide, more in a gesture of welcome than a reference to the tortures of the Cross. The Cross's brilliant blue color itself evokes a scene in the skies, in Heaven, rather than the gruesome reality of Calvary. It reminds us that the Cross is ultimately about light and love, not darkness and hate.

Jesus is welcoming us to Heaven. And the route there is through His beautiful Cross.

As we enter the church, let's make the Sign of the Cross together. We're on a pilgrimage to Heaven.

Say a Prayer in Silence

Once we enter the church and arrive at our pew, or bench, many use the time before the Mass begins to say some personal prayers in silence. Sometimes for a special intention, sometimes for something that is troubling our hearts, and sometimes just to settle ourselves down. For an introspective image about this moment, we will turn to one of the great prayer warriors of the Church, St. Jerome. He's in Heaven right now, but we have a pretty good picture of him in Baltimore.

Walters Museum of Art, Baltimore. Evelyn and I have stopped at the Walters Museum on our trip south to see two particular pieces of art. One is the stained glass window illustrating the martyrdom of St. Vincent of Saragossa, whose relics we referenced on our little trip to Conques; the story of this window and how it came to be in Baltimore is for another time.[19] The second is for the painting we

St. Jerome in the Desert, Bernardino Pinturicchio, 1475–1480, Walters Museum of Art, Baltimore

stand before now: Pinturicchio's portrait of St. Jerome in prayer, which may have inspired Leonardo da Vinci's later, unfinished *St. Jerome* hanging at the Vatican Museums. It's a painting about prayer and silence and offers a useful attitude to reflect on while we're waiting for the arrival of the priest.

A Closer Look

The similarities of Pinturicchio's *St. Jerome* with Da Vinci's are striking; almost certainly Da Vinci used Pinturicchio's for inspiration. Like many of Da Vinci's masterpieces, this one was never finished.

St. Jerome Praying in the Wilderness, Leonardo da Vinci, 1480–1490, Vatican Museums, Rome, Italy

St. Jerome is best known for translating the Bible into Latin for the first time. Before he did so, after being confronted by the Lord in a dream about the sin of pride and his poor use of time, Jerome left for the desert, to spend four years in prayer and penance. We see him here, gaunt and humbled, enraptured by the crucifix before which he kneels. The Cross is tied to the small evergreen tree in front of him.

Jerome is alone, at the entrance to a cave, surrounded by the silent, colorless landscape around him. An open book lies on the ground to his left; the museum's catalog tells us scholars have deciphered that the writing represents an inspirational letter to him in the desert from St. Augustine. Jerome's bright red hat, the only article of clothing recognizable from his former life as a Church scholar, lies on the ground to his right, alongside another book, presumably the Hebrew Bible that he would soon translate to Latin; the hat seems to have been tossed there carelessly. Jerome is guarded by a lion, a symbol of the saint's legendary temper and fiercely polemical writing style. Over the years, the lion became a loyal companion to Jerome after the saint healed him by pulling a thorn from his paw. The evergreen tree to which Jerome has fixed the Cross was often used by painters at this time to represent eternity, which stands in stark contrast to the abyss of death before and below the saint.

Interestingly, as we peer closer at the corpus of Christ on the Cross, the body almost seems alive, as if Jesus is talking back to Jerome. A light is emanating from Jesus on the Cross as the interaction between Him and the saint deepens.

Silent prayer can have this effect. You can begin to hear the voice of God.

In today's hurly-burly world, entering the mystery of the Mass can be difficult. We bring so many deadlines, anxieties, and "places we need to get to" with us, and these can often distract us from the mystery. It happens to me a lot. One antidote is this image of St. Jerome in prayer. Put your cares aside for a moment. Take off that fancy hat of yours, from your life "out there." Enjoy the quiet around you. And enter spiritually into a simpler world alone with Jesus.

In the silence, listen for His soft, gentle voice.

The prophet Elijah described one of his great prayer moments in a way that must have inspired Jerome himself. It's a prayer about the power of silence.

"Then the LORD said: Go out and stand on the mountain before the LORD; the LORD will pass by. There was a strong and violent wind rending the mountains and crushing rocks before the LORD — but the LORD was not in the wind; after the wind, an earthquake — but the LORD was not in the earthquake; after the earthquake, fire — but the LORD was not in the fire; after the fire, a light silent sound. When he heard this, Elijah hid his face in his cloak and went out and stood at the entrance of the cave. A voice said to him, Why are you here, Elijah?"

— 1 Kings 19:11–13

The Entrance

Sing Praise to the Lord!

As we're kneeling in prayer before the Lord, getting into a St. Jerome kind of focus, suddenly the organ starts up and everyone stands to join in song. At least, *theoretically* we all join in song. Not to generalize, but we Catholics are not particularly good at singing together. Some of us (myself included) are worried about carrying a tune. Others can't find the page in the hymn book. And for others, it's just maybe embarrassment. My advice: Get over it! We're here to celebrate the great feast of the Mass, a little slice of Heaven! And what better way to celebrate Heaven than to join the angels there, who are among us now in the church, in songs of praise to God. After all, that's what angels do! And to inspire us, we've enlisted one of the Vatican Museums' special angels.

Vatican Museums. We are in the Pinacoteca of the Vatican Museums, which gets less foot traffic than the major attractions of Raphael's Loggia and Michelangelo's Sistine Ceiling. One of our reasons for coming here is to see the angels of the spectacular Renaissance-era ceiling frescoes of the Church of the Twelve Apostles, near Trajan's Forum.

The ancient church of *Dodici Apostoli* has undergone many renovations in its sixteen-hundred-year history, and one of them, a Baroque-period redo in the 1700s, brought the angels here, to the Vatican Museums. The Renaissance master Melozzo degli Ambrosi (Melozzo da Forlì) painted them as part of a large fresco in the former apse. When it was pulled down in 1700, the pope had the good sense to save the frescoes, which were carefully detached from the ceiling and re-mounted here at the Pinacoteca.

These angels, so beautiful, so bright and colorful, and, well, so joyful, literally "sing for themselves." I'll just sprinkle them around when we break into song during the Mass.

Musician Angel, Melozzo da Forlì, 1480, Pinacoteca (Vatican Museums), Rome, Italy

For now, let's imagine ourselves with the angels in Heaven, joining in praise of God. God's minister or intermediary, the priest, is marching down the aisle to greet us.

The opening hymn for our Mass is an old favorite. It's about coming to a place of rest in Jesus from the world outside.

"I Heard the Voice of Jesus Say"

I heard the voice of Jesus say, "Come unto Me and rest;
"Lay down, O weary one, lay down, your head upon my
breast."
I came to Jesus as I was, so weary worn and sad;
I found in him a resting place, and he has made me glad.

I heard the voice of Jesus say, "Behold I freely give
The living water, thirsty one, stoop down, and drink and
live."
I came to Jesus and I drank of that life-giving stream.
My thirst was quenched, my soul revived, and now I live
in him.

I heard the voice of Jesus say, "I am this dark world's light;
Look unto me, your morn shall rise, and all your day be
bright."
I looked to Jesus, and I found in him my star, my sun;
And in that light of life I'll walk till my traveling days are
done.[20]

Sign of the Cross

"In the name of the Father, and of the Son, and of the Holy Spirit."

"Amen."

It Begins

As soon as the opening music stops, the priest celebrating the Mass with us leads us in a collective signing of the cross, "in the name of

The Crucifix at Santa Croce, Giovanni Cimabue, 1265, Basilica di Santa Croce, Florence, Italy

the Father, and of the Son, and of the Holy Spirit." With this first collective prayer as one community in faith, the Mass begins.

To help us enter prayerfully the beginning of the Mass, we want to turn to our third Cross, Cimabue's thirteenth-century masterpiece, *The Crucifixion*. It's located at Florence's Franciscan Basilica, Santa Croce. This image was taken prior to the 1966 flood damage.

A Closer Look

The Crucifix at Santa Croce, Giovanni Cimabue, 1265, Basilica di Santa Croce, Florence, Italy (post recent restoration)

The flood of 1966 severely damaged many great masterpieces in Florence, perhaps first among them Cimabue's *Crucifix*. Restorations have been ongoing ever since, but the restoration of the *Crucifix* was particularly difficult due to the very extensive damage it endured. The very modern, haunting approach taken in the restoration is spectacular in effect but still pales before the original. This is what it looks like today.[21]

The Basilica di Santa Croce, Florence. We are here early one morning to visit the great Franciscan Basilica di Santa Croce, almost as important to the Florentines as the Duomo itself. Many of their most famous poets, painters, and musicians (like Dante, Ghiberti, and Rossini) are buried here. Even Michelangelo, who asked to be buried in Rome where he died, was carried instead by the Medici back here to Florence for internment. We've come for many reasons, but first and foremost to see this crucifix, now kept at the Basilica's adjacent museum. More than any other painting of Christ crucified, this Crucifixion image changed the course of Western art forever. A full fifteen feet high, it was damaged severely in the great flood of 1966, and the restoration created an even more haunting figure. For our purposes, let's focus on the image as it hung before the flood, in its full glory.[22]

Although two of Cimabue's most famous pupils, Giotto and Duccio, would eventually outshine their master, it was Cimabue who first broke out of the medieval Byzantine formula of two-dimensional iconography pointing to Heaven. Rather, he wanted to show God on earth and Heaven at the same time—what I have called "the Emmanuel Moment in Art,"[23] which would lead eventually to the Renaissance. And this crucifix was the apex of his new way of thinking about art, God, and the mystery of the Faith.

Here we have a scene that isn't terribly pretty, at least on the surface. No longer do we have here the Heaven-centric, symbolic crucifixes of the Byzantine/Medieval period, such as the Conques crucifix that we used as we entered the church. In Cimabue's revolutionary rendition, we have a real man, Christ, suffering in a very real way on a very real Cross. His mother and His best friend John, "the disciple whom Jesus loved," look on mournfully from either side, almost in despair. When we see Jesus, our Good Shepherd, twisting in agony as He tries to lift Himself up for a last breath, it hits us.

This really happened. This is not an interesting story written down two thousand years ago by someone with a good imagination. This sacrifice actually happened; it was at once horrific and almost beyond our comprehension. And as we are about to witness, it is in some ways happening still. The sense of twisting movement up there on the Cross only magnifies the mystery; the Crucifixion almost seems to be happening in real time.

This is not any ordinary ceremony or ritual we are about to enter into. This is a lot bigger. We better get focused. And we're going to need some help.

GREETING

"The Lord be with you."

"And with your spirit."

Enter the Holy Spirit

As the priest finishes the Sign of the Cross, he greets the faithful.

"The Lord be with you."

And we reply, "And with your spirit."

Sometimes we say this prayer so quickly and absentmindedly, we forget what we're doing: we are invoking the arrival of the Holy Spirit, the third Person of the Trinity, to inspire the priest for the celebration of the Mass ahead. In the early days of the Church, as the liturgy of the Mass was being formed and developed, the Holy Spirit seems to have been especially active. In Luke's history of the early Church, the Acts of the Apostles, the Holy Spirit is mentioned more than sixty times! Throughout the story, the Spirit seems to be communicating with and through the apostles, and they listen to His directives with little hesitation. He's in charge.

When it comes to painting the working of the Holy Spirit within and through human beings, there is one painter who soars alone. Domenikos Theotokopoulos (El Greco). Time to pay him a visit.

Pentecost, El Greco, 1612–1614, Museo del Prado, Madrid, Spain

Museo del Prado, Madrid. We are back in the Prado with Carlos and Maria. While for Maria "my Velasquez" is her all-time favorite Spanish painter, El Greco probably follows. Technically, El Greco was not Spanish; he migrated as a young artist to Spain from Crete and its Byzantine icon tradition. That tradition, blended with the "new style" Renaissance art flowing into Crete from its Venetian rulers, exerted a deep influence on El Greco's art throughout his life. Still, the vast body of his work was produced within the deeply Catholic Counter Reformation culture of late sixteenth-century Toledo, and the Prado holds many of his greatest works. We are standing before one of his most famous ones now.

El Greco painted *Pentecost* in 1600 as part of an altarpiece for a church in Madrid, Our Lady of Aragon. He was sixty years old and entering the final decade or so of his long career. By now, the three mighty cultural rivers that influenced his art — Eastern icon tradition, Western Renaissance/Mannerist painting, and Spanish Catholicism — had fully matured and blended into a unique style that became his hallmark. El Greco sought to paint humanity as both the outer man and the inner soul — on earth, but in Heaven at the same time. As he aged and grew ever closer to Heaven, his art seemed to evolve with him on this journey. By the time he reached the turn of the seventeenth century, his images almost appeared "inside out." On the surface, the soul itself; beneath, the body. *Pentecost* was one of the paintings at this time that launched him even higher into the skies.

Before us we have an image of the scene described by Luke in Acts 2:

> *"When the time for Pentecost was fulfilled, they were all in one place together. And suddenly there came from the sky a noise like a strong driving wind, and it filled the entire house in which they were. Then there appeared to them tongues as of fire, which parted and came to rest on each one of them. And they were all filled with the holy Spirit and began to speak in different tongues, as the Spirit enabled them to proclaim."*
>
> — *Acts 2:1–4*

In El Greco's rendition of the scene, the apostles are huddled together in the Upper Room. Still terrified for their lives, they are praying, awaiting "The Advocate" whom Jesus had promised He would send. Mary is at the center of the crowded scene, the Jewish mother holding the terrified men together, leading them in prayer (see Acts 1:14). Suddenly, the Spirit arrives in the form of tongues of fire. As Mary and the apostles look up, they are transfixed by the image of the dove, the Holy Spirit, descending dramatically upon them. They are bathed in a cool, translucent, and heavenly light. As we meditate before the painting, we can almost see the Spirit transforming them from terrified followers of Christ to bold proclaimers of the Faith.

"Maria," Evelyn perks up. "I can see their souls!"

Amazingly, even while we can see clearly the structure of the disciples' earthly bodies beneath their cloaks, somehow, glowing on the surface of their cloaks, El Greco has painted their souls, now afire with the Holy Spirit!

"Not just *their* souls," Maria adds. "We are all part of this mystery; we've all been baptized with the Holy Spirit. El Greco makes this point with the apostle next to Peter in the foreground, whom we can only see from behind. He is there as a stand-in for us, as a vehicle to help us imagine ourselves in the scene."

Then, as if to underscore the present-day nature of *Pentecost,* El Greco adds one last twist — he's painted himself into the image, as the third apostle standing to Mary's left, bearing the pointed beard with which he was typically identified.

"Yes, Steve, that's my guy! That's El Greco himself!" "Angeles" exclaims.

So, like everything about the Mass, Pentecost is not just some event that happened once two thousand years ago. To some degree, it happens every day. It's happening now. The Holy Spirit is alive and with us. That same Holy Spirit, as we invoke Him in our simple response, "and with your Spirit," has just come down upon all of us, here at Mass.

It has truly begun.

THE PENITENTIAL ACT

(Confiteor)

"Brethren, let us acknowledge our sins and so prepare ourselves to celebrate the sacred mysteries."

As soon as we've greeted each other and invoked the Holy Spirit, the priest immediately initiates a series of prayers called "The Penitential Act." Together, we reflect on where we have failed God, and we seek His forgiveness. This prayer is situated to put us in an attitude of humility as we enter the mystery of the Mass — and in a better position to receive the graces offered.

The prayer itself varies somewhat with the liturgical years and seasons. Sometimes, we use the short form, called the Kyrie, repeating three times, following promptings from the priest,

"Lord, have mercy."

"Christ, have mercy."

"Lord, have mercy."

Other times, we use the long form, called the "Confiteor" from its first Latin word, which many Catholics know by heart:

"I confess to almighty God and to you, my brothers and sisters, that I have greatly sinned, in my thoughts and in my words, in what I have done and in what I have failed to do, through my fault, through my fault, through my most grievous fault; therefore, I ask blessed Mary ever-Virgin, all the Angels and Saints, and you, my brothers and sisters, to pray for me to the Lord our God."

Mary Magdalen, the grave sinner turned devoted saint, has been an icon used by the Church for centuries to promote the value of a good Confession and the graces it confers. Most images of the "Penitent Magdalen," such as La Tour's painting we visited earlier, have a serenity and peacefulness associated with them that always moves and inspires me.

For this moment in the Mass, though, we decided to use a real bone rattler. The first time I saw it, more than forty years ago, it left me shaken to the root. It still does.

Penitent Magdalen, Donatello, ca. 1455, Museo dell'Opera del Duomo, Florence, Italy

Museo dell'Opera del Duomo, Florence. Following the disastrous flood of 1966, many of the treasures of Florence's Duomo, once restored, were moved inside the newly rebuilt museum behind the cathedral. That's where we are visiting with the *Magdalen* now, instead of inside the baptistery, where she stood for centuries; this baptistery is where new entrants to the Faith were baptized before entering the church next door. All of Florence was familiar with and loved this image of Mary Magdalen. She was almost an alter ego of another great Florentine sculpture, Michelangelo's *David*. We'll be visiting *David* soon enough, but for this moment as we pray the Kyrie, we need the *Magdalen*.

Sculpting her from a block of wood late in his storied career, Donato di Niccolò di Betto (Donatello) reveals Magdalen to us almost bigger than life, a little over six feet tall. Anatomically, she's perfectly proportioned and entirely realistic. Spiritually, she appears repentant and sorrowful for her past, standing before God in an attitude of utter humility. Rather than the beautiful young woman normally portrayed as Magdalen, Donatello has cast her as an older, gaunt woman, dressed in rags. Though thin, her muscle tone suggests an inner strength. Having spent years in the desert in penance for her sins, she now stands before God, a changed person from the young woman who had led a life of sin before she met Him. Mary is both humble before God and confident in His forgiveness.

As I contemplate the *Magdalen*, what seemed jarring and unappealing when I first viewed her many years ago now leads me to a deeper thought about sin and why it so offends God. God created Mary, and all of us, to be perfect — beautiful — full of dignity, lovable. When we fall into sin, it disfigures our soul. It stains us. God alone can restore us to the perfect beings He created, and He wants to. But we, like Magdalen, need first to recognize what's happened and to seek His forgiveness and healing.

Donatello's *Magdalen* is a cry across the centuries for healing and forgiveness. We use it here during the Confiteor to remind ourselves of this profound need for forgiveness within our own souls. At the same time, we, like Mary, stand confident in Jesus' love and forgiveness, even as we admit our faults. We know His mercy is bigger than our sins. We know He still loves us.

As we pray the Confiteor, let's remember that as we enter more deeply into the Mass, we need to enter it with the attitude of the *Penitent Magdalen*: as sinners seeking redemption, in need of the graces to come in the Mass that has begun. And, as we pray this prayer of reconciliation collectively as a community, let's remind ourselves that all of us are in the same boat. We all need Him.

The Absolution

Just after we beat our chests, repeating the prayer "Through my fault, through my fault, through my most grievous fault," we hear the Lord's powerful response: the reminder that He does forgive us and that we remain His beloved children. That He's about to put a shiny new cloak over our shoulders so we can enter the feast, like He did with the prodigal son. Indeed, whatever form of the Penitential Act the priest uses, the priest's concluding prayer is always the same. Day after liturgical day, year after liturgical year, he says:

"May Almighty God have mercy on us,
forgive us our sins,
and bring us to everlasting life."

Msgr. Landry explains, "The reason the priest's response is always the same is because God's is too: He never tires of forgiving us. By keeping the priest's prayer of absolution identical in all three versions of the Penitential Act, the Church emphasizes this. We might stumble and fall, but His response never changes. It's always pure love. Mercy. Forgiveness. And although for grave sins we need to go to the Sacrament of Reconciliation, the Penitential Act reminds us that we're far from perfect and need God's mercy and forgiveness."

Let's go get that shiny new cloak. It's in a small museum in Strasbourg, France.

Forgiveness

Strasbourg, France. When I think of the prodigal son, Rembrandt's masterpiece always comes to mind: a young man kneeling before his father "while he was still a long way off," (Luke 15:20), utterly contrite.

The Return of the Prodigal Son, Rembrandt, 1667, Hermitage Museum, St. Petersburg, Russia

A Closer Look

Rembrandt's last painting, *The Return of the Prodigal Son,* offers a poignant image of mercy and forgiveness. Here we see a young man kneeling before his father as he first sees him, seeking his forgiveness, utterly contrite. The father's hug is far greater than the son had hoped for. The figure at the right of the canvas is presumed to be the older son, who later in the story refuses to enter his father's house for the feast welcoming the prodigal home. *The Return of the Prodigal Son* was the artist's last painting, which was done for himself without commission.

Return of the Prodigal Son, Michel-Martin Drölling, 1806, Musée des Beaux-Arts de Strasbourg, Strasbourg, France

Rembrandt's image is at a slightly earlier point in the son's journey home than we are now at Mass, so instead we've traveled to Strasbourg on a cold December day to visit a humbler, less famous image: Michel-Martin Drölling's *Return of the Prodigal Son.*[24]

In Drölling's version, the son and his father are just outside the father's house, minutes after the son has attempted to spit out his confession. I say "attempted" because in Luke's Gospel, before the son can even begin his well-rehearsed speech of contrition, the father interrupts him:

> *"So he got up and went back to his father. While he was still a long way off, his father caught sight of him, and was filled with compassion. He ran to his son, embraced him and kissed him. His son said to him, 'Father, I have sinned against heaven and against you; I no longer deserve to be called your son.' But his father ordered*

his servants, 'Quickly bring the finest robe and put it on him; put a ring on his finger and sandals on his feet.' "
— Luke 15:20–22

What we are seeing here is the father embracing the son soon after he has barely mouthed the words, "Father, I have sinned." The father is now proactively leading his son the rest of the way home. Understanding that the son's very presence implies contrition, the father has already forgiven him! He loves him totally!

Sometimes when I'm at Mass and wondering why the priest doesn't give me enough of a pause to think through all my transgressions perfectly before praying the Confiteor, I just smile and think of the parable, and Drölling's take on it. God loves me completely. He's so happy to see me here, back in His home. And He knows I love Him.

Yes, I am a beloved child of God. I'm home again. And I am anxious to hear His words of wisdom for me — a lot better than the false prophets who once had me confused.

Then we take a deeper look at Drölling's diminutive masterpiece. There are some other characters in the story. Whom do these people in the painting represent? Who is the servant with his arms upraised in joy? Who is the second servant near him on his left, looking confused that the father has forgiven the prodigal? Who is the man with the shepherd's staff on the right side of the canvas, turning away back towards the fields?

In a sense, they are the people around us now, here at Mass; they might even be me. For sure, our varied reactions to the Father's forgiveness happening now are probably similar to the reactions that Drölling envisions for us in *The Return*. Some of us are overjoyed to be here and to feel the Father's love and mercy being dispensed on us and also to our brothers and sisters around us at Mass; as we imagine this, our arms and spirits literally rise to the heavens in joy. Others are surprised at how readily the Father forgives, and they almost can't believe He has; we are the servant on the far left of the canvas. There are days at Mass when I suffer this myself, in disbelief that I've been forgiven — as if my sin were bigger than the Father's heart!

And still others, while grateful for having been forgiven, cannot bring themselves to forgive someone in their lives, someone (they feel) who should be an exception to this prayer for Absolution. That is the attitude of the older brother later in the story, who most certainly is the man on the right side of the canvas, staff in hand, turning away from the scene. Do I harbor any feelings of resentment towards someone in my life, possibly here at Mass, who has wronged me in some way? If I do, now would be a good time to let it go — and to love my brother however much of a prodigal he's been. Then I will come to the Feast with a clean slate.

As our hearts fill with love at this special moment, there are others also present: the angels! They're celebrating our return!

We are about to hear them. And if we look up, we might even see them.

Glory to God

(The Gloria, or Angels' Hymn)

My years as a missionary on the streets of New York have taught me many things about our Faith that have helped me penetrate its beauty. One idea stands out above all others: the transformative power of God's forgiveness on the human soul. Time and again, whenever a long-lost soul is brought home to the Church through the Sacrament of Confession, that soul glows in a special way. Having felt, almost surprisingly, the depth and power of the Lord's love and mercy, they are suddenly restored. Most seem to float out of the confessional, wearing a special halo we missionaries call "the Confession glow."

So, as we close out the Penitential Act, let's remember what's just happened. We've once again met the Lord in His mercy and now we feel deep gratitude and love back; we are drawn toward Him. Exuberant, we lift our voices together with the angels in an ancient hymn said to be based on the one — at least at the beginning—the angels sang at Bethlehem when Jesus was born![25] The Gloria! Let's sing it out every Sunday and feast with the same joy that we feel after a good Confession! Or, as AnnaMaria Cardinalli recommends in her glorious book, *Music and Meaning in the Mass,* we should "remember how on Christmas, with all the sparkle and trappings of the day surrounding you, moved with joy, you probably sing *Gloria in excelsis Deo* with all your heart!"[26]

"Glory to God in the highest,
and on earth peace to people of good will.

We praise you, we bless you,
we adore you, we glorify you,
we give you thanks for your great glory."

Church of St. Ignatius, Rome. When Evelyn and I first visited the Church of St. Ignatius, we gasped as we looked up. We knew, intellectually, that we were looking at a solid barrel-vaulted ceiling over the enormous nave of the church. Yet, for a moment, we felt like we were looking into an open ceiling, soaring toward the heavens.

Through a careful use of a painterly technique developed in the Renaissance called "foreshortening," Pozzo creates the illusion that we are viewing images rising vertically above us. At the edges, "closest" to us, we see people being thrown violently back to the earth, their souls not prepared to enter the heavenly gates. Above them, angels and saints soar ever higher, on an upward vertical path that seems to be infinite. All of them are heading to the central point of the nave, where yet further above them appears our risen Lord, Christ, effortlessly holding His Cross with a few fingers of one hand, triumphant. Even as St. Ignatius soars ever higher, Jesus seems to be flying toward St. Ignatius, leading him on the last mile toward home, toward Himself. I like to imagine myself in St. Ignatius's place, being led by Jesus, the Good Shepherd and the triumphant Cross Bearer, leading me to His Father in Heaven. All I can think of at this moment is the Gloria. Glory to God in the Highest! Indeed!

St. Ignatius Being Received in Heaven, Andrea Pozzo, 1685, Chiesa di Sant'Ignazio di Loyola, Rome, Italy

THE COLLECT

(Opening Prayer)

"Let us pray."

As the Introductory Rites end and we get ready for the Liturgy of the Word, the Church inserts a special prayer each day, tailored to the liturgical season or feast day being celebrated. It's called the "Collect" because it's meant to bring together the Church's prayers and intentions for that particular Mass. For example, on the Memorial of Our Lady of Mount Carmel, the priest prays the following "Collect":

"May the venerable intercession of the glorious Virgin Mary come to our aid, we pray, O Lord, so that, fortified by her protection, we may reach the mountain which is Christ. Who lives and reigns with you in the unity of the Holy Spirit, God, forever and ever."

"Amen."

And with our Amen, The Liturgy of the Word begins.

Part II

LITURGY OF THE WORD

"Were not our hearts burning within us while he spoke to us on the way and opened the scriptures to us?"

—Luke 24:32

– 3 –

How to Listen to God

"In the beginning was the Word, and the Word was with God, and the Word was God. He was in the beginning with God. All things came to be through him, and without him nothing came to be. What came to be through him was life, and this life was the light of the human race."

—*John 1:1–4*

The Liturgy of the Word, as proclaimed to us in the Scriptures, is very much alive, and it operates during the Mass within each of us in a very special way. The readings are literally the Word of God, given a voice by a human intermediary, for sure, but nonetheless the living Word of God to each of us in that moment of that day.

At a mysterious level, the Word, as suggested by John's capital "W" in John 1, is God Himself. That is why the book of the Gospels bearing the Word is so respectfully carried from the altar to the pulpit, or ambo, by the priest.[27] And as He characteristically does in all things, God is simultaneously, through His Word, talking to each of us personally.

Still, perhaps because the Liturgy of the Word is largely read to us, with few active prayers on our parts, we sometimes get distracted. We don't always open our ears enough to hear God's special message for us today. So in the moments after the priest reads the Collect and the lector approaches the ambo, it's a good practice to get tuned in. To sit down and listen. To God.

For inspiration on how to do this, let's turn to two people from the time of Christ who are with us at today's Mass. Both were model listeners.

The first, no surprise, is our Blessed Mother herself. To see the image I have in mind, we'll have to make a short trip to Siena. Well, not exactly Siena. Sassetta's *Annunication* now hangs conveniently at the Met.

Lean into Your Angel . . .

The Annunciation, Sassetta, 1435,
The Metropolitan Museum of Art, New York

Siena, early fifteenth century. Siena in the early fifteenth century remained an important center of arts and culture in Tuscany, though it was gradually eclipsed by its larger and still wealthier rival, Florence. At that time, painters in Siena were painting highly stylized, almost two-dimensional images in a style called "International Gothic," even as Florence was already shifting towards the three-dimensional, earthbound images of the Renaissance. Siena's leading light, who later in his career would himself adopt a more Renaissance artistic style, was Stefano di Giovanni, known commonly as "Sassetta." A pious, devout man, his greatest works were the altarpieces he painted for the city's churches. This is a wing of one such altarpiece,[28] which we're visiting at the Met.

Like most of the hundreds of paintings of the Annunciation in the fourteenth and fifteenth centuries, Sassetta's composition holds just two figures: Mary and the archangel Gabriel sent by God to seek her willing compliance, her fiat, to God's plan of salvation. That plan involves a very difficult mission for her, and we'll reflect on that later with another painter, Fra Angelico. Here, though, Sassetta is drawing us into something else: the way Mary listens.

The message, for sure, is a difficult one for her: to bear the Son of God. Yet, in his very delicate, gentle way, Sassetta depicts Mary as simply listening. Or rather, leaning—leaning into the Word of God, delivered through the angel.

In most Annunciation images, Mary is tilted backwards, sometimes in shock, other times in humility. Or if she is peering in, she does so while maintaining her poise and composure, focusing with her eyes but not necessarily her body. In Sassetta's altarpiece, Mary's entire body is tilted forward, towards the Word of God. She's intently focused on the angel, or in our context here at Mass, on the reader who is approaching the ambo. Mary doesn't want to miss one precious word. She wants to, and does, live on every word that comes from the mouth of God.

She's "all in."

The next time you're at Mass and about to slump back into your pew to let the lector do all the work, remember Mary and the angel.

Sit up — and lean in. Something very important, a message unique to you, is about to be read. It's a Word from God.

And if this doesn't help, try taking notes, like St. Matthew did.

. . . *And Take Notes*

St. Matthew and the Angel, Guido Reni, 1635, Pinacoteca (Vatican Museums), Rome, Italy

Vatican Museums, Rome. We're back at the Pinacoteca and, with Sr. Francesca's help, have found Reni's masterpiece, *St. Matthew*

and the Angel. By Church tradition, St. Matthew is often painted in the presence of an angel, who's inspiring him as he's writing his Gospel; the Met has one such image, by Giovanni Girolamo Salvado. Caravaggio painted at least two versions, one of which was accidentally destroyed in World War II. But my favorite is Reni's rendition, painted after Caravaggio's and probably inspired by him. It has found its way here, to the Vatican.

St. Matthew is hard at work, writing down the Gospel story. We are years after the events of Christ's public ministry, Passion, Death, and Resurrection; Matthew is no longer the young tax collector converted by Christ to be one of the twelve apostles. His hair has turned silver-grey, his face wrinkled. Yet, the rosy flesh of his cheeks and the fullness and brightness of that white head exude energy and youthful exuberance. He's inspired.

The inspiration is very close at hand. An angel of the Lord has nestled up intimately beside him, squeezed between the evangelist and his notebook. The angel is speaking to Matthew, who is listening so animatedly we can almost hear the two going back and forth as Matthew tries to find the right words. And as he captures those words, he's writing them down feverishly, taking notes.

What Matthew is doing here goes way beyond passive listening. This is active listening! Hanging on every word, writing each down, and feeding back to the speaker what he's hearing. Not just the precise words, but more deeply, their meaning.

Whenever I'm about to zone out, I try to remember Reni's *St. Matthew and the Angel.* I want to listen like this: animated, energetic, contemplative, active. Or as Bishop Robert Barron is fond of saying, as if "the Word is on fire."

And now we're ready to listen to the Word of God. *Shhh!* The lector has begun to speak. The sample first reading is going to remind us of our forefathers' failure in the Garden of Eden. This is a good time, perhaps, to re-imagine that idyllic scene in the left panel of Bosch's *Garden of Earthly Delights,* which portrays the Eden before the Fall.

The Garden of Earthly Delights (left panel detail),
Hieronymus Bosch, ca. 1495, Museo del Prado, Madrid, Spain

– 4 –

First Reading

For Masses on Sundays and holy days, we're blessed with three Scripture readings prior to the reading of the Gospel. Except for special seasons such as Easter, and certain feast days, the first two readings are from the Old Testament, drawn from the collected Scripture readings of the Hebrews. The first comes from one of the Old Testament's forty-six books, the second almost invariably from the Book of Psalms. The Old Testament is a virtual spiritual treasure trove. Msgr. Landry helps us find the thread that holds the whole trove together.

"The Old Testament's central core of readings present the history of God's relationship with man up to the time of Christ. It begins with the story of creation and original sin, and then focuses on God's actions to restore us to the loving relationship with Him that He had originally created us for. It is a history of salvation, presenting the ups and downs of our spiritual forebearers in their attempts to follow God, run from Him, then reunite with Him. As ancient as some of these texts are, they remain incredibly relevant to our own struggles in relationship to God. Throughout salvation history, we witness God's persistent love for us despite all our failures, as He sends leader after leader, prophet after prophet, to try to bring us back to our senses. He repeatedly forms covenants with us, eternal promises within a personal loving relationship like marriage; then we repeatedly break those covenants, and a new solution is required."

"In other words, we seem to always find a way to screw up," I add helpfully.

"You could certainly use that phrase, Steve! But here's the point: God never gives up on us. In fact, through the entire Old Testament, He is preparing the way for His Son. Eventually, God reveals His divine plan to save us and make eternal life with Him possible; He comes down to earth Himself, in the person of His Son. Or in the words of St. Paul, 'When the fullness of time had come, God sent forth His Son, born of a woman, born under the law, to ransom those under the law'" (Gal. 4:4–5).

This story, the story of the New Covenant, is reserved for the main readings of the day from the New Testament. The most important is the Gospel, which comes last in sequence. The other is a letter from one of the apostles, like Peter, Paul, or James, applying the teachings of the Gospel to the life of the first Christians.

One of the beautiful mysteries of our Faith concerns the parallels between the stories and prophesies of the Old Testament with Jesus' Life, Death, and Resurrection as told in the New Testament. To highlight this mystery, on Sunday and major feasts, the Church normally selects Old Testament readings that link to the Gospel reading for that day; all the readings for Sunday Mass, in fact, are carefully planned over a three-year cycle to correspond in this way and to make sure that every three years, we cover most of the Bible. But if you want to make sure you don't miss anything, you can go to Mass daily or as a minimum incorporate the daily Mass readings within your prayer routine!

As Evelyn, Msgr. Landry, and I pondered how to use art to visualize the readings in the Liturgy of the Word, we were confronted with a very big issue: the readings are different every day, and only rarely repeated within any three-year cycle. We couldn't even attempt to think about providing an image for each reading of every Mass. We'd have to present a sample to help us get into the practice of trying to visualize the scene of the reading. To make ourselves present there, to experience it personally. And in that way, to let the Lord touch us.

The samples we chose are some of the most archetypical images of the Scripture readings that take place during Mass, in the hope that collectively they will provide a helpful visual backdrop to the readings on any given day.

For the Old Testament readings, we've selected three representative passages to reflect on. Each is about someone you already know.

Old Testament Reading (Sample 1)

The Fall of Man

The story of the Fall of man is familiar to all Catholics, and the restoration of man from the Fall, salvation history, begins here. This reading is normally read at Mass within the Church calendar at the beginning (the fifth Friday) of Ordinary Time every second year, but parts of the story appear frequently at other Masses.

"A reading from the Book of Genesis."

Now the snake was the most cunning of all the wild animals that the LORD God had made. He asked the woman, "Did God really say, 'You shall not eat from any of the trees in the garden'?" The woman answered the snake: "We may eat of the fruit of the trees in the garden; it is only about the fruit of the tree in the middle of the garden that God said, 'You shall not eat it or even touch it, or else you will die.'" But the snake said to the woman: "You certainly will not die! God knows well that when you eat of it your eyes will be opened and you will be like gods, who know good and evil." The woman saw that the tree was good for food and pleasing to the eyes, and the tree was desirable for gaining wisdom. So she took some of its fruit and ate it; and she also gave some to her husband, who was with her, and he ate it. Then the eyes of both of them were opened, and they knew that they were naked; so they sewed fig leaves together and made loincloths for themselves. When they heard the sound of the LORD God walking about in the garden at the breezy time of the day, the man and his wife hid themselves from the LORD God among the trees of the garden.... The LORD God therefore banished him from the garden of Eden, to till the ground from which he had been taken.

— *Gen. 3:1–8, 23*

We Deny Ourselves Paradise on Earth

Brancacci Chapel, Chiesa di Santa Maria del Carmine, Florence. Evelyn and I are here this early autumn afternoon to meditate on Masaccio's famous fresco of human grief and regret: his *Expulsion from the Garden of Eden.*

Expulsion from the Garden of Eden, Masaccio, 1425, Brancacci Chapel (Church of Santa Maria del Carmine), Florence, Italy

The *Expulsion* sits on the upper left side of the chapel and, with the mirror image on the opposite wall of Adam and Eve in the Garden of Eden, frames the chapel's large fresco cycle of the life of St. Peter. A variety of artists were involved in the greater cycle; Tommaso di Ser Giovanni Cassai (popularly known as "Masaccio") was just 21 years old when he got involved as an apprentice to the-then-more famous Masolino, but soon began working on his own. One of the very first images created in the new Renaissance style, the sense of realism and space created by the young artist, complete with light and shadows and mathematically precise perspective, have made it a "must see" for art historians studying the Renaissance. But that's not why we're here.

We're here to contemplate the consequences of sin. Of trying to make ourselves God.

As told in Genesis, God created humankind as perfect images of Himself, with one exception: He alone could judge good and evil. Perhaps wanting to avoid a repeat of the disastrous rebellion of Satan and his band of followers, God created us and the world around us to be a peaceful, beautiful, perfect paradise — like Heaven on earth. To keep it that way, we simply had to live according to the way God had made us, according to the rules He inscribed within us, which He put in place as a gift to keep us from falling and hurting ourselves spiritually. This was the first covenant.

Unfortunately, our original parents, Adam and Eve, wanted to make their own rules, to decide for themselves what was good and what was evil. They wanted to "be like gods." They took a bite of that iconic apple,[29] the fruit of the tree of the knowledge of good and evil. And when they did, the first covenant was torn asunder. God's original plan was disrupted.

The expulsion that follows necessarily from their defiance is no small thing. Now scarred by sin, they are no longer in a state of communion with God and cannot remain in the garden where all their earthly needs had been provided. To exist, they'll now need food, clothing, and shelter. And they'll have to toil daily to provide it for themselves and their offspring. Moved, we can assume, to something beyond divine tears, God stitches together their first set of clothes before they are expelled from the garden: "The LORD God made for the man and his wife garments of skin, with which he clothed them" (Gen. 3:21).

Some scholars have observed that Masaccio's take on the Genesis story is not entirely accurate; for one, they are shown being expelled without clothes, even though God, as we have just seen, had created clothes for them. What he does capture, though, is the overwhelming grief they share at the consequences of their very big mistake. And he does so in both a very physical, present way, while also somehow penetrating deeply into their distraught spirits. Eve scrambles to cover herself and laments bitterly, with a deep primordial scream that we can almost hear jumping off the wall of the chapel. Adam, utterly distraught, hangs his head in shame as he cries his eyes out for his sin. Behind them, we see a well-constructed portico of a wall, presumably the wall around the garden. Its perfect symmetry is not just reflective of early Renaissance artistic style; rather, it stands for the well-ordered world they are now leaving, as they enter the bleak and untidy landscape of the world outside the garden, the world in which they will now have to try to survive on their own, without God.

While it's easy, with the distance of time, to look back on Adam and Eve and judge harshly their Original Sin, this image also forces me to consider occasions in my own life when I've sinned like this, and regretted like this soon after. This usually happens when I try to rationalize away some behavior or rule that God handed down for my own good and I temporarily decide to abandon it for something "better." The "better" never comes; the fruit that looks so tasty on the outside is usually rotten within.

Our collective failure in the garden, breaking the very first covenant, would not finally be fixed until God created the New Eve, Mary, and through her sent the New Adam, Jesus, to form the New Covenant that we are celebrating today. We'll be hearing more about this when we get to the Gospel reading, but for now we need to try to learn something from another one of our forebears, Noah.

Old Testament Reading (Sample 2)

The Flood and Its Aftermath

The story of Noah and the flood is normally read within the Church calendar every third year on the first Sunday of Lent and every second year on the sixth Thursday of Ordinary Time.

"A reading from the Book of Genesis."

I will remember my covenant between me and you and every living creature — every mortal being — so that the waters will never again become a flood to destroy every mortal being. When the bow appears in the clouds, I will see it and remember the everlasting covenant between God and every living creature — every mortal being that is on earth. God told Noah: This is the sign of the covenant I have established between me and every mortal being that is on earth. The sons of Noah who came out of the ark were Shem, Ham and Japheth. Ham was the father of Canaan. These three were the sons of Noah, and from them the whole earth was populated. Noah, a man of the soil, was the first to plant a vineyard. He drank some of the wine, became drunk, and lay naked inside his tent.

— Gen. 9:15–21

Beware of Spiritual Success

Sistine Chapel, Vatican. The first time I visited the Sistine Chapel ceiling more than forty years ago, I had no idea what I was looking at. For sure I was captivated, as I had been instructed to be in my art history classes, by the sheer perseverance and vision of Michelangelo painting in fresco, upside down on his back, over the course of four years, mostly at night.[30] When I first saw it, and even today, I marveled at this genius, who had barely ever painted anything and then painted one of the largest compositions ever attempted before or since. And while he built on the techniques of other greats before him, he truly invented a new, grand style of art for the ages. Way up high, soaring nearly seventy feet above us, his images seem to have almost been sculpted out of the ceiling. Gigantic and bursting with energy, they dominate whole, uncluttered spaces, proclaiming their stories to us spectators far below.

Still, it's taken many visits since, with some of Rome's greatest guides such as Liz Lev and Sr. Francesca, to appreciate more fully the mysteries of the ceiling. We're not going to begin to try to unlock them all here; today we're going to reflect with Liz Lev on one element that appears over the course of the Mass's readings cycle: the great flood and God's covenant with Noah.

Liz is one of the foremost art historians in Rome today and Rome's best pilgrim guide. She knows the Sistine Ceiling better than anyone. Her energy, humor, and insights, laced with a rich conviction in her Catholic Faith, make her tours of the Sistine life-changing.

As we look up at the main panel, we can see the waters of the flood coming for humanity, which had by now in the Genesis story sunk into a very deep and ingrained form of spiritual chaos. After our ancestors repeatedly and intentionally ignored God and the natural law of moral behavior, God sends a flood to destroy them

The Flood, Michelangelo, ca. 1508, Sistine Ceiling (Vatican Museums), Rome, Italy

and to "start over." The one man who obeys God and heeds His warnings, Noah, builds an ark as instructed, to preserve the necessary elements of God's creation. We see him on the ark with "every creature," floating off safely in the distance of the main panel, as the rest of humanity scrambles belatedly to try to find refuge from the flood about to destroy them.

As dramatic as this scene is, our focus today as we look up is not on the main panel, but on the small one above it, called "The Drunkenness of Noah." Noah's entire story takes up five chapters in Genesis, and just eight verses of one of these chapters mentions the drunkenness of Noah. Yet, Michelangelo chose to devote an entire panel of the Sistine Ceiling to these eight verses.

"Noah at this point is literally on top of the world," Liz explains. "Only he and his immediate family have survived, and, by the subtraction method, he's in charge. God has just developed for him a new covenant to replace the failed one with Adam and Eve and, in return for Noah's obedience and faith, God promises never again to destroy the earth. He's literally in spiritual Heaven. And then what does he do?" "He immediately goes off and gets drunk!" Evelyn answers.

The Drunkenness of Noah, Michelangelo, ca. 1515, Sistine Ceiling (Vatican Museums), Rome, Italy

Michelangelo displays him here, languidly reclining within a tent on high ground, larger here in size than nearly the entire multitude of drowning sinners in the adjacent panel of the flood. One of his sons is trying to cover him, or perhaps is mocking him. The Scripture is unclear, though some theologians say the latter could be taken as a foreshadowing of the mocking of Christ during His Passion.

Looking up there at poor Noah, so drunk he doesn't even know where he is, my first reaction is pity. After all, the guy was trying his best, and he had done everything the Lord wanted him to do. Didn't he deserve a little party, perhaps?

"Well, he was probably exhausted," I mused. "Deserved a break."

But the "little party" soon turned into a "big party" and then a complete breakdown, reducing the once-noble Noah to this undignified mess.

We can't help but start wondering why Michelangelo chose to highlight this story at all.

"After all, as big as the ceiling is, space in a way was 'limited'—in total, the main panels of the central narrative are only nine in number," Liz points out.

It does seem odd that, with only nine panels of space available, Michelangelo devoted one of them to eight verses of the epic story of Noah.

Then comes my second reaction: When has the same thing happened to me? It's called "spiritual complacency." Just when my spiritual life seems on track, when things are going well, I'm caught off guard. And I slip. Thank goodness for the Sacrament of Reconciliation.

Now, I'm back in Mass. As I listen to the often-vivid and very human stories of the Old Testament, rather than simply considering them important history lessons, I try to place myself in the scene. And rather than chuckle at the foibles and mistakes of the main characters, blowing up yet another covenant with God for what seemed like a little well-deserved entertainment or perhaps just a "break," I reflect on how similar we are. And how much, even more, I need God.

We have one last Old Testament reading about another key figure in salvation history. You all know him.

OLD TESTAMENT READING (SAMPLE 3)

David and Goliath

This story of an underdog who becomes a hero with the backing of God is popular even outside the Catholic liturgy. Within the liturgy, this story is usually read once every other year in January, on the Second Wednesday of Ordinary Time.

"A reading from the Book of Samuel."

With his shield-bearer marching before him, the Philistine advanced closer and closer to David. When he sized David up and saw that he was youthful, ruddy, and handsome in appearance, he began to deride him. He said to David, "Am I a dog that you come against me with a staff?" Then the Philistine cursed David by his gods and said to him, "Come here to me, and I will feed your flesh to the birds of the air and the beasts of the field." David answered him: "You come against me with sword and spear and scimitar, but I come against you in the name of the LORD of hosts, the God of the armies of Israel whom you have insulted. Today the LORD shall deliver you into my hand; I will strike you down and cut off your head. This very day I will feed your dead body and the dead bodies of the Philistine army to the birds of the air and the beasts of the field; thus the whole land shall learn that Israel has a God. All this multitude, too, shall learn that it is not by sword or spear that the LORD saves. For the battle belongs to the LORD, who shall deliver you into our hands." The Philistine then moved to meet David at close quarters, while David ran quickly toward the battle line to meet the Philistine. David put his hand into the bag and took out a stone, hurled it with the sling, and struck the Philistine on the forehead. The stone embedded itself in his brow, and he fell on his face to the ground.

— 1 Sam. 17:41–49

David Triumphs

Galleria dell'Accademia, Florence. We're here once again at the Galleria dell'Accademia. Ever since I first visited Florence many decades ago, the art history lover in me just can't escape the magnetic draw of Michelangelo's masterpiece in marble. It stands more than seventeen feet high, towering over all who look on. In art circles, it's considered the greatest sculpture ever created in the Western World, or at least since classical antiquity.

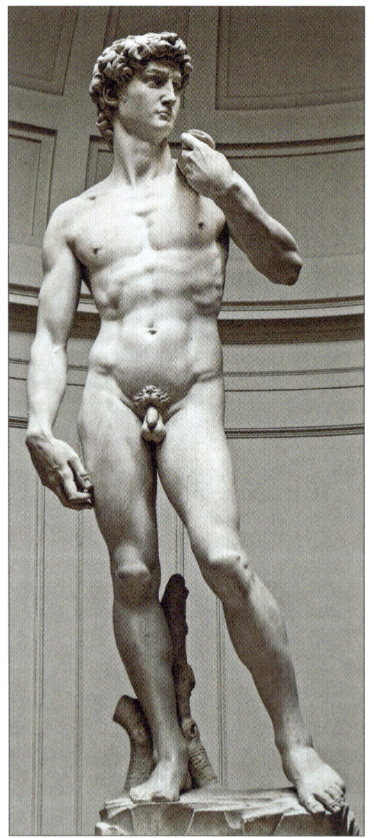

David, Michelangelo, 1504, Galleria dell'Accademia, Florence, Italy

Technically, it's a wonder. Simply managing to carve a block of marble so large, and then creating from it an image of someone standing on two feet in classical *contrapposto* form, was spectacular and unprecedented. Incredibly, nothing supports the weight of the grand form of David but the stub of a "tree" immediately behind David's right leg! Beyond this marvelous feat of engineering, Michelangelo chooses a truly unique perspective: He carves David without the usual symbol of his triumph, the bloody severed head of his opponent Goliath. Instead, he chose a more interesting moment, the moment before the battle.

To accomplish this so realistically, Michelangelo somehow had to convey a psychological portrait of the young shepherd boy, who'd never been in a big fight before, as he faced the most terrifying warrior of the time — armed with nothing more than a slingshot, held casually over his left shoulder while his right hand clasps the one stone he'll have to do the job! David appears completely still, but the veins popping on his arms as his body turns towards his foe tell us all we need to know of the fierce struggle before him. The quiet confidence, the stored energy as David measures up his unseen foe, made this sculpture the rave of Florence when it was first unveiled in 1504, and it has been so ever since.

But none of this, Evelyn reminds me, is why we are here today. We are here to consider the driving force behind David's quiet confidence, his poise under pressure, his belief in the future. More precisely, his faith in God.

David's quiet confidence, which defies all logic given his circumstances, is supernatural. It is rooted in his deep connection with the Lord, as he himself tells Goliath just moments before he slays him: "Today the Lord shall deliver you into my hand" (1 Sam. 17:46). Earlier, he had told King Saul pretty much the same thing during the frantic minutes before heading out to his appointed duel with Goliath: "The same LORD who delivered me from the claws of the lion and the bear will deliver me from the hand of this Philistine" (1 Sam. 17:37).

David is in, what I call in the spiritual life, "the zone." Through a life of quiet prayer tending sheep on the countryside (another New Testament foretelling, by the way), David has developed a very close connection with God. And God with him. Together, David knows they can take on anything.

Like Noah, he's at the top of his spiritual game.

Uh-oh.

– 5 –

Responsorial Psalm

Of the two Old Testament readings normally at Sunday Mass, the second is taken from the Psalms, the ancient Jewish poetry set to music that the Jews used to sing in liturgies and on pilgrimages.[31] During Sunday Masses, a psalm reading always separates the first reading from the Old Testament and the readings from the New Testament. At daily Masses, it comes after the first reading, whether from the Old or New Testament, and then the Gospel follows.

The Psalms were composed over centuries by the Hebrew prophets and sacred writers as a form of worship and passed down for centuries through an oral tradition. They were sung at the Temple of Jerusalem. We can think of the Psalms as an ancient prayer songbook, and when we pray them, it is sometimes helpful to remember how many of our forefathers, both Christian and Hebrew, prayed these very same words. Some of the psalms are songs of praise and adoration, while others remind us of the Lord's work in salvation history, of His covenants with us and of our frequent departure from those covenants. Jesus even quoted the Psalms as He hung on the Cross. We chose two psalm readings for our journey into the Mass. One is a penitential psalm, written by our friend of "David and Goliath" fame. We'll get to that momentarily. But first, a psalm of praise.

PSALM READING (SAMPLE 1): A SONG OF PRAISE

The Good Shepherd

This most iconic of psalms is read often within the Church liturgy: seven times each year during Sunday Mass, and six times at daily Mass, not to mention those times, like at baptisms, funerals, and weddings, when people ask for them to be read. Most Christians know it by heart.

The LORD is my shepherd; there is nothing I lack.
In green pastures he makes me lie down;
to still waters he leads me; he restores my soul.
He guides me along right paths for the sake of his name.
Even though I walk through the valley of the shadow of death,
I will fear no evil, for you are with me;
your rod and your staff comfort me.
You set a table before me in front of my enemies;
You anoint my head with oil; my cup overflows.
Indeed, goodness and mercy will pursue me
all the days of my life;
I will dwell in the house of the LORD for endless days.

— Ps. 23

Our Protector in Times of Trouble

One of the most common themes of the psalms is praise and adoration of God and of the possibility of our relationship with Him. Given that the Good Shepherd started all this by guiding us out of the cold into the Mass, now might be a good time to reflect on the psalm that most Christians can recite almost from memory. It presents one of the great images of our faith, the Lord as our Shepherd — Our Good Shepherd. To see the earliest image of Him, we're going to have to go underground, to the Catacombs of Domitilla.

The Good Shepherd, 100–300, Catacombs of Domitilla, Rome, Italy

Catacombs of Domitilla, Room Q10, Rome. Psalm 23's image of the Lord as our Shepherd, who guides us through the difficulties of life, the joys, temptations, falls, and recoveries, is one that has enlivened the Christian conscience from the very early days of the Faith. We've already had the chance to reflect on one of the early fourth-century sculptures of the Good Shepherd, standing in the Pio Cristiano at the Vatican. Now, we've descended deep into one of the catacombs of Rome to view an even earlier version, from the second century, painted on the walls of this early Christian tomb and occasional refuge.[32] In this version, the Good Shepherd is not only carrying the wayward sheep home on His shoulders; the rest of the flock — representing us — is contentedly looking up to Him as He guides them through "the valley of the shadow of death" to "green pastures." This simple painting of Jesus is the earliest-known man-made image of Him that we have. (The *Shroud of Turin* is likely older but not man-made.[33])

As the Good Shepherd, Jesus stands firmly before us, the sheep, and gently prods us with His rod. Seeing His rod in this context helps remind us of its purpose: not to punish, not to harm, but to lead us to the green pasture of Heaven. He has one of us, perhaps the wayward one, tenderly wrapped around His broad shoulders. Two others, nearest Him, look up adoringly. "Just tell us what to do!" we seem to be saying. Another, on the far right, is already enjoying the fruits of following Him, the green pasture He's led us to.

In today's world, when the Faith at times seems under attack, reflecting on Psalm 23 at Mass, considering this image from an ancient catacomb, consoles me. This is not the first time in the history of the Faith that we've faced our challenges, and it's unlikely to be the last. Fortunately, we have the Good Shepherd to guide us and keep us safe. We just have to let Him.

As much as we love our Good Shepherd, who has rescued us so many times, we humans sometimes fall anyway. We just can't seem to help ourselves. Even the best of us, the most blessed, find a way to fall, just like one of our great spiritual forefathers did, King David.

We were last with King David as he slew Goliath. That was kind of fun. The next part of the story isn't as good. To see it we'll have to hop a quick flight back to Paris.

Psalm Reading (Sample 2): A Penitential Psalm

Repentance from a Fall

Psalm 51 is sung within the church liturgy each year four times at Sunday Mass and twelve times at daily Mass. It's prayed every Friday by priests, religious, and lay people who pray Morning Prayer or Lauds. It is often given as a penance after Confession. The psalm is believed in tradition to have been composed by David as his own penance following his fall from grace with Bathsheba.

Have mercy on me, God, in accord with your merciful love;
in your abundant compassion blot out my transgressions.
Thoroughly wash away my guilt; and from my sin cleanse me.
For I know my transgressions; my sin is always before me.
Against you, you alone have I sinned;

I have done what is evil in your eyes
So that you are just in your word,
and without reproach in your judgment.
Behold, I was born in guilt, in sin my mother conceived me.
Behold, you desire true sincerity;
and secretly you teach me wisdom.
Cleanse me with hyssop, that I may be pure;
wash me, and I will be whiter than snow.
You will let me hear gladness and joy;
the bones you have crushed will rejoice.
Turn away your face from my sins; blot out all my iniquities.
A clean heart create for me, God;
renew within me a steadfast spirit.
Do not drive me from before your face,
nor take from me your holy spirit.
Restore to me the gladness of your salvation;
uphold me with a willing spirit.
I will teach the wicked your ways,
that sinners may return to you.
Rescue me from violent bloodshed, God, my saving God,
and my tongue will sing joyfully of your justice.
Lord, you will open my lips;
and my mouth will proclaim your praise.
For you do not desire sacrifice or I would give it;
a burnt offering you would not accept.
My sacrifice, O God, is a contrite spirit;
a contrite, humbled heart, O God, you will not scorn.
Treat Zion kindly according to your good will;
build up the walls of Jerusalem.
Then you will desire the sacrifices of the just,

burnt offering and whole offerings;
then they will offer up young bulls on your altar.
— Ps. 51:1–21

Bathsheba Receives a Letter She Doesn't Want

Bathsheba at Her Bath, Rembrandt, 1654, Louvre Museum, Paris, France

The Louvre, Paris. Today we're standing before one of Rembrandt's late-in-life masterpieces, a cousin of an earlier painting on the same subject we had previously encountered on our art tour at the Met. That painting, *The Toilet of Bathsheba,* transformed our art tour at the Met into a pilgrimage in search of God, some fifteen years ago.

The Toilet of Bathsheba, Rembrandt, 1643,
The Metropolitan Museum of Art, New York

A Closer Look

The Toilet of Bathsheba predates *Bathsheba at Her Bath* by a decade. This first Bathsheba — mysterious, alluring, almost flirtatious — initially scandalized viewers. Rembrandt portrayed her as a modern woman, and the garter on the model's left calf indicates she was someone he knew personally; presumably, she is the tutor he was illicitly joined with at that time.

Although his audience would have been quick to blame the lady, Rembrandt probably knew better, as she was under his employ. And so his second *Bathsheba*, painted eleven years later, may have been his attempt to clear up the mixed message. Note the expression of the second Bathsheba, possibly modelled by Hendrickje Stoffels, his housekeeper and companion. Had she instigated the affair, her invitation from the king would have represented a moment of triumph. But that is not what we see in Bathsheba's countenance, for she appears to be conflicted, even sad, over what she is about to do — what she has been ordered to do. "Yes, I'm having an illicit affair," Rembrandt seems to be saying. "And it was my idea." Thus, in a sense, *Bathsheba at Her Bath* may have been Rembrandt's own personal version of Psalm 51.[34]

It is 1654 and Rembrandt's life and career have taken a difficult turn. His beautiful wife Saskia van Uylenburgh had died twelve years earlier, and a subsequent, possibly concurrent, dalliance with his son's tutor had ended in a messy separation. A longer-lasting affair ensued with his housekeeper, Hendrickje Stoffels. His unmarried, live-in arrangement with Stoffels created a scandal within Rembrandt's Dutch Reformed congregation, but for shadowy reasons, perhaps financial arrangements, he never consecrated the arrangement with a marriage.

As his style grew ever more introspective and realistic in its portrayal of the messy interior life of his subjects, along with their physical appearances that were not always perfect, Rembrandt's early-career popularity had waned. Commissions grew scarce; bankruptcy loomed. In fact, scholars suspect *Bathsheba* may have been painted "on spec," without a commission from a known, paying patron.

For all this, the Louvre's *Bathsheba* is numbered by many as among Rembrandt's finest works. The mystery here is rich and pulls us into an uncompleted narrative. Before us, filling almost the entire canvas, rests a beautiful young woman at her bath, accompanied only by a maid servant washing her feet. The woman stares pensively toward the maidservant but seemingly into the dark room around her, as she considers the contents of a letter she holds loosely in her right hand. Clearly, we have joined the action here *in medias res*; something important must have happened before, leading to this letter. And something even more dramatic appears to be about to happen; we can sense it in the quiet tension that ripples beneath the surface of what should otherwise be a peaceful domestic scene.

The seventeenth-century viewers of Rembrandt's *Bathsheba at Her Bath*, unlike many standing with us at the Louvre today, would know the back story that provides some of the clues to unwrapping the mystery. That story, from 2 Samuel 11, tells of David's adulterous affair with Bathsheba that led, eventually, to David's arranging the assassination of Bathsheba's husband. Given the painting's title, we are clearly nearer the beginning of the story, when David spies Bathsheba at her bath. But what is the letter in her hand?

David, who appeared earlier as the God-given hero to the Israelites in their battle with the Philistines, has now been appointed king. The Israelite army is once again at war, and nearly all the men of military age are on the battlefields to the north. All, that is, except for David. He has stayed behind, and from the turret of his tower, he's looking upon Bathsheba; he's in the wrong place, at the wrong time. We know from the biblical account that his next move was to invite Bathsheba to his palace, where they would have an affair. This letter, not mentioned in the biblical account, is presumably his invitation to her to come over to the palace for dinner.

Here Bathsheba is in deep contemplation, as Rembrandt helps us peek into the struggle within her own soul. She's just received a personal letter from the hero of Judea, the king himself. As flattering and exciting as such a letter could have been, Bathsheba seems far from excited. In fact, she looks downright melancholy. She knows that if she goes to the palace, it's not going to be just a fancy meal. The affair that is likely to ensue presents for her a particularly thorny problem, for she's married. Worse, she's married to a loyal lieutenant of the king, currently up on the front lines defending the country from the Ammonites.

On the other hand, should she turn down the king's invitation in the name of her moral integrity, he's not likely to be happy with her, or her husband, for that matter. The consequences could be dire. What to do, what to do?

To Bathsheba's left, a large portion of the canvas is devoted to her white robes, symbols of purity and virtue. As she struggles with her decision, she almost seems to clutch them, maybe even gesturing to pull them toward her to cover her naked body for modesty's sake. But she doesn't do that. She's thinking about it.

The maidservant continues to bathe her, perhaps preparing her for her now-pending visit with the king. And Bathsheba doesn't stop her. She just stares forlornly into space.

Around her, darkness reigns. And it is into this darkness that she eventually heads in the next act of the story. She and David are already on the slippery slope of sin, and soon things will get far worse. Adultery, an unwanted pregnancy, and finally the murder of Bathsheba's husband, an officer in the army. In a short period of time, David, the king, will be sunk. And she will be sunk with him. She might even be blamed for it.[35]

As we envision this story playing out, we can choose whether to view it as ancient history, a morality tale gone wild, or to personalize it. I often hear on the streets of New York, "Well, I haven't committed murder! So, I'm ok, right?"

We don't have to commit murder — or adultery — to cut ourselves off from God. All it takes is some premeditated act of defiance to do something we know that is not ultimately going to be good for us and that He doesn't want us to do. When have I been in Bathsheba's shoes? Or David's? And when, in some way, have I sinned like them?

Fortunately, David's story didn't end here, and neither must ours. Once he'd been brought low by pursuing his own passions and desires, David found a way back to God. He confessed his sin and sought God's forgiveness. God, who loved David, forgave him for even this.

David left us the prayer he wrote to God at this moment. It's Psalm 51. The choir is singing it now in Mass, as today's psalm reading.

Have mercy on me, God,
in accord with your merciful love;
in your abundant compassion
blot out my transgressions.

— *Ps. 51:3*

– 6 –

Second Reading

The early years of the Church — including the time when the image of the Good Shepherd was painted in the catacombs — were a time of great struggle, for sure. The Church grew and expanded at an almost exponential rate, from twelve apostles cowering with Mary in the Upper Room before Pentecost[36] to a Church of more than six million souls by the fourth century.

What is often called the "second reading" of the Sunday Liturgy[37] is normally drawn from the writings of the early apostles during this period, either the Acts of the Apostles, the early Church's "history book," the letters of the apostles to the expanding Christian communities, or the Book of Revelation, an apocalyptic account of Heaven from which elements of the liturgy of the Mass itself were partially drawn.[38]

Of the New Testament writings, a key figure is the apostle Paul, originally Saul of Tarsus. Although not technically one of the original twelve apostles, when the time was right for the early Church to expand beyond the confines of Jerusalem, God turned to him to lead the evangelization outside of the Jewish diaspora, to the "Gentiles," or non-Jewish people of the empire. God recruited Saul dramatically, on Saul's trip to Damascus. If you weren't there, don't worry. The story is recounted early in the Acts of the Apostles, and the lector is about to read it to us.

Second Reading (Sample 1)

The Conversion of St. Paul

The story of Paul's conversion is read every year on January 25, the Feast of the Conversion of St. Paul, as well as the third Friday after Easter.

"A Reading from the Acts of the Apostles."

Now Saul, still breathing murderous threats against the disciples of the Lord, went to the high priest and asked him for letters to the synagogues in Damascus, that, if he should find any men or women who belonged to the Way, he might bring them back to Jerusalem in chains. On his journey, as he was nearing Damascus, a light from the sky suddenly flashed around him. He fell to the ground and heard a voice saying to him, "Saul, Saul, why are you persecuting me?" He said, "Who are you, sir?" The reply came, "I am Jesus, whom you are persecuting. Now get up and go into the city and you will be told what you must do." The men who were traveling with him stood speechless, for they heard the voice but could see no one. Saul got up from the ground, but when he opened his eyes he could see nothing; so they led him by the hand and brought him to Damascus. For three days he was unable to see, and he neither ate nor drank.

—Acts 9:1–9

Along the road to Damascus from Jerusalem, ca. 36 A.D. Soon after Pentecost, Christianity—what the early followers of Jesus called, "the Way"—was spreading quickly. The apostles, on fire with the Holy Spirit, were proclaiming to the Jewish people the story of Jesus, the long-awaited Messiah who had come to rescue them. They'd been expecting a political rescuer to free them from the Romans, but Jesus was a lot better than that—the spiritual rescuer, God Himself, sent to save them from themselves and their own sinfulness. He made with them the "New Covenant."

As more and more of the Jews converted, the Jewish authorities determined to stamp out what they viewed as a dangerous, non-conformist Jewish sect. One of the Jewish leaders of this persecution was Saul of Tarsus, who first appears in Acts, leading the execution of one of the Church's first deacons, St. Stephen. They "laid down their cloaks at the feet of a young man named Saul" (Acts 7:58).

Saul was one of the rising stars of the Jewish establishment. Schooled by the premier Jewish scholar of the day, Gamaliel, Saul was a Roman citizen raised in Tarsus; he was probably at least trilingual in Greek, Hebrew, and Latin. Saul was going places. Following the dramatic stoning of St. Stephen, Saul led the first major persecution of the followers of Jesus. Having cleaned up Jerusalem, he was on his way to Damascus, where reports of another Christian community were cropping up. As St. Luke tells the story in Acts, and St. Paul recounts himself in his letters, something very dramatic happened on the way: he had an encounter with Jesus outside the gates of Damascus.

Dozens of artists have depicted this story from Acts over the centuries, including Giovanni Battista Tiepolo, Jacopo Tintoretto, and even the great Michelangelo himself. Most show the scene as it more likely occurred, with a variety of confused soldiers and attendants surrounding Saul, who presumably had an armed retinue with him to round up the Christians in Damascus. And nearly all have an image of Jesus above Saul, to help us imagine the conversation that changed Saul's life forever.

And then, there's Caravaggio's version. It's in church near one of the old gates of Rome. We'll go there now. Get ready! It's literally a lightning bolt from God.

Paul Gets Knocked Off His High Horse

Conversion on the Way to Damascus, Caravaggio, 1600, Cerasi Chapel, Santa Maria del Popolo, Rome, Italy

Santa Maria del Popolo, Rome. We are standing now before one of Caravaggio's masterpieces, *The Conversion on the Way to Damascus*. Caravaggio is one of those mysteries of the art world. As a boy, Michelangelo Merisi (Caravaggio) grew up on the streets of Milan as an orphan, and his short life was often characterized by violence and darkness. At the same time, his deep spirituality and love of God burst through the dramatic canvases he painted throughout Rome, Naples, and elsewhere. Above all, his paintings speak of the battle of light and darkness in which all of us are engaged, and with which he was particularly familiar in his own tumultuous life.

What makes Caravaggio's *Conversion* so provocative and engaging is that he shows none of the helpful contextual details that his artistic forbears provided. No image of Jesus is hovering above, no band of soldiers and other witnesses surround Saul. Rather, Caravaggio presents us with the full emotional and spiritual drama of the moment and only provides hints to the rest. He forces us to participate actively in the story, to fill in the visual blanks ourselves.

As we stand before this great painting, the first thing we notice is that we are at ground level, with Saul, looking up. The figures have been dramatically foreshortened, an artistic trick to create the effect of a figure thrusting towards us from inside the scene. Saul has been literally kicked off his high horse,[39] thrown to the gritty, dirty brown ground around him. His symbols of earthly authority, his sword and his helmet, have been tossed aside to his left and right, respectively. As if to emphasize Saul's sudden fall from earthly leader to a humbled servant, Caravaggio devotes more than half the canvas to Saul's horse, transformed from the steed of a warrior into the workhorse of a farmer for ploughing his fields.

And, importantly, we don't see Jesus at all.

We know He's there. Somewhere up above, in the blinding white "light up in the sky" that is reflecting off the horse. Saul is looking straight at Him, his arms outstretched before God, in a cry for mercy that almost seems to be transforming into a loving embrace right before our eyes. This is happening even as Saul loses his physical eyesight. He'll get that back later in the story; for now, he's blind, but he finally sees. He sees Jesus, in the light. And in that moment, his transformation from Saul to St. Paul begins.

Just as we are absorbing all this spiritual mayhem, I notice one last little Caravaggesque detail that cuts me right to the heart: the man tending the horse.

He's in the scene, but he isn't. Busy keeping the horse from running off, he seems completely oblivious to what is going on around him. He's focused on what he thinks is something more important, keeping the horse on track. And in so doing, he's literally, and spiritually, in the dark.

Most of us have never had a calling from God quite like this, literally getting knocked off our horse. Or have we?

Is it possible, at some point along the way, something like this happened to us? A health crisis, perhaps? A career wrong turn? A failed relationship? At that moment, were we too busy addressing what seemed like the more important details of keeping things on track? Those details probably were pretty important. But did we look up — to the Light?

SECOND READING (SAMPLE 2)

Christian Love

Paul's first letter to the Corinthians, chapter 13, is one of the most famous passages of all his letters. It is often read at Nuptial Masses, and it is also read on the Fourth Sunday in Ordinary Time, Year C, and the Twenty-Fourth Wednesday of Ordinary Time, Year II, during the daily Mass cycle.

"A reading from the First Letter of St. Paul to the Corinthians."

If I speak in human and angelic tongues but do not have love, I am a resounding gong or a clashing cymbal. And if I have the gift of prophecy and comprehend all mysteries and all knowledge; if I have all faith so as to move mountains but do not have love, I am nothing. If I give away everything I own, and if I hand my body over so that I may boast but do not have love, I gain nothing. Love is patient, love is kind. It is not jealous, [love] is not pompous, it is not inflated, it is not rude, it does not seek its own interests, it is not quick-tempered, it does not brood over injury, it does not rejoice over wrongdoing but rejoices with the truth. It bears all things, believes all things, hopes all things, endures all things. Love never fails. If there are prophecies, they will be brought to nothing; if tongues, they will cease; if knowledge, it will be brought to nothing. For we know partially and we prophesy partially, but when the perfect comes, the partial will pass away. When I was a child, I used to talk as a child, think as a child, reason as a child; when I became a man, I put aside childish things. At present we see indistinctly, as in a mirror, but then face to face. At present I know partially; then I shall know fully, as I am fully known. So faith, hope, love remain, these three; but the greatest of these is love.

— 1 Cor. 13:1–13

The Letter of Love

The Acts of the Apostles, which the Church proclaims almost in its entirety during the fifty days that follow Easter Sunday, is teeming with high drama throughout, and the conversion of Saul to Paul is for sure one of the highlights. The New Testament reading, though, is more often from one of the twenty-one letters or epistles of the first Church leaders to the early Christian communities. Paul's are the most numerous and, of all the letters, one chapter is probably the most treasured by Christians around the world: 1 Corinthians 13.

Painting a state of mind is never easy, much less one as complex and varied as the Christian ideal of "Love" or "Caritas." One favored image during the sixteenth and seventeenth centuries, usually titled "Charity," was of a mother caring for three children at one time. The unselfish and undying love of a mother is something most people can relate to in a very visceral way, and a mother juggling three needy children at once communicates the total giving of self that Paul's *agape* or "all-giving" love is all about.

Here at Mass, preparing for the Liturgy of the Eucharist that is ahead, we need a painting that doesn't just describe Charity, but also reminds us of its source. The one we're thinking of is in London.

Charity, Anthony van Dyck, 1627, The National Gallery, London, England

The National Gallery, London. When we first visited Anthony van Dyck's take on *Charity,* I told Evelyn I didn't like it. "She looks too stressed out. Overwhelmed! I like Reni's version better."

"That's *you* talking again, Steve. You keep thinking it's all on you. And that's what van Dyck is reflecting on. It's not all on us. It's on Jesus!"

As in Reni's and most other depictions of Charity, we see her here embodied in the form of a young mother, nurturing three active little boys simultaneously. One she cuddles gently to her chest with her left arm; he reciprocates the favor by teasingly pulling on her hair. The other, on her right, seems to be playing hide and seek with her and just now re-appears with a "boo!" from behind her back. The third clings to her neck, watching carefully what his mischievous sibling to his mother's right is up to, even while pawing at her for attention. We want the mother to demonstrate her calm cool demeanor, but what we see instead is something more normal, more human. She's completely at her wits' end.

And then, instinctively, she does something all of us sometimes do in a situation like this. She looks heavenward, to God. "Lord, help me please!" she seems to be saying. "Help me give more than I have to give! Help me to love like you."

It took a second visit (okay, a third visit) with *Charity* to see what happens next.

Jesus responds.

We see Him in the form of the heavenly light piercing the dark clouds behind her, as she looks up and prays. And we see Him in her eyes!

They are glistening with tears, which might have started out as tears of distress but somehow Jesus, through van Dyke, has converted them to tears of joy, tears of love.

We all want to think we can love unselfishly, like Jesus did, and as St. Paul describes in 1 Corinthians 13. We want to believe that we can persevere through all difficulties with our own wits and strength. That we can just simply tough it out with what I like to call "the white-knuckle method." And some of us can do this, at least for a time.

Except for one minor problem.

In the very process of employing the "white-knuckle method," we lose our joy, we lose our center, we lose our charity. We end up nurturing, perhaps, but nurturing without joy, without love. We're just doing a job. And the people on the receiving end of this "love" know it and react accordingly: "Ungratefully!"

A Closer Look

Many images of Charity, such as the one by Guido Reni that we used in *The Pilgrimage to the Museum,* show an idealized, perfect image of love. All-giving, and, at the same time, calm and joyful. These ideal images remind us that when we can bring ourselves to give everything we have to another, we will find peace and joy, not pain and sorrow.

Charity, Guido Reni, 1630, The Metropolitan Museum of Art, New York

The other way to find Charity in our soul, and then give it to others, is what I call "the Holy Spirit method." Ask Jesus for it. Ask Him to work through us perfectly, to use us to give His love to others. Look up to Heaven and beg Him, if necessary. Like this young mother in van Dyke's rendition as she instinctively turns to God. She's praying to Him to learn how to "*bear all things, believe all things, hope all things, endure all things.*" She's learning to love. To sacrifice herself completely.

The harsh reality is, to "be perfect as our heavenly father is perfect," we need Jesus. Only He can love like this. The way He loved on the Cross.

As we stand before *Charity,* we consider again those puzzling last two verses of 1 Corinthians 13, and an important foundation of our Faith finally sinks in: When we get to the afterlife, to eternity, we will no longer need faith: God will be before us, we will know Him and will see Him face-to-face. We will no longer need hope in the eternal — because we will be there. But we will need pure love to stand in the presence of pure Love. This is the love we lost in the Garden of Eden. This is the love that is within the Eucharist.

The crosses we bear along the way, that Jesus asks us to carry, such as the cross this young mother is bearing now with those three overactive munchkins, are ... a training ground. They help us form the habit of love that we'll need to be in Heaven with God.

Jesus doesn't ask us to carry our crosses to punish us, or because He wants us to suffer for suffering's sake. He asks us because He loves us and wants us to be with Him for eternity. And for that to happen, we need to learn to love like Him. He needs us to form the instinctive habit of love and imprint it in our soul so we can carry it with us to Heaven.

The route to learning to love is through the Cross.

Msgr. Landry sums it up: "The Cross is not so much a sign of excruciating pain and suffering, but of the love that willingly bore even that much pain and suffering to save us. It's the greatest love sign of all time, which Jesus Himself validated when He said no one has greater love than to lay down his life for his friends. The Cross shows us that greatest love."

And the food for our way of the Cross is the Eucharist, Christ's pure love. Pope Benedict, after Jesus' words to St. Margaret Mary Alacoque, called the Eucharist "the Sacrament of Love," the efficacious external sign that communicates to us what it points to, namely the burning love Jesus has for us.

Maybe that's why we Catholics make the Sign of the Cross so many times during Mass. We're soon going to make three more. Time to stand up! Here is the priest approaching the ambo now! Alleluia!

– 7 –

Gospel Proclamation

"Alleluia, Alleluia!"

Musician Angels (from the Fresco Paintings of the Basilica dei Santi Apostoli), Melozzo da Forlì, ca. 1480, Pinacoteca (Vatican Museums), Rome, Italy

As the priest approaches the ambo, we all rise and — except for the season of Lent, when a different acclamation is sung — the congregation sings, "Alleluia, alleluia!" *Hallel* is one of only three Hebrew words in the Mass,[40] and it has been sung as a song of praise to God from well before the time of Christ.[41] We use it here because God, through the voice of the priest, is about to speak to us in the climactic reading of the Liturgy of the Word. We stand to listen to the Gospel reading, in which we believe the living Jesus speaks to us! This is a time for great joy within the assembly and, to mark it, we've thrown in a whole collection of the Vatican's angels. As our collective voice rises to the heavens, we know that they, too, are joining joyfully with us in this moment.

Then, as the chorus ends its Alleluia prayer, the priest breaks the silence to announce which section of which of the four Gospels he's about to read. Just before he begins the reading, something special happens.

Three More Crosses

Silently, without saying a word, the priest makes a Sign of the Cross three times: Once on his forehead, once on his lips, and once on his chest. Everyone at Mass, without responding verbally, does the same: traces the cross upon our forehead, to purify our minds and open them to the Word; upon our lips, to remind us to listen and not talk and prepare us to share what we hear; and upon our hearts, to help us to receive the words with love for God and others. It's the only moment in the Mass where priest and congregation pray a prayer with each other but never mouth a word. And what better place to reflect on the Cross in silence than the Convent of San Marco.

St. Dominic Adoring the Cross, Fra Angelico, 1439–1443, Convent of San Marco, Florence, Italy

Convent of San Marco, Florence. The Dominican Observants, a conservative order of the Dominican friars, assumed control of the Convent of San Marco in 1438, on the at-that-time-swampy outskirts of Florence; shortly after, they commissioned one of their own, Fra (or Brother) Giovanni from Fiesole, to fresco the forty-four cells or small dormitory rooms in the upper floor of the convent. Giovanni's work at San Marco, at once austere and emotionally charged, raised the emerging "Renaissance art" of the early fifteenth century to a new level and would bring him worldwide fame. It was probably not long after completion of the San Marco frescoes that the Florentines, believing the devout religious's artistic masterpieces to be divinely inspired, began referring to him as "Fra Angelico" (the Angelic Friar). He was beatified by Pope St. John Paul II in 1982 and two years later was declared the patron of Catholic artists.

The most elaborate of Fra Angelico's San Marco frescoes were executed on the walls of the guest rooms, in the hallway outside them, and in the rooms of the senior members of the community. We'll view two of these later, but for our crosses, we are now going to visit the cells of the novices. These were the most simply painted of all the cells and receive the least attention from visitors.

At first glance, it seems that Fra Angelico painted the exact same image in each cell: the order's founder, St. Dominic, adoring the crucified Christ as His blood streams down from the Cross. Each image has certain common features. Christ is the central one, literally dying in front of us as He hangs there, the last drops of His blood pouring out of Him as He makes the ultimate sacrifice to save us, His beloved. The other figure is the order's founder, Dominic, who is on his knees, alone, before Him. The landscape is otherwise barren, devoid of any other people or images.

As we inspect the paintings more carefully, however, we begin to see that Fra Angelico has done something very special by painting the same subject six times (the seventh cell has a different adorer, Jesus' mother, Mary): He's given us a roadmap to various ways and attitudes we can take as we cross ourselves each day. All are ways to meditate on Jesus' sacrifice on the Cross and all correspond to seven of the nine forms of prayer of St. Dominic popularized by the Dominican order.[42]

I've chosen three here that roughly parallel the three Signs of the Cross we make silently before Christ just before the Gospel reading. Let's put ourselves into the scene like St. Dominic as we silently make the Sign of the Cross on our forehead, lips, and heart.

First, a drop of Jesus' blood falls onto our foreheads as we kneel at the foot of the Cross, and we cross our forehead and implore Him to open our minds to His Word.

Second, we cover our face with our hands as we cross our lips, asking Him to keep our lips and minds silent as we focus on His Word and to equip us to use our mouths to proclaim the Word that we hear.

Third, we cross our hearts as we ask Him to strengthen our love so that we can fully receive His Word and act on it.

"And the Word became flesh
and made his dwelling among us,
and we saw his glory,
the glory as of the Father's only Son,
full of grace and truth."
—John 1:14

The proclamation of the Gospel reading for the day at Mass represents the apex of the Liturgy of the Word. Unlike most prayers in the liturgy, each day's Gospel reading is special to that day, with only a few readings repeated over the three-year cycle. Mysteriously, each reading speaks to us differently, according to our circumstances and dispositions at the time. If you take notes one day from a particular reading, then do it again three years later, you'll be surprised how different those notes are! So even if you "know" the story from a previous reading, avoid the temptation to zone out. Instead, lean in, like Mary. The Lord has a special message for you, today. To hear it, you have to listen actively.

The Gospels incorporate a rich variety of stories and sayings from the life and ministry of Christ, and the Gospels' drama-filled passages have inspired some of the most profound artistic masterpieces of all time. In curating the passages and paintings we would use for the Gospel reading, we chose for you seven that cover most of the key elements of Jesus' ministry on earth and that appear regularly on the liturgical calendar: calling the apostles, forming them with His teaching, explaining the Faith through parables, performing miracles and signs of His divinity, healing the sick, calming the storms, and sacrificing Himself in His Passion. Together, let's envision ourselves in each story and try to hear more clearly the Holy Spirit's individual message for us as we listen to it today at Mass.

Gospel Reading (Sample 1)

The Calling of St. Matthew

"A Reading from the Holy Gospel according to Matthew."

As Jesus passed on from there, he saw a man named Matthew sitting at the customs post. He said to him, "Follow me." And he got up and followed him.

—Matt. 9:9

In all four gospels,[43] the apostles are called by Christ to follow Him. Some of these accounts are longer and more detailed than others. One that resonates with many of us in the business world is Christ's calling of Matthew, the tax collector. The story of the calling of St. Matthew is in each of the three synoptic gospels: Matthew, Mark, and Luke.[44] St. Matthew's account is appropriately read on the Tenth Sunday in Ordinary Time (A). It's also read four times each year at daily Mass on several prescribed dates, so it's an important one for sure. [45]

Matthew's job was the kind of profession with which a guy like me, working on Wall Street, might identify: collecting money. It's one of my favorite Gospel stories, and Caravaggio's interpretation of it is one of my all-time favorite paintings. To see it, we'll head back to Rome to a small church, not far from the Piazza Navona.

An Unexpected Visit from God

The Calling of St. Matthew, Caravaggio, 1599–1600,
Chiesa di San Luigi dei Francesi, Rome, Italy

Contarelli Chapel, Near Piazza Navona, Rome. One of our first stops in Rome whenever we arrive is the Chiesa San Luigi dei Francesi (Chiesa Francesi), the little "Church of the French," near the Piazza Navona. Although the Baroque period church itself is beautiful, our purpose is always the same: to visit Caravaggio's masterpiece, *The Calling of St. Matthew.*

As we enter the painting, we find ourselves in a dark room where Matthew the tax collector is doing business at a table. A tax collector in Jesus' day would have been something like a spy for the occupying Romans. He would know the locals, who of them had money and how much they made, and therefore what they owed Caesar in taxes. The tax collectors were paid a lucrative commission by the Romans for finding and collecting the cash, and as such the Jewish community considered them traitors who had "sold out" their countrymen. A dark, sinful business. And it's pretty dark in here with Matthew.

Matthew is the older man, finely dressed in the trappings of his profession. He is surrounded by four other men, whom no one has definitively identified. The one at the far left of the painting, counting the money, seems to be one of Matthew's accountants, as might be the older man standing above the money counter. The two younger men are either apprentices in Matthew's business or possibly taxpayers who have come to settle up. Some modern historians assert that Matthew is one of these peripheral figures, but Liz Lev, in her brilliant *How Catholic Art Saved the Faith*, argues in favor of the bearded man in the center of the grouping.[46] I'm with Liz.

Things are going just fine for Matthew, another dark day at the office, when suddenly Jesus shows up, unexpected. Jesus has a halo over His head, marking Him as holy. The man who enters the room with Jesus, with his back to us, is most often identified as Peter, who had been previously called as an apostle. Art historians believe Peter was painted into the composition after its completion, to highlight the importance of the chief apostle to Christ's mission.[47]

The only light in the dark room is coming from an unknown source behind and above Christ; it seems to have burst onto the scene simultaneously with Him. We assume the light is coming from God the Father, who has sent Jesus on this mission to enlist Matthew and who is referenced by Jesus' halo. That light of God is shining directly on Matthew's face, a face that until now has been staring into the darkness. It's the same divine light that Caravaggio would highlight later in his *Conversion on the Way to Damascus*.

I can't help but focus on the two pointing fingers in *The Calling*. Jesus' extended index finger seems drawn from the famous finger of God in Michelangelo's Sistine Ceiling; Caravaggio would of course have been very familiar with it, as would all of his contemporary

Roman audience, so he's "quoting it" here. But instead of bringing Adam to life, that same finger is now bringing Matthew to a new life in Christ.

And then, the ultimate irony. In the Sistine's *Creation of Adam,* a half-awake Adam manages to reach out his hand to connect with God, or more accurately, God energizes Adam's hand to reach out to Him. But in *The Calling,* Matthew, unprepared and focused elsewhere, turns his pointed finger in the opposite direction—away from God. Ambiguously, it's not clear where his finger is pointing; some say to himself, others to the man counting money to his right.

Within this ambiguity, Caravaggio captures for many of us the two most frequent excuses most of us give to God whenever, like Matthew, we hear His call. "Who, me? You must be joking! I'm not holy enough!" and "Oh, you must mean him! His problem, not mine!"

Yet, as Matthew bathes in the light of Christ, that light seems to be transforming him before our eyes. Matthew can't escape the light of grace, penetrating the darkness. It falls directly on his face. "It's you Matthew," Jesus seems to be saying. "It's you!"

Back at Mass, as the priest reads Jesus' simple words to Matthew, "Follow me," I am suddenly transported here, to the Chiesa Francesi. I am in that darkened room, trying to point Jesus in a different direction. And I, too, can hear His words:

"It's you Steve. It's you. Follow me!"

Gospel Reading (Sample 2)

The Sermon on the Mount—The Beatitudes

After Jesus called His disciples, He began teaching them. One of the most prominent of all the "teaching" Gospel readings at Mass is the sermon Jesus gave on what is now called the Mount of the Beatitudes, sometimes called "The Greatest Sermon Ever Given." It's a summary of all of Jesus' teachings in one long passage. This Gospel finds its way into the liturgy every year. It's read on the Fourth Sunday in Ordinary Time (A), as well as on All Saints' Day every November 1 and on Monday of the Tenth Week in Ordinary Time.

Let's read it together:

"A Reading from the Holy Gospel according to Matthew."

When he saw the crowds, he went up the mountain,
and after he had sat down, his disciples came to him.
He began to teach them, saying:
"Blessed are the poor in spirit,
for theirs is the kingdom of heaven.
Blessed are they who mourn, for they will be comforted.
Blessed are the meek, for they will inherit the land.
Blessed are they who hunger and thirst for
righteousness, for they will be satisfied.
Blessed are the merciful, for they will be shown mercy.
Blessed are the clean of heart, for they will see God.
Blessed are the peacemakers,
for they will be called children of God.
Blessed are they who are persecuted for the sake of
righteousness, for theirs is the kingdom of heaven.
Blessed are you when they insult you and persecute you
and utter every kind of evil against you [falsely]
because of me. Rejoice and be glad,
for your reward will be great in heaven.
Thus they persecuted the prophets who were before you."

—Matt. 5:1–12

The Greatest Sermon Ever Given

Sermon on the Mount, Jan Brueghel the Elder, 1598, J. Paul Getty Museum, Los Angeles

Mount of the Beatitudes, Galilee, ca. 30 A.D. Early in His earthly ministry, shortly after gathering various disciples around Him, some of whom He would later send out as apostles, Jesus began healing and preaching throughout the region of Galilee, today northern Israel. Galilee at this time consisted largely of rural "working class" people who earned their living farming and fishing. It was distant from the center of power at that time in the Jewish world, Jerusalem.

One day, out in the countryside, a huge gathering of people came to Him all at once. Some were looking for healing, others were seeking political leadership against the Roman oppressors, and others were probably there out of curiosity.

Once the crowd had settled, Jesus began talking. His tone was quiet, loving, and peaceful. It exuded great awareness of who He was and why He'd come. The Sermon on the Mount absorbs three full chapters of Matthew's Gospel, though the first twelve verses of

Matthew 5, known as "The Beatitudes," outline the key elements. Those elements summarize all of Jesus' teaching in twelve short verses. Many Christians can recite most of the verses by heart; they are that important to our Faith. Jesus' simple words are like His own version of the Ten Commandments; rather than tell us what *not to do*, Jesus focuses on what *to do*.

"What to do" seems simple enough, until we examine it closely. Poverty of spirit is easy to aim for, but hard to accomplish in a world where success is measured by the number of zeroes in your bank account. "Meekness of heart," both in the rough-and-ready world of Palestine in the first century and in today's hurly-burly one, seems more a recipe to get run over than to succeed. "Cleanness of heart" sounds good in theory, until the next Bathsheba moment or racy commercial comes along.

None of what Jesus teaches is easy. On the surface, it seems pleasant and simple enough, but, if you really think about it, it's a very tough message and hard to accept.

Jan Brueghel the Elder's small painting of the Sermon on the Mount captures this very powerful tension between the beauty of Christ's message on the surface, and the difficulty of applying it in our day-to-day lives. Using a technique called copper plating, with paint applied over a copper surface, Brueghel's painting seems almost incandescent as you approach it. He's imagined for his Dutch audience an idyllic, contemporary scene somewhere in the Dutch countryside. A large crowd has gathered. They are dressed in a range of modern clothes recognizable to his Dutch viewers as those worn by the gamut of folks, poor and rich, who might have been at the scene had it happened in seventeenth-century Holland. Jesus Himself is almost hard to find until you look carefully. We spot Him with His yellow halo near the center of the crowd, surrounded by His apostles. He is dressed more simply than even the poorest of the colorful multitude surrounding Him.

What's so curious about the composition of Brueghel's *Sermon*, an ode to "The Greatest Sermon Ever Given," is the reaction of the crowd. Had we been there, most of us would like to imagine that we and the thousands around us would have been fixed in rapt attention, hanging on Jesus' every word.

But that's not what we see as we examine the painting carefully.

Some for sure appear to be in just that kind of focused attitude, particularly the ones closest to Jesus, in the "front pew." As they look up at Him and consider His words, they express a variety of reactions. Some seem fearful, others in awe, others at peace, others full of joy and rapture. So, while not yet fully signed on to Jesus' revolutionary program, they at least are listening and considering. To emphasize their readiness to hear the message, Brueghel paints them within the circle of light that seems to be coming from the heavens above, spotlighted on Christ.

To the right, we can see stragglers arriving late to find out what all the hubbub is about. Or are they standing at a distance, considering the cost of entry? We're not sure.

Those in the dark, literally and figuratively, are another matter. Near the center of the group in the shadows, a man in a blue tunic engages in an animated conversation with a man next to him wearing a red hat. Nearby, a beggar and a young boy seek alms from a finely dressed man in a white hat; had the gentleman been listening to Jesus about being "poor in spirit," he might have been more inclined to help. A woman seated, dressed in a fashionable yellow dress, pets her dog with her right hand while considering buying a pretzel to snack on with her left, and she's not looking too "hungry." Others chat with their neighbors about the weather or some other banality. Some simply stare off blankly into the distance.

All in all, not entirely the reaction we have come to expect from "The Greatest Sermon Ever Given."

Before we pull a Saul and jump on our judgmental high horse, it might be time to ask this question: If I had been blessed enough to be at the Sermon on the Mount, which person in this crowd would I have been?

Or, today, here at Mass as the priest proclaims Matthew's Gospel message, which of Brueghel's characters am I?

Gospel Reading (Sample 3)

The Parable of the Good Samaritan

Later in His ministry, Jesus expanded on His Sermon on the Mount with practical stories or parables that illustrated for His disciples and for us what it means to live the Beatitudes in daily life. One of the greatest of these parables is the Good Samaritan. The Parable of the Good Samaritan is to the parables what the Beatitudes are to Jesus' teachings: iconic and diffused throughout our broader Western culture. It appears in the Gospel of St. Luke and is read at Mass on the Fifteenth Sunday of Ordinary Time every third year and each Monday of the Twenty-Seventh Week in Ordinary Time.

"A Reading from the Holy Gospel according to Luke."

But because he wished to justify himself, he said to Jesus, "And who is my neighbor?" Jesus replied, "A man fell victim to robbers as he went down from Jerusalem to Jericho. They stripped and beat him and went off leaving him half-dead. A priest happened to be going down that road, but when he saw him, he passed by on the opposite side. Likewise a Levite came to the place, and when he saw him, he passed by on the opposite side. But a Samaritan traveler who came upon him was moved with compassion at the sight. He approached the victim, poured oil and wine over his wounds and bandaged them. Then he lifted him up on his own animal, took him to an inn and cared for him. The next day he took out two silver coins and gave them to the innkeeper with the instruction, 'Take care of him. If you spend more than what I have given you, I shall repay you on my way back.' Which of these three,

in your opinion, was neighbor to the robbers' victim?"
He answered, "The one who treated him with mercy."
Jesus said to him, "Go and do likewise."
—Luke 10:29–37

Psychiatric Asylum of Saint-Paul-de-Mausole, Saint-Rémy-de-Provence, France. Evelyn and I are in southern France to visit the small countryside hospital where Vincent van Gogh spent nearly a year trying to recover from his debilitating depression—and where he created some of his greatest works. Raised by a Methodist minister, van Gogh began his adulthood as a pastor of a small parish in France, but his struggles with relationships made him a poor fit for the job. When that didn't work out, Vincent told his brother Theo he would turn to art as a way to find God in his life.[48]

His unique style of "Impressionism," with thick, tactile brushstrokes and brilliant colors drawn from the French countryside, was unappreciated during his lifetime; he's since become one of the most popular painters in history. His most prolific period, shortly before his tragic early death by suicide, happened here, in his stay at this former psychiatric hospital. There is a quiet beauty about the place, set in the rolling countryside of Provence. If there were any place for van Gogh to find God, this was probably it.

His paintings such as *Starry, Starry Night* and *Wheatfield with Cyprus* suggest his relationship with God was a stormy one, even a little scary. But in *Good Samaritan,* painted here at Saint-Rémy, we see something more hopeful. It's a story about love—where love meets the road.

Where Love Meets the Road

The Samaritans, one of the original "lost tribes of Israel," were looked down upon by the Jews of Jesus' day as non-believers and, more or less, as rabble. Though they lived in an area adjacent to

The Good Samaritan, Vincent van Gogh, 1890, Kröller-Müller Museum, Otterlo, Netherlands

Judea and Galilee, relations between the two peoples were poor, at best. They avoided all contact and interaction with each other, each basically pretending the other didn't exist.

In St. Luke's account of Jesus' parable, the Samaritan comes upon a Jewish man who's been accosted by robbers along the road, severely beaten, and left for dead. Already two prominent Jewish travelers have passed by the man and have done nothing to help. Looking the other way, they just kept moving. The unlikely Samaritan is the one who steps in and saves him. After bandaging him up and tending to his wounds, he loads the Jewish stranger on his animal and carries him to a nearby inn, where he pays the innkeeper to care for him. Then he moves on with his interrupted trip.

This is a story about the Beatitudes in action. Ironically, it's not one of those well-dressed high society types in Brueghel's painting who saves the day. It's one of the poor guys blurred within the crowd who's been trying to draw closer to Jesus.

Van Gogh's image, based on earlier versions by Rembrandt and Delacroix, vibrates with a colorful intensity that amplifies the physical energy the Samaritan needed to save the half-dead traveler found in the ditch. The Samaritan literally bends over backward to hoist the man to his horse, using every muscle in his back and legs to keep himself from falling over with the man still gripped in his arms. Although Jews believed it was unholy even to touch a Samaritan, van Gogh paints the Samaritan and the Jew as almost one flesh, no separation between them. The Samaritan's beard presses up against the nearly naked man's bare chest, as the Jew's near-lifeless arms wrap themselves around the Samaritan's broad shoulders.

This is the kind of love that Christ preaches about in the Sermon on the Mount. Agapeic love that gives totally of the self, without thought to consequences. This parable, and van Gogh's painting, are also about the other side of *agape*—the beaten man's fellow countrymen who were too busy to stop to help: me, and you.

We see one of them in the far upper left of the painting, walking safely away to his destination. Seemingly unmoved by the traveler's distress, uninterested in the Samaritan's heroics, and uncaring even about helping the Samaritan hoist the man on his horse. In his own little world, "he passed by on the opposite side."

As I put myself in the scene, hoping I will have the courage and determination to love like this, I consider the times on the streets of New York that I haven't, when I "passed by on the opposite side." So focused on getting to my "destination" that I forgot about my real destination.

Gospel Reading (Sample 4)

The Multiplication of the Loaves

Jesus taught some of his greatest lessons over a good meal. There is something intimate about sharing a meal together, and the Gospels record many such moments: the wedding at Cana, meals at the house of St. Peter, the hospitality of Martha and Mary, the encounter with sinners at Matthew's house, and Jesus' surprising self-invitation to dine at Zacchaeus's place. Then of course there is the meal we are celebrating here, the Eucharist itself, the Last Supper.

Aside from the story of that most special of meals, there is only one other of Jesus' meals that appears in all four Gospel accounts: the time Jesus fed five thousand men, not counting women and children. And He made the whole thing Himself, with a little help from the apostles and a boy with barely enough food for lunch.

"A Reading from the Holy Gospel according to John."

After this, Jesus went across the Sea of Galilee of Tiberias. A large crowd followed him, because they saw the signs he was performing on the sick. Jesus went up on the mountain, and there he sat down with his disciples. The Jewish feast of Passover was near. When Jesus raised his eyes and saw that a large crowd was coming to him, he said to Philip, "Where can we buy enough food for them to eat?" He said this to test him, because he himself knew what he was going to do. Philip answered him, "Two hundred days' wages worth of food would not be enough for each of them to have a little [bit]." One of his disciples, Andrew, the brother of Simon Peter, said to him, "There is a boy here who has five barley loaves and two fish; but what good are these for so many?" Jesus said, "Have the people recline." Now there was a great deal of grass in that place. So the men reclined, about five thousand in number. Then Jesus took the loaves, gave thanks, and distributed them to those who were reclining, and also as much of the fish as they wanted. When they had had their fill, he said to his disciples, "Gather the fragments left over, so that nothing will be wasted." So they collected them, and filled twelve wicker baskets with fragments from the five barley loaves that had been more than they could eat. When the people saw the sign he had done, they said, "This is truly the Prophet, the one who is to come into the world."

—*John 6:1–14*

Boiling It Down to the Key Elements

Vatican Museums, Rome. We are back in Rome with Sr. Francesca, standing before "The Dogmatic Sarcophagus." Discovered in

The Dogmatic Sarcophagus (front face), c. 340 AD, Pio Cristiano (Vatican Museums), Rome, Italy

the nineteenth century, the sarcophagus is named after a detail located in the upper left of the full panel, which shows all three persons of the Holy Trinity creating Eve from the body of Adam. It is one of the very early Christian images of the Triune God, leading scholars to date the sarcophagus's creation to the period after the Council of Nicaea in 325 A.D.

In today's Gospel reading, our focus is on the upper right (see "A Closer Look" feature below): an image of the multiplication of the loaves.

A Closer Look

Images of loaves and fishes were very popular in early Christian art, providing the faithful with an ever-present reminder of one of Jesus' greatest miracles, while also referencing the Eucharist itself. (Below is another example.) Indeed, because this miracle involved "the breaking of the bread," its connection with the eucharistic feast was not lost on the faithful.

Eucharistic Fish and Loaves, Catacomb of Callistus, 2nd–4th century, Rome, Italy

Sarcophagus sculptors, presented with requests to carve multiple aspects of the Faith on one relatively confined space, were forced to reduce each scene down to its essential elements. While sacrificing the realism of a broader canvas, the result focuses our attention like a laser beam on what is happening spiritually in the scene.

Multiplication of the Loaves, The Dogmatic Sarcophagus (detail) ca. 340 A.D., Pio Cristiano (Vatican Museums), Rome, Italy

In the multiplication of the loaves section, the sculptor has included just three figures, even though we know from the Gospel account that there were five thousand men present, along with thousands more women and children. At the center is Jesus, flanked by two apostles, who stand in for the Twelve. The apostle at Jesus' right is probably Andrew, who had come back from the crowd with a meager five loaves and two fishes. He presents one loaf to Jesus, in what appears to be a basket; the other four loaves and two fish sit in baskets at Jesus' feet. On Jesus' left, another apostle, possibly Philip, who had cautioned Jesus of the impossibility of feeding a crowd this large, cradles in his arms a now "broken" loaf, miraculously transformed from the one Andrew gave Jesus. So, as we focus on the scene, we literally are watching the miracle occur, frame by frame, right in front of us. Five loaves and two fish, transformed into food for thousands.

We can pause to reflect on why this miracle of Jesus was so important to the early Christians that images and symbols of it recur over and over in Christian art. Here, the very limitations presented by attempting to illustrate multiple stories on one relatively small stone can give us a clue to the essential elements of the miracle that impressed them so.

The first takeaway for me, as a missionary, is that Jesus wants us involved — for our own sakes. While the sculptor left out most of the apostles, and could have left out all of them, he included two to stand in for us all. Jesus didn't need the apostles, nor does He need us, to perform the miracle.

"But He nevertheless drew the apostles into the story and let them be a part of it," Sr. Francesca emphasizes. Why? "Maybe it was a way of curing their lack of faith that feeding more than five thousand was even possible. Involving them, involving us, in His mission to feed the multitudes was Jesus' way of allowing us to participate in His mission and to share in His joy of what happens when we feed people, physically and especially spiritually."

As any missionary will tell you, the chance to work alongside the Lord in growing His Kingdom, in watching Him perform miracles of grace around and through you, is itself transformative. In the miracle of the loaves, the apostles initially urge Jesus to send the people home, believing that feeding them would be impossible in such a remote place. At the end of the story, their faith in Jesus, and in themselves as apostles, has itself been raised to an entirely new level.

Another big takeaway is the broken loaf in the arms of Philip. To the early Christians, the words in Luke's Gospel account of the multiplication of the loaves, "Taking the five loaves and the two fish, and looking up to heaven, he said the blessing over them, and gave them to the disciples to set before the crowd" (Luke 9:16), must have made a very strong impression, especially the breaking of the bread. It was that phrase that was typically associated with the Sacrament of the Eucharist, the same words used by Christ at the Last Supper and at the Supper at Emmaus.

"So, for them and us, this miracle of the loaves was itself a reference to the Eucharist — the Eucharistic Meal," Sister concludes.

Back here at Mass, as the priest proclaims the Gospel of John, I have one last thought, a question. Maybe it's the question Jesus is asking me through the priest's proclamation:

Do I love the Eucharist enough to have an image of it carved onto my gravestone?

GOSPEL READING (SAMPLE 5)

The Curing of the Paralytic at Bethesda

Another prominent theme in the Gospel accounts of Jesus' ministry is His many miracles of healing. In a very profound way, Jesus' entire mission on earth was to heal the human race. He did so not only on a macro level with His death on the Cross, but also at a micro level, one person at a time. These personal encounters of Jesus with people who were suffering are some of the most poignant moments in the Gospel accounts. The priest is going to read one now. It's from the Gospel of John. It is normally read every year at daily Mass during the fourth week of Lent.

"A Reading from the Holy Gospel according to John."

After this, there was a feast of the Jews, and Jesus went up to Jerusalem. Now there is in Jerusalem at the Sheep [Gate] a pool called in Hebrew Bethesda, with five porticoes. In these lay a large number of ill, blind, lame, and crippled. One man was there who had been ill for thirty-eight years.

When Jesus saw him lying there and knew that he had been ill for a long time, he said to him, "Do you want to be well?" The sick man answered him, "Sir, I have no one to put me into the pool when the water is stirred up; while I am on my way, someone else gets down there before me." Jesus said to him, "Rise, take up your mat, and walk." Immediately the man became well, took up his mat, and walked.

—*John 5:1–9*

Jesus the Healer

Christ Healing the Paralytic at the Pool of Bethesda, Murillo, 1667–1670, The National Gallery, London, England

The National Gallery, London. We are back in London and standing before one of a series of eight paintings completed by the great Spanish Baroque artist Bartolomé Esteban Murillo for the

Hospital de la Caridad in Seville. Ironically, it is here in London, not in Seville, because four of the paintings in the series were looted by Napoleon in the early eighteenth century and somehow, in the post-Napoleonic war reparations treaties, the British got it. It is an image of one of Jesus' great healings, the curing of the paralytic at the pool of Bethesda.

One artistic element of the *Healing* that strikes me right away is the perspective from which Murillo painted it—lying flat on his back, next to the paralytic, looking up at Christ. With this little painterly trick that you almost don't notice until you think about it, Murillo invites us to imagine ourselves as alongside the paralyzed man, in need of a cure. After all, most of us do need a cure. But sometimes we're afraid to ask for one.

As I lie there next to the paralytic, and he complains to Jesus that he can't get to the curing waters of the pool, an uncharitable thought crosses my mind. "For goodness' sake, man! You're able to crawl around begging for food with those two arms of yours. You mean to tell me that over the course of thirty-eight years you haven't managed to get yourself into the pool?"

That's when I go home after Mass and reread the Gospel of John. In the footnotes to chapter five, I discover "the missing verse." Modern "originalist" Bible scholars eliminated it some time ago. They established that it was not written by John and was added to the Greek original sometime in the second or third century. That missing verse, as explained in the footnote, included a helpful explanation of why the paralytic could not get to the pool on his own: "For [from time to time] an angel of the Lord used to come down into the pool; and the water was stirred up, so the first one to get in [after the stirring of the water] was healed of whatever disease afflicted him." So, the paralytic's problem isn't that he can't get to the healing waters, he just can't get there fast enough to be the first one in.[49]

Now I see the point.

While the apostles to Jesus' right view the paralytic somewhat skeptically, Jesus looks with love and compassion toward the man on his back. He's come to cure everyone, not just those who work hardest and crawl fastest. He's here for all of us. And Murillo sees the point, too. In the upper right frame of the painting, he imagines the "one and done" healing angel up in the sky above the pool, flying back toward Heaven — exiting stage right. The Big Healer, the Son of God, is taking over.

To be healed, I need to lie humbly on my back, arms spread wide before God, and answer one question in the affirmative:

"Do I want to be well?" Or, said differently, *"Do I need Jesus?"*

Gospel Reading (Sample 6)

The Storm on the Sea of Galilee

Having helped Jesus feed the five thousand, and then witnessed so many of His miraculous cures, the apostles must have been on a spiritual high of sorts. They were coming to realize that Jesus was the Messiah, the Savior of the Jewish people. Things were going really well.

And then they sailed into a storm. Today's reading is about just that, a storm on the sea of Galilee. It appears in all three Synoptic Gospels (Matthew, Mark, and Luke) and is read at Sunday Mass every third year on the Twelfth Sunday in Ordinary Time, as well as twice at daily Mass. Today's reading is taken from Matthew's Gospel.

"A Reading from the Holy Gospel according to Matthew."

He got into a boat and his disciples followed him. Suddenly a violent storm came up on the sea, so that the boat was being swamped by waves; but he was asleep. They came and woke him, saying, "Lord, save us! We are perishing!" He said to them, "Why are you terrified, O you of little faith?" Then he got up, rebuked the winds and the sea, and there was great calm. The men were amazed and said, "What sort of man is this, whom even the winds and the sea obey?"

—Matt. 8:23–27

Jesus in the Storm

The Storm on the Sea of Galilee, Rembrandt, 1633, current whereabouts unknown

In the home of the thief, location unknown. In 1990, two thieves disguised as police officers entered the Isabella Stewart Gardner Museum in Boston and stole one of Rembrandt's early career masterpieces, *The Storm on the Sea of Galilee*. Although the FBI continues to pursue the case, to this day *The Storm* has not been recovered. Since we can't visit with it, we'll have to imagine doing so with the photo taken before it disappeared. I hope and pray that whoever has *The Storm* in his living room right now is reading this book. Because *The Storm* is a story about Jesus saving us all — even thieves.

The Storm is one of Rembrandt's largest oil paintings, measuring more than five feet high and more than four feet wide. It depicts the scene described in Matthew 8 when, shortly after performing a series of healing miracles, Jesus crossed the Sea of Galilee in a boat with the apostles. While at sea, after Jesus had fallen asleep, a sudden storm rolled in, sending everyone into panic — except Jesus. Once they rouse him, He calmly orders the storm to pass and saves the boat. Then He goes back to sleep. Whew!

As art historians like to point out, one element that made Rembrandt's painting of this Gospel story so valuable was that it was one of the artist's only seascapes, which are notoriously difficult to paint due to the translucency of the water. Rembrandt does so with aplomb and gives us water in a variety of conditions: light, dark, churning, and even still.

What intrigues me about *The Storm* is not, however, this painterly proficiency. Rather, it's how Rembrandt zeroes in so directly on the variety of reactions of the different apostles to the life-threatening situation they suddenly find themselves in. Caught in a sudden storm, they all respond differently.

Broadly, Rembrandt divides the disciples into three groups. In the bow, a group of five apostles are trying desperately to adjust the sails into the wind. They are led by Peter, identifiable by his white hair and beard. Ever the man of action, Peter's trying to get through the storm using what we called earlier the "white-knuckle method": simply grit your teeth and outpower the storm. Fight through it. Regrettably, things don't seem to be going too well for Peter and the group around him; even as we cheer them on, the main sail is torn asunder, flapping hopelessly in the gale.

In the middle of the boat, three men are in various stages of disbelief or denial. One vomits over the side; one stares out blankly with his back to us, down into the bow; and the third simply looks out towards us, away from the entire scene, disengaged.

In the back of the boat, where the darkness of the storm is deepest, we find five apostles. The only light is the one that seems to be glowing out of Christ. One apostle is manning the oar; like the group with Peter, doing everything he can to steer the hapless boat through the storm. But even as he does so, he's got one eye on the only person who can really fight and win: Jesus. The other four are in different phases of surrender to the Lord. One is literally on his knees praying before Jesus, probably John. He's utilizing "the Holy Spirit method" of confronting the storm: turning to God and trusting He'll get them out of this. Another has his hands folded in prayer but seems somewhat distracted by the happenings in the boat; he's looking away from God. Two others, perhaps in the "trust but verify" mode, interrupt their prayers to literally accost Jesus and urge Him to hurry up.

As they do so, the Lord expresses His disappointment over their lack of faith. Then, He orders the wind to stop. Almost instantly, a break opens in the clouds, and suddenly a patch of blue sky appears on the upper left. The storm is already beginning to clear, but Peter and his band up front don't even realize it; their backs are to the light.

So, let's see, five in the front, three in the middle, five in the back—thirteen. Wait! Thirteen? There were only supposed to be twelve apostles in the boat! That's when I start looking at the faces one more time and see something familiar in the man staring straight out at us—it's Rembrandt, whose visage we know well from his many self-portraits. Rembrandt has put himself into the boat. He's placing himself in the scene of the story—and maybe even inviting us to join him.

As I imagine myself on the Sea of Galilee in the storm, after having just witnessed Jesus perform several of His great miracles, I like to think that I would have been there with John, on my knees praying for deliverance. After all, Jesus is God. If anyone was going to get the apostles out of this jam, it was He.

But as I meditate on the others in the boat and think of the many storms I've encountered in my life, I realize that, at one time or another, I have reacted in all the ways they did. Certainly, I've been there with Peter many times, trying to simply fight my way out. "Type A's" like me are prone to that; the sin of pride, I suppose. Other times, I've just been too terrified to think, and have vomited over the side. On other occasions, I've given up and stared blankly into the abyss.

And sometimes, when I've been "in the zone," I've confidently gotten down on my knees to put the thing in the hands of God.

As we listen at Mass today to the proclamation of the storm on the Sea of Galilee, we can imagine ourselves in that boat with Jesus, in the midst of the storm. In our journey to eternity, we've all attempted to still the storm using every one of the methods Rembrandt has imagined for us in his masterpiece. Finally, through the trial-and-error method, we realize that the path out of the storm is always smoother when we engage the Lord, when we seek His help. He's there in the boat with us; we just have to turn to Him — to drop to our knees in the boat, or here at Mass, in the pew.

Evelyn adds, "With a prayer like this: 'Lord, my life is so rocky right now. I'm in a storm. Please set my boat aright.'"

It's that simple.

Gospel Reading (Sample 7)

The Agony in the Garden

The story of Jesus' Passion and Death on the Cross is another story that appears in all four Gospels. "Appears" is too light of a term; the story dominates all four Gospels and collectively accounts for thirty of the eighty-nine chapters included in the Gospel accounts. While elements of the Passion accounts are read at different points in the

Church calendar, these readings completely dominate the readings during Holy Week, the highest point of the Church calendar. When we were curating the samples of the Gospels to include in the Mass we are imagining today, we knew we needed to draw one reading from the Passion accounts, which are read every year during Holy Week.

"A Reading from the Holy Gospel according to Matthew."

Then Jesus came with them to a place called Gethsemane, and he said to his disciples, "Sit here while I go over there and pray." He took along Peter and the two sons of Zebedee, and began to feel sorrow and distress. Then he said to them, "My soul is sorrowful even to death. Remain here and keep watch with me." He advanced a little and fell prostrate in prayer, saying, "My Father, if it is possible, let this cup pass from me; yet, not as I will, but as you will." When he returned to his disciples he found them asleep. He said to Peter, "So you could not keep watch with me for one hour? Watch and pray that you may not undergo the test. The spirit is willing, but the flesh is weak." Withdrawing a second time, he prayed again, "My Father, if it is not possible that this cup pass without my drinking it, your will be done!" Then he returned once more and found them asleep, for they could not keep their eyes open. He left them and withdrew again and prayed a third time, saying the same thing again. Then he returned to his disciples and said to them, "Are you still sleeping and taking your rest? Behold, the hour is at hand when the Son of Man is to be handed over to sinners. Get up, let us go. Look, my betrayer is at hand."

—Matt. 26:36–46

We Fall Asleep When Jesus Needs Us

The Agony in the Garden, Andrea Mantegna, 1455–1456, The National Gallery, London, England

The National Gallery, London. Christ's Passion, Death, and Resurrection, recorded in the Gospel accounts, is what distinguishes Jesus from simply a holy man who was a healer and preached a new way of living life on earth. The Gospels indicate who Jesus is, the Son of God who came to save us. It's that mysterious salvific act that we are celebrating now, in the Mass.

The climax of the Passion accounts is Jesus' Crucifixion, which is incorporated throughout the Mass. We have already visited several of these Crucifixion images, with more to come. Today's Passion reading, though, is from the beginning of the story, Jesus' struggle in prayer in the Garden of Gethsemane. Adam and Eve had their own struggle in a garden, as we've seen. They lost. Jesus didn't.

One of the most dramatic images of Jesus' struggle in the Garden is before us now: Andrea Mantegna's Renaissance masterpiece, *The Agony in the Garden.*

The Agony places Jesus in the Garden just moments before His arrest. The foreboding, dark sky on the horizon tells us it is early evening. Day is fading. Darkness is approaching. Jesus is at prayer in the Garden, speaking with His Father.

"He advanced a little and fell prostrate in prayer, saying, "My Father, if it is not possible that this cup pass without my drinking it, your will be done!" (Matt. 26:39).

Jesus is isolated, alone; the landscape around Him is bare and rocky. A barren tree frames the painting on the right; on its branch is poised a black crow, harkening death. Before and above Him are a group of angels attending Him; they offer not relief, but the symbol of His coming mission, a cross. Sent by His Father, these harbingers of suffering are the answer to Jesus' prayer, not necessarily the response for which Jesus in His humanity was hoping. Jesus is conforming His human will to His Father's. An impossible ask, yet He is doing so out of love, trusting even now in His heavenly Father.

Do I pray like this? Or, when I get back the answer I don't want, do I ignore the reply?

Over Jesus' right shoulder, in the middle ground of the painting, Judas the betrayer and a crowd of assorted thugs and temple guards are hurriedly approaching. His defenders, especially the closest of all the apostles — Peter, James, and John — have fallen asleep at the critical moment. Hmmm.

"How could these guys have possibly fallen asleep just when Jesus needed them?" I ask.

"At the critical hour!" Evelyn adds.

Then we look at each other, and ask together, "When have I fallen asleep at the critical hour in the Mass? Or, out in the world, fallen asleep just when Jesus needed me to help Him?"

One last detail in this painting underscores for us the reality that the Liturgy of the Word is alive and present today, not just a story about something heroic that happened "a long time ago, in a galaxy far, far away." It's the city in the background of the painting. That's supposed to be Jerusalem, but it's not! It's Mantegna's contemporary Florence.[50]

The Word of God we've been listening to is present, current, and real. It applies to us today, in our own twenty-first-century life. We just need to listen — actively. To place ourselves in the scene and hear the special message that the Lord has for us this day as He speaks.

Having heard His Word, it is now time for us to respond. Good time to go back to Emmaus.

– 8 –

Responding to the Word

FOLLOWING THE PROCLAMATION of the Word of God, it's time for us to respond. Sometimes at this stage, we're in a bit of a daze. Maybe the parable is confusing. Or we can't figure out how the readings are connected. Sometimes, unfortunately, we just drift off.

Fortunately, before the Liturgy of the Eucharist begins, the Church gives us in the structure of the Mass some help to formulate our personal response. The first, the homily, unpacks the Word, helps us deepen our reflection on it, and seeks to help us to apply its lessons to our life. The next, the "Profession of Faith" (the Creed) is our chance to respond to God's Word by publicly reaffirming our Faith in Him and in all that He has revealed to us through the Word. And finally, in the Universal Prayer, commonly called the "Prayer of the Faithful," we respond to the Word by asking the Lord's help and grace to achieve the mission He's just given us.

The homily's place in the Mass is said to be of "apostolic origin"[51]; it was probably inspired by a story late in the Gospel of Luke. It was Jesus' "homily" to two of His discouraged disciples on Easter Sunday. Let's imagine ourselves there now.

HOMILY

"Then beginning with Moses and all the prophets, he interpreted to them what referred to him in all the scriptures. Then they said to each other, 'Were not our hearts burning [within us] while he spoke to us on the way and opened the scriptures to us?' "
—Luke 24:27, 32

The Road to Emmaus, Robert Zund, 1877, Kunstmuseum, St. Gallen, Switzerland

Road to Emmaus, 33 A.D. I sometimes like to imagine myself on the road to Emmaus on the first Easter Sunday. I suppose I'd be "the other disciple," unnamed by Luke. I'd have been in despair. The "Messiah" with whom I'd spent three long years, the man in whom I'd placed all of my hope, had just been executed in the most horrific, humiliating way. It was a crushing blow to those of us who had put so much faith in Him, the man we'd thought would be the long-awaited King to save us from the Romans.

When we bump into this stranger, we don't recognize Him and, at first, we dismiss Him brusquely. "Are you the only visitor to Jerusalem who does not know of the things that have taken place there in these days?" (Luke 24:18). Jesus is unfazed. He proceeds to break open the Liturgy of the Word, citing passages from "Moses and the prophets" (the "Old Testament") and showing how those holy writings prophesied the stories of His own life, Passion, and Death. As He does so, the deeper truth of what's happened becomes perceptible to the discouraged disciples. A light begins to dawn.

All of this had a much bigger meaning than they could have imagined. And maybe, just maybe, the Lord is still alive!

Which brings us to Zund's painting of Jesus' homily on the road to Emmaus. At first glance, the painting seems inconsistent with the details of Luke's story. After all, the countryside around Jerusalem is largely barren, dry, treeless, particularly in the spring, around the time of the Passover. Yet Zund paints an almost-bucolic scene, full of bright sunlight and green trees.

That's when we realize Zund is not trying to paint the road to Emmaus as it was in 33 A.D. He's painting the transformed hearts of the disciples, as they walk happily alongside Jesus and listen to His "homily." It's a picture of the joy and light that should be in our hearts as we listen to the priest's homily this morning at Mass.

The priest's homily is the one section of the Mass that is not entirely prescribed, and as a result, the quality is not always uniform. Pope Francis has made counseling his priests in how to give a good homily a key focus of his pontificate. The homily was actually one of the leading topics of his first encyclical, *The Joy of the Gospel,* where he urged his priests to renew their efforts to deliver life-giving sermons that deliver God's words to the people in a way that touches their hearts and minds and become "an intense and happy experience of the Spirit, a consoling encounter with God's word, a constant source of renewal and growth."[52]

We lay Catholics often have our own advice for priests. "Make it shorter, more to the point!" "Stay on topic!" "Give us more real-life examples!" "Stick to the Gospel!" Sometimes, we even choose the Mass we go to depending on which priest is going to give the homily.

Another way to think about the homily, whether it is "good" or "bad," is whether it helps us to have a personal conversation with God and, through that dialogue, prepares us for the communion with Him that lies ahead. As he preaches the homily, the priest encourages us to contemplate a thought or a phrase that struck him from the readings that he hopes will strike us, too. Sometimes it does, and sometimes it doesn't. But if we're listening with open hearts, the homily will almost always help us to get the conversation going. To taste fully the fruit of a good homily, we need to listen — actively. We need to stay engaged.

Or, as Evelyn so succinctly puts it, "Maybe it's your fault, Steve. Stop blaming the priest! Get engaged. God is trying to tell you something through that priest!"

So the next time you perk up your ears as the priest begins his homily, whether with eager anticipation or somber dread, try to conjure up Zund's *Road to Emmaus*. Open your heart. Let the light in. You're having a joyful conversation with the Lord.

THE CREED

(Profession of Faith)

Immediately following the homily on Sundays and special feast days, the laity respond to the Word of God with a prayer that affirms many of the elements of our Faith that are contained in that Word. The prayer is called the Creed, and its origins go all the way back to the very earliest days of the Church.

Council of Nicaea, 325 A.D. Not long after Constantine's unification of the Roman Empire under one Emperor following the Battle of the Milvian Bridge in 312, he legalized the practice of Christianity throughout the empire with the Edict of Milan of 313. Already there were an estimated six million Christians at that time; by the end of his reign, scholars estimate the Christian population expanded fivefold.

Ironically, as the Faith continued to spread across the vast area incorporated within the empire and beyond, differences in practice and even theology had begun to emerge among the followers of Christ. Differences that did not seem to matter during the previous age of persecution came to the fore. To ensure that the Faith remain true to the teachings of Christ and His original apostles, Constantine convened the first great ecumenical council to clarify the fundamental beliefs of Christianity, which until then were summarized in the much shorter "Apostles' Creed."

Most bishops and church leaders were present at the council, which was convened in Nicaea. From it emerged the statement of our universal beliefs as a Church, called the "Nicene Creed." The Nicene Creed built on and elaborated upon the earlier Apostles' Creed and specifically addressed theological controversies that had arisen since, particularly on the divinity and humanity of Christ.[53] The recitation of the Creed by the faithful was incorporated into the Mass as our collective response to the Word of God; it is a statement in full on the question, "What does it mean to be a Christian?" Following the homily, we normally pray as a congregation the Nicene Creed, although sometimes we may pray the shorter Apostles' Creed or do so in response to questions, as we renew our baptismal promises.[54]

To help the faithful remember the Creed, medieval church builders and artisans often chiseled and painted it into the walls of the churches themselves. To see how they did this, let's go back to Orvieto.

Orvieto Cathedral, Orvieto. During our visit to Orvieto Cathedral to see the Signorelli frescoes, Evelyn and I were struck unexpectedly by the depth and complexity of the art built into the sacred edifice over the course of its construction and decoration from the thirteenth through sixteenth centuries. The façade alone, with its four pillars of relief sculptures detailing nearly the entire history of the Faith from Genesis through the Book of Revelation, presents the faithful who enter its doors a kind of illustrated Bible. Within, the frescoes and statuary carry on the narrative, complementing it with useful and colorful incremental details. The more we probe

Façade (Orvieto Cathedral), 13th–16th century, Orvieto, Italy

and study the art there, the more we realize that our idea to create a book illustrating the Mass with art was hardly a new one. That's precisely what the designers of Orvieto Cathedral had already done centuries before!

So as we pray the Creed together, here is the art of Orvieto Cathedral to help us see. As you view it and pray, try to put yourself in the church in the thirteenth century, "reading" the Creed on its walls.

"I believe in One God, the Father Almighty, maker of Heaven and Earth, of all things visible and invisible."

Creation of Adam and Eve (Orvieto Cathedral, first pier), 1310–1330, Orvieto, Italy

In the first pier, which covers the Genesis story, the first image our eye catches is the panel at the base: God lovingly bringing Adam to life from sleep, and then very carefully and painstakingly drawing Eve out of Adam's side. Do I realize how much God the Father loves me, how much care and attention He put into creating each of us?

"I believe in one Lord, Jesus Christ, the Only Begotten Son of God, born of the Father before all ages, God from God, Light from Light, true God from true God, begotten, not made, consubstantial with the Father; through him all things were made. For us men, and our salvation, he came down from heaven, and by the Holy Spirit was incarnate of the Virgin Mary and became man. For our sake, he was crucified under Pontius Pilate, he suffered death, and was buried . . ."

The Life of Jesus (Orvieto Cathedral, third pier), 1310–1330, Orvieto, Italy

We contemplate the third pier, the highlight reel of Christ's life on earth: the Annunciation to Mary His mother, His nativity and the flight into Egypt, the raising of Lazarus, the betrayal by Judas, the sacrifice of His Passion and Death on the Cross. As we gasp in awe before this pier and contemplate the mystery of Christ's Incarnation through His willing submission to death, we stand in awe. Our almighty God, who could have left us to wither away in a world without love, instead sent His beloved Son to us — to save you, and to save me — to teach us how to love.

"... and rose again on the third day in accordance with the Scriptures. He ascended into heaven and is seated at the right hand of the Father."

Resurrection of Jesus (Orvieto Cathedral, third pier), 1310–1330, Orvieto, Italy

Then, all the way up there in the top panel of the third pier, triumph! We see the image of Mary Magdalen and the other women at the empty tomb, with the angel. To the right, the apostles meet and adore the risen Lord. Alleluia! The Lord is risen! Alleluia!

"He will come again in glory to judge the living and the dead, and his kingdom will have no end."

Last Judgment, (Orvieto Cathedral, fourth pier), 1310–1330, Orvieto, Italy

Now we focus in on the fourth pier, carved both to inspire and terrify. At the very top of the pier, Christ sits on His throne in Heaven, surrounded by angels and saints; at the very bottom, and closest to us, are the gruesome scenes of Hell and, in the row just above that, the condemned being sent to an eternity without God. In between are the souls in Purgatory, being encouraged to sanctity by the angel of God, and above them, the just, in Heaven. As we contemplate the reality of Heaven and Hell before us, and in the verse of the Creed we are now reciting, we are reminded that in the end, our destination for eternity is a choice. A choice that only we can make.

"I believe in the Holy Spirit, the Lord, the Giver of Life, who proceeds from the Father and the Son, who with the Father and Son is adored and glorified . . ."

Annunciation and *Baptism of Christ*, (façade of Orvieto Cathedral), 1350–1390, Orvieto, Italy

The Holy Spirit infuses His life and love throughout the stories on the façade, and at least two images of Him as a dove are discernible in the mosaics above the left portal depicting the Annunciation and beneath, Christ's Baptism by John. It is that same Spirit that gives life to each of us.

"... who has spoken through the prophets."

Old Testament Prophets (Orvieto Cathedral, second pier), 1310–1330, Orvieto, Italy

Over decades, four piers were carved for the façade of Orvieto Cathedral. One of the four was dedicated entirely to this one line of the Creed we are praying now: the messianic prophesies. There are so many of them in the Old Testament! As we stand before the sometimes jumbled and confusing second pier, it first and foremost reminds us of just how important this article of the Creed was, and is, to the Church.

"The New Covenant does not stand alone as the beginning of history, but rather is in the middle of it; it's part of God's grand plan for our salvation," Msgr. Landry explains. "The New is concealed in the Old and the Old revealed in the New. It's similar with the articles of the Creed. They stand not only on Jesus' revelation of Himself in His Life, Death, and Resurrection, but also on the teachings and words of the prophets before Him, inspired by the Holy Spirit."

That link to the past, to the unveiling of salvation history, is what the second tier is all about. It reminds us continually that our connection to God and His plan to save us goes back deep into the times of our ancestors.

"I believe in one, holy, catholic and apostolic Church."

Rose Window Surrounded by Apostles (façade of Orvieto Cathedral), 1310-1330, Orvieto, Italy

Sometimes skepticism is so prevalent in the world around us, it is easy to forget how deep and rich the Catholic Faith is. Throughout her two-thousand-plus-year history, the Church, founded by Jesus Himself, has endured attacks, survived, and flourished on the rock of truth. Like the institution of the Mass itself, the Church wasn't a fabrication of a few popes. It is a holy institution, guided through history by the Holy Spirit of God.

As we stand here before the façade of Orvieto Cathedral and look up at its great rose window, the entire institution of the Church looms before us. At the very center of the window is the face of Christ, her founder. Surrounding Him, in stone and reliefs, are the great leaders and proclaimers of the Faith over history: the evangelists and apostles, martyrs and saints, popes and prelates, and of course us, as we prepare to enter the church. Sometimes, surrounded by others with different beliefs or none at all, we can forget just how remarkable Jesus' Church is, and how long and deep its roots extend.

"I confess one baptism for the forgiveness of sins . . ."

Baptismal Font of Orvieto Cathedral, 1310–1330, Orvieto, Italy

The Sacrament of Baptism, which removes from us the stain of Original Sin as well as the stains of any personal sins we may have committed, is the first sacrament that Catholics receive; it's the sacrament that makes us Catholic. You will find a baptismal font in every Catholic church in the world, some more elaborate than others. Orvieto's, not surprisingly, is anything but invisible. It stands proudly just off the nave, near the entrance to the church. It's a reminder to us of the power of Baptism in restoring grace.

"and I look forward to the resurrection of the dead . . ."

The Resurrection of the Flesh (Orvieto Cathedral),
Luca Signorelli, 1499–1502, Orvieto, Italy

This article of our Faith, the resurrection of the flesh, is sometimes overlooked or dismissed by the laity as a kind of spiritual allegory rather than the real deal. It is certainly a mystery, which Paul tried to clear up in his First Letter to the Corinthians, some of whom were expressing doubts in this core belief. "If there is no resurrection of the dead, then neither has Christ been raised. And if Christ has not been raised, then empty [too] is our preaching; empty, too, your faith.... For the trumpet will sound, the dead will be raised incorruptible, and we shall be changed" (1 Cor. 15:13–14, 52). To help us visualize this mystery of the Faith, Signorelli painted it high on the wall of the San Brizio Chapel. Just as St. Paul described it!

"... and the life of the world to come. Amen."

The Elect in Paradise (Orvieto Cathedral), Luca Signorelli, 1499–1502, Orvieto, Italy

Across the chapel from his painting of the resurrection of the dead, Signorelli painted images for us of the life of the world to come — one of Hell, and this one of Heaven. That's what we are all aiming for: Heaven, with our loved ones in tow. Frolicking there with the angels, adoring God above, in eternal happiness. That's why we're here at the

Mass, for a taste of Heaven here on earth, and for the graces we will need to get there — the graces that flow from the Eucharist.

Now, having heard the Word, reflected on its message for us, and reaffirmed our Faith in God and His Church, it's time for one last prayer before we enter into the eucharistic liturgy: the Prayer of the Faithful. This is our chance to put our needs before God, including the ones we just realized we need as we reflected on the Word.

Prayer of the Faithful

(Universal Prayer)

"Lord, hear our prayer."

So often many of us approach prayer the way children anticipate a visit with Santa Claus: we provide God with a list of our "wishes" and hope He gives us what we want. And while Jesus encouraged His disciples to ask anything in His name (see John 14:13), before we rush to do so, we need to put His assurance in its proper context. As my friend Fr. Shawn Aaron[55] likes to remind me, "Prayer is the process of discerning the Father's will, and conforming your will to His."

In the Agony in the Garden, Jesus gave us a perfect example of what an "ask" in prayer should look like. "Father, if it is possible, let this cup pass from me; yet, *not as I will, but as you will*" (Matt. 26:39).

That's why it's a good idea to tune in to the Prayer of the Faithful, also called the Universal Prayer, at the end of the Liturgy of the Word. In addition to special prayers for the Church, for leaders in government, for the sick and the faithful departed, most parishes include petitions to help us all to live out the mission set forth in that day's readings. It is a collective prayer from those in the congregation in response to the Word, seeking the graces of the Holy Spirit to help us find the will to live out that mission.

Shake Shack, Midtown, New York City. It's 9:00 p.m. on a Sunday night and I'm sitting down to a late dinner with a new friend, Dony MacManus. Dony is a skilled and inspired modern artist devoted to the Church and to the New Evangelization. Born in Dublin and art-schooled in New York, he's dedicated his life to creating Catholic imagery that emotes the spirit of the Faith while being relatable to the modern culture around him. Dony has started art schools in Dublin, Florence, and Washington, D.C., and we are here in New York to talk about art and God. As the discussion rambles long into the night, Dony and I, coming from distinctly different directions, excitedly realize we've arrived at the same place: that art, when you boil it all down, is about man's search for God and God's search for man. Somehow, within this almost fourth-dimensional world of the spirit, art is a place where the Creator and the created can meet.

"Steve, you are inside my head. The way you describe how El Greco painted is exactly what I'm doing when I sculpt. I'm sculpting the person inside out. I'm trying to sculpt his spirit!"

To inspire us during the Prayer of the Faithful, where we seek the Spirit to help us conform our will to the Father's, we'll turn now to one of Dony's most intriguing works, *Pentecost — The Birth of the Church.* To find it, we will need to take a short thirty-minute Uber ride to the outskirts of Rome. Or if you're going there after a Sunday morning Mass in the catacombs with a priest, like we did, you can ask him to drive you.

The Chapel of the PRABB, Rome. Dony created *The Birth of the Church* as the altarpiece for a chapel in Rome at the Campus Bio-Medico, following in the tradition of the great altarpieces created for the churches of Rome from the Middle Ages onward. In the spirit of the Byzantine icon painters, he and his assistants began and ended each day during the creation of *The Birth* in prayer for guidance from the Holy Spirit. The result was a modern masterpiece about the power of prayer and the role of the Holy Spirit in it.

Pentecost — The Birth of the Church, Dony MacManus, 2013, The Chapel of the PRABB (Campus Bio-Medico), Rome, Italy

As we enter the semi-circular chapel, our eyes are drawn immediately to the shining bronze altarpiece that dominates the quiet, brightly lit room. At its very center rests the tabernacle, where the precious Eucharist is kept. Just beneath the image of Mary, it seems to rest on her lap. Atop the tabernacle is the dome of St. Peter's Cathedral. The tabernacle references the "Holy of Holies" of the Old Testament, while the dome represents the New Testament and the Church being born at this moment.

Above the church/tabernacle sits Mary, the mother of Christ and of the newly born Church beneath her. She is surrounded by disciples, including ourselves, as together we lift our arms in a collective prayer for the Spirit's arrival. As we do so, the Holy Spirit bursts onto the scene, shooting tongues of fire to each of us. While His fire comes from a central source, importantly it then reappears above the head of each person, speaking to them in a unique way.

I wasn't sure about the figure with wings, on whose back the entire grouping rests; he doesn't correspond to any similar image in the tradition of Western art. To figure it out, I cheated. I called Dony.

"Steve, you're right. That winged figure beneath the tabernacle is not from the Western tradition. It was actually inspired by the Orthodox iconographic figure of 'Cosmos.' Cosmos is featured often at the base of iconographic depictions of the Pentecost event. He represents the world being embraced by the Holy Ghost as He holds the world in His wings. The Holy Spirit is thus not just above the group, He is beneath them as well, supporting them."

Like I said, Dony's work in many ways is in the spirit of the great Byzantine icon painters or, as they call themselves, "writers of the Holy Spirit."

Take a moment to meditate on the disciples. Most images of Pentecost show the twelve apostles with Mary and perhaps one or two additional figures such as Mary Magdalen. In Dony's rendition, he's included seventeen disciples with Mary.[56] The extra disciples help us place ourselves in the scene, as the congregation here at Mass. And each person portrayed seems to be an individualized portrait of someone that may have modeled for the artist, rather than an iconic image from history. Each is reacting differently to the personalized message the Spirit is sending them, even as they pray as a group in communion with each other and the Church—"As a body is one though it has many parts" (1 Cor. 12:12).

So, as we lift our voices together in the Prayer of the Faithful, let's remember to involve the Holy Spirit. He will guide us to ask what God wants of us, rather than what we want simply for ourselves. Then He will send us out empowered to do His will, just as He did on the first Pentecost the day the Church was born.

And here's the good news. He will join us in the journey.

The way He does that is through the Eucharist. The climactic part of the Mass, the Liturgy of the Eucharist, is about to begin.

PART III

LITURGY OF THE EUCHARIST

"And it happened that, while he was with them at table, he took bread, said the blessing, broke it, and gave it to them. With that, their eyes were opened and they recognized him."

Luke 24:30–31

– 9 –

Preparing to Enter the Sacred Mystery

As the Liturgy of the Eucharist gets underway, a certain energy takes hold around the church. The priest, deacon when present, and acolytes prepare the altar, while the ushers begin distributing baskets for contributions to the Church. Members of the laity walk to the back of the church to get the gifts of bread and wine that will be offered at the altar. As they bring the gifts forward, they stand in for all the assembled laity, presenting their offerings at the table of the Lord. The whole church seems abuzz. The Messiah is coming, and we need to prepare gifts to present to Him!

Offertory Hymn

As the gifts are collected, an Offertory hymn is normally sung, adding to the unified energy of the moment. Here is one of our favorites, about giving our hearts to God. We'll be visiting with a king soon, who does just that.

Angel Playing the Lute, Melozzo da Forlì, 1480, Pinacoteca (Vatican Museums), Rome, Italy

"Be Thou My Vision"

Be Thou my Vision, O Lord of my heart. Naught be all else to me save that Thou art.

Thou my best thought by day or by night, waking or sleeping, Thy presence my light.

Be Thou my Wisdom, and Thou my true Word; I ever with Thee, and Thou with me, Lord.

Thou my great Father, I Thy true son. Thou in my dwelling, and I with Thee one.

Riches I heed not, nor man's empty praise. Thou mine
inheritance now and always.
Thou and Thou only first in my heart. High King of
Heaven, my Treasure Thou art.

High King of Heaven, my victory won. May I reach
Heaven's joys, O bright Heaven's Sun!
Heart of my own heart, whatever befall, still be my Vision,
O Ruler of all.[57]

Contributing to the Offering

As we become engaged with the Offertory hymn, we sometimes forget about the hardworking usher with that collection basket! In the early days of the Church, the practice of contributing the gifts extended to the bread and wine itself, along with a collection for the poorer members of the community. Now, our part in the Offertory is relegated to the collection basket, and so what we give has both practical and symbolic meaning.

As we look up from our hymnal, we see the usher approaching. While we are considering what to put in it, this could be a good time to visit with our friend from *The Garden of Earthly Delights* in chapter 1, Hieronymus Bosch. His image of what happens to misers might be a good one to reflect on before the collection basket gets any closer.

Don't Be a Miser!

National Gallery of Art, Washington, D.C. I am here at the National Gallery with a colleague from work. On our way to see a client in D.C., we drop in to the the National Gallery to spend a half hour with *The Miser.* Ok, let me say right up front, *The Miser* is not one of my favorite paintings. However, it serves a useful purpose: I use it to help me remember why generosity with the Lord, and his beloved poor, is so important. It was painted more than five hundred years ago—but it still speaks to all of us, especially us Wall Street types.

Coming to Mass is a high calling, a chance to experience Heaven on earth, to be with our Lord, to hear Him and feel Him; to commune with Him; to be nourished by Him. Another reason is to prepare for the time when we will leave this earthly life, to head for the eternal life God promises us all. Eternal life is obviously more important, but because it's less tangible, less "immediate," we all tend to focus in-

Death and the Miser, Hieronymus Bosch, ca. 1516, National Gallery of Art, Washington, D.C.

stead on the present life. That can lead us at times to be less generous with others, including God Himself. We also tend to hoard our favorite "things," be they our God-given talents or our earthly riches.

Our friend the miser here has been doing just this. We see him lying on his death bed, his room cluttered with stuff he's stored for the future rather than shared with others. Worse, scholars suspect that the goods and wealth overflowing his storage chest were most likely ill-gotten, that Bosch's miser might have been a modern-day loan shark.[58] A mysterious figure, with a rosary hanging from his belt, is busy depositing gold coins into a chest at the foot of the bed, even as the "owner" lies dying.

On this third visit to *The Miser,* as I look more closely at the figure's face, I realize the person storing the gold is a slightly younger image of the same man now dying in bed! Bosch has split the scene into multiple periods of time, a technique sometimes used by artists at this time to enrich their narrative.

Given the unkempt scene around him, we sense that the miser is about to take a disorderly exit from life. Death is near; we see its shadow opening the closet door, coming for him, its arrow pointed at the miser's heart. His deathbed is receding into darkness. The moment is not far away now.

The devil, with whom he's presumably been doing deals for a while, offers him one last bag of gold from behind the curtain, to the miser's right.[59] In fact, the whole room is infested with evil spirits; one is holding open the gold bag within the chest, another is in the canopy, two more are on the floor among his things.

But hold on! All is not lost! God, ever hoping to change our hearts, has sent one of His angels down to the miser, even at this last and final moment. The angel is there on his left, trying to get the miser's attention. He's pointing him to a ray of light that is beaming down from Heaven, right through that crucifix hanging in the window far above.

Incredibly, the miser, though he presumably grasps the gravity of the moment, just can't help himself. His lifelong practice of grabbing the bag of gold, and running from the crucifix, seems too strong to resist, even at this late date. Although the outcome is not certain even now, the general effect of the scene is chilling. "Oh my! He's taking the bag of gold."

Then our eye is drawn back again to one of those devils on the floor amongst the miser's earthly possessions. The one in black clothes, with wings.

As we look more carefully, we see a familiar face. It's the miser's.

That must be his soul, a few minutes from now, flying from the scene, dressed in black — heading into the darkness of Hell. Gulp!

A bitter irony now occurs to us, and we are stirred.

The miser believed in God. At least, he had amongst his things on earth symbols of God — the rosary hanging from his side, the crucifix on the window. Is it possible that even as he lived a life of miserliness, sinfulness, he believed in the end he'd have a chance for one last Confession on his deathbed? That he'd put it all straight at the end and still get to Heaven?

That hope was not entirely misplaced. God loves us deeply and His mercy and forgiveness are on offer to all of us, always. He is so in love with us, so wanting us with Him in Heaven, that if we just turn back to Him in contrition, even if it's at the very last moment of life, He takes us in. We saw that in *The Return of the Prodigal Son.*

He'll even send His angels to help guide us at that moment, as He does here for the miser.

But if the man in the painting was counting on this, Bosch reminds him, and us, of the hitch in that plan. What if, when we're lying on our death bed, when we're operating by instinct, what if the lifelong habit of turning from God is too difficult to overcome?

Maybe I should be more generous now, so the habit of generosity will be more ingrained later, when the devil appears with a bag of gold at the last minute.

Here comes the basket! Practice makes perfect.

⊰⊱

Presentation of the Gifts, Preparation of the Altar, and Prayer Over the Offerings

"Blessed are you, Lord God of all creation, for through your goodness we have received the bread we offer you: fruit of the earth and work of human hands, it will become for us the bread of life."

Once the collection is completed, the ushers and/or other members of the congregation process up the aisle to present our offering — our collective gifts — to the priest as we enter the mystery of the Eucharist. The most important gift is, of course, the bread and wine; these are normally carried up by the laity and received by the priest, who lays them upon the altar and blesses them with the prayer over the gifts.

The formality of presenting gifts to Christ is probably best expressed in art through images of the Adoration of the Magi. And no better place to see an Adoration of the Magi painting than the Uffizi Gallery in Florence, where this image and tradition was closely linked with the Renaissance city's most prominent leading family, the Medici.

Uffizi Gallery, Florence. Lorenzo Monaco painted in Florence in the early part of the fifteenth century, when the highly stylized and cursive international gothic style was at the peak of its popularity. At the same time, the more realistic and solidly three-dimensional Renaissance style of artists such as Masaccio, whose *Expulsion* we visited earlier, was just arising. Monaco bridged these two styles and used them to communicate images of both great style and visual appeal, while also projecting a presence here on earth.

When you overlay all this with his early training as a manuscript illustrator, you get a third dimension that makes standing before a fully cleaned and restored Monaco a thrilling experience. We have a magnificent Monaco at the Met that we use on our pilgrimage there, but it has yet to be cleaned and fully restored. Imagine my surprise when Evelyn and I arrived before the image we now have upon us; fully restored, four feet high and six feet wide, it literally bursts off the wall, shimmering with life and color. The perfect antidote to *The Miser.*

Giving with Humility and Love

Adoration of the Magi, Lorenzo Monaco, 1420–1422, Uffizi Gallery, Florence, Italy

In Monaco's *Adoration of the Magi,* the kings from Matthew's Gospel (Matt. 2:1–3) have arrived at last following their long journey from the east and their unsettling meeting with Herod. They are accompanied by a retinue befitting their worldly status, and Monaco's exotic depiction of the entourage emphasizes just how far they've travelled.

Although the scene immediately before us is soaked in a bright light that sparkles off the colorful cloaks of the kings and their retinue, we know that light is supernatural and divine; the darkness of the distant landscape from whence the kings travelled tells us that. A new era dawns. In the distant dark on the mountainside, we can see the angel Gabriel awakening the shepherds, proclaiming the birth of the Christ.

The three kings have clearly come from a great distance to find the long-awaited Christ. The emotions of love and adoration in their facial expressions, along with the variety of attitudes and postures of the people in the retinue, leave us with the impression that the group represents all of humanity — including us.

Interestingly, it's the oldest — and presumably the most important — who's leading the way. He's the first to kneel before Jesus, the true King, the King of Kings. As he does so, we can see that he's been generous. That unidentified gift he's placed before the Lord would surely have cost "a king's ransom." According to Church tradition, the first of the three gifts was gold, a symbol of Jesus' kingship; followed by frankincense, a symbol of His divinity; then myrrh, a reference to His coming Passion and His mortality. Monaco's fellow Florentines would have known all three to be wildly valuable.

That's when I notice the crown, or rather, don't notice the crown. The ultimate symbol of worldly wealth and power, it's not on the king's bald head as he kneels before the Lord. Where is it?

Evelyn spots it first. "There it is Steve, on the ground to his left! He's taken off his crown to adore the true King! He's left it in the dirt!"

Now I see it. On the ground by Joseph's feet. The king has tossed it aside. It's of no use to him now. He has found his North Star, Jesus. No need for a crown. He's given his heart to Christ.

As the gifts are presented on the altar, and just as I'm congratulating myself for the fat check I just put in the basket, I imagine that king and his gift. Am I prepared to give my heart to Jesus?

As I respond to the priest's prayer over the gifts, I pray for my heart to be as "all in" as we acclaim,

"Blessed be God forever."

THE WASHING OF HANDS

(Ablutions)

"Wash me, O Lord, from my iniquity and cleanse me from my sin."

Having received our gifts in front of the altar, the priest performs a rite that many of us overlook during the Mass: He washes his hands with water. The ritual washing of the hands by the priest is a custom that dates from before Christ and was a practice common among the Jewish priests as they entered the "Holy of Holies" in the Temple.[60]

At the first Mass, the Last Supper, Jesus carries the washing with water even further, symbolically washing the feet of the apostles. As He explains to Peter, this is to ensure that they are not only physically clean, but also spiritually pure, before entering the mystery of the Eucharist (John 13:10). In some ways, then, the ritual of the priest washing his hands is a reenactment of the Sacrament of Baptism itself, when the priest uses the holy water to purify the soul and wash away the stain of sin.[61]

Fortunately, we're in Florence at the Uffizi — just a few galleries away from one of the most famous paintings of the most famous Baptism that ever happened. Let's rush over there now.

Da Vinci rooms, Uffizi Gallery. Poor Andrea del Verrocchio. For one of his most famous works, *The Baptism of Christ,* he will forever share credit with one of his young pupils who aided him in the work, Leonardo da Vinci. Art historians love this kind of stuff and argue forever about which elements of *The Baptism* were born from the youthful hand of da Vinci. Most of them see da Vinci's emerging style in the kneeling angel on the far left of the panel. Evelyn did, too.

"Steve, it must be the angel on the left! She is so exquisitely drawn. So beautiful, so joyful, so innocent. She's a perfect little angel."

The Baptism of Christ, Andrea del Verrocchio and Leonardo da Vinci, 1472–1475, Uffizi Gallery, Florence, Italy

I had to agree. The delicate and soft "sfumato" manner he has painted her face and hair seems quite similar to his later, independent work, such as the *Mona Lisa*. Ditto the fading atmospherics of the distant landscape. Within the studio of a major artist such as Verrocchio at the time, it would not have been unusual to hand off peripheral figures, such as the angel or background landscapes, to an apprentice. He just wasn't supposed to outdo the master!

Returning my attention to the painting, I could certainly see some similarities with the faces and hair of both the angel and Mary in his *Annunciation*, his first solo act. "Let's go see it," I say to my wife. "It's hanging right over here, and it was painted at almost the same time." *The Annunciation*, painted shortly after his contribution to *The Baptism*, now hangs in the same gallery. Viewed side by side, it is easy to see da Vinci's hand in *The Baptism*'s angel.

The Annunciation, Leonardo da Vinci, 1472, Uffizi Gallery, Florence, Italy

Once resolving this issue, we begin to settle down and take in the whole exquisite composition of *The Baptism*. One of the first Florentine paintings to use the new medium of oil that had been popularized in the Netherlands, *The Baptism* has a richness and depth to it that the more traditional fresco technique sometimes lacks. Perfect to reflect on as we're watching the priest wash his hands to prepare for the coming miracle of the Eucharist.

Christ is about to begin His ministry. He has arrived at the Jordan River to be baptized by John who, as the final prophet before the coming of the Messiah, has been sent to Judea to prepare the Jews for Jesus' coming. He is calling for them to repent and be cleansed in the Jordan by a ritual Baptism.

The sinless Christ is in no need of repentance, but nevertheless asks John to baptize Him. John reluctantly agrees. This humble act both acknowledges and blesses John, while also serving as an example and witness to us all. If even Christ asked for a Baptism, what does that say about the rest of us? And does it not infuse new meaning to this moment of the Mass, when we witness Christ's priests washing their hands with the water of grace?

The clarity and richness of Verrocchio's composition pull us quickly into this scene. Both Christ and John are standing in the clear, pure waters of the Jordan. Jesus is posed humbly, with His legs tilted towards John as He bows and prays to His Father for what He needs to fulfill His coming mission. John's legs are spread, as if to brace himself for the impossible task of "baptizing" God; his facial expression is one of determination and focus to do the best possible job he can. (Can you imagine what this must have been like? Talk about a "clutch moment!")

John, Jesus, and the two little angels all bear halos, but only the Lord's has within it a red cross, referencing His coming mission, Passion, and Death. Likewise, the palm tree on Jesus' right and the evergreens on His left refer to salvation and eternal life, respectively. The scene appears to be taking place at dawn, the dawn of a new age.

As John pours the water over Jesus' head, the hands of God the Father above them send the Holy Spirit towards Jesus; only He can truly anoint the Son of God. John is just an instrument.

Then God the Father bestows the blessing; His words are referenced on the scroll hanging from John's cane:

"This is my beloved Son, with whom I am well pleased."
—Matt. 3:17

After the washing of hands, the priest is ready to enter the sacred mystery. We send him off with one last communal prayer:

"May the Lord accept the sacrifice at your hands, for the praise and glory of his name, for our good and the good of all his holy Church."

– 10 –

Sacrifice and Triumph

The Eucharistic Prayer

We have now entered the most sacred part of the Mass: The Eucharistic Prayer, when the bread and wine are transformed into the sacred Body and Blood of Christ. As transubstantiation occurs, Christ's sacrifice on the Cross and His triumph over death is relived across time and space, into the present moment.

As a lay person, I sometimes get mixed up as the priest prays the series of prayers that make up the "Eucharistic Prayer." The Church calls for different versions of each prayer at particular times of the liturgical season, and the celebrant has discretion as to which version of the Eucharistic Prayer he uses. For these reflections, we will draw on expressions from various Eucharistic Prayers, making note of them as we do.

As the Eucharistic Prayer begins, the priest urges the laity to lift our hearts up to God. Our Lord and God is in Heaven. We are on earth. And soon we will be together in the sacrifice on the altar. This first part of the Eucharistic Prayer is called the "Preface." It begins with a familiar dialogue between us and the priest, the same at every Mass, and concludes with a final prayer that varies according to which Preface is being used that day. Its purpose, from apostolic times, is to introduce the Liturgy of the Eucharist and focus all of us on the coming mystery.[62]

PREFACE

"The Lord be with you."

"And with your spirit."

"Lift up your hearts."

"We lift them up to the Lord."

"Let us give thanks to the Lord, our God."

"It is right and just."

"It is truly right and just, our duty and our salvation,
always and everywhere to give you thanks,
Lord, holy Father, almighty and eternal God,
through Christ our Lord."

Over lunch in Rome, Evelyn and I discussed with Sr. Francesca the best image to focus our minds and hearts on during this important moment in the Mass. Sister insisted on Raphael's masterpiece, *Disputation of the Holy Sacrament*. "Steve, this painting above all others incorporates the entire theological underpinnings of the Eucharist. You must start there!"

Since Catholic grammar school, I learned never to disagree with a nun. So off we go with Sr. Francesca to see the *Disputation*, still on the wall onto which Raphael frescoed it in the "Room of the Signature" in the Vatican Palace.

Room of the Signature, Rome, ca. 1510. Rome was absolutely bustling in 1510, and no place was bustling more than the Vatican. Pope Julius II, a noted patron of the Renaissance arts, was determined to rebuild Catholic Rome with more grandeur than its imperial past and had called to Rome most of the great Italian artists of the day to participate in the project. Michelangelo, whose *David* had made him famous but who had scarcely ever painted anything, was assigned the task of painting the expansive ceiling of the Sistine Chapel. And Raphael, his fellow Florentine and artistic rival, was assigned the task of painting Julius II's apartments, just a short distance away within the Vatican complex.

Unlike Michelangelo, Raphael was a natural painter. He had a linear style of drawing his subjects, then painting them as idealized images of their true selves, that made him the master of the painters of his generation. His paintings were orderly, symmetrical, and harmonious. He painted perfection, perfectly. Everything fit together precisely. On some level, Raphael was painting creation through the eyes of God, a creation that was perfect, balanced, complete.

But I do need to admit something before we get too far into the *Disputation*. Something I didn't admit to Sr. Francesca.

I find Raphael a little boring.

A little *too* symmetrical, a little *too* staged, a little *too* academic.

Boring or not, Raphael's fresco serves us well as we pray the Preface and enter the mystery of the Eucharist. In fact, it was designed by Raphael, with his patron Pope Julius II, to explain the theological underpinnings of the mystery.

By way of context, the *Disputation* is frescoed onto one of the four walls of the room that at the time was the pope's office. Directly across from it is the equally famous *School of Athens*, which portrays all the great classical and medieval scholars in search of ultimate truth through the study of philosophy. The outcome of all this study and discourse was ultimately the classical virtues that were adopted into the Catholic faith and that brought mankind part of the way towards the discovery of God: prudence, justice, fortitude, and temperance.

"But the classical philosophers could only get mankind so far. They needed Christ for the rest," Sr. Francesca explains. "While they concluded from observing the world that there must be a god of some kind behind it, it is only through Divine Revelation that we know the truth about God: that He is Father, Son, and Holy Spirit and that in that Host there is the Real Presence of Christ. This

School of Athens, Raphael, 1508–1511, Room of the Signature (Vatican Museums), Rome, Italy

miracle comes about through transubstantiation that occurs during the Holy Mass through the power of the Holy Spirit. This Revelation is what Raphael is imagining for us here in the *Disputation*."

The *Disputation of the Holy Sacrament* is Raphael's painting of the theology of the Eucharist. At the very heart of Catholic theology is Jesus Christ, both in Heaven in His resurrected body, and on earth in His eucharistic presence.

As we stand before the *Disputation*, having reviewed *School of Athens* and now with our backs to it, we can see visually that Raphael has divided the composition horizontally, using a bank of clouds. Above the clouds, Christ reigns in Heaven with God the Father immediately above Him. Jesus is surrounded by the prophets, apostles, and saints who each played a role over the course of salvation history in preparing the world for Christ or in proclaiming His gospel. Some of the particular saints included with Christ here seem obvious.

For example, St. Peter, the first pope, on Christ's far right, holding the keys to Heaven; John the Evangelist, the unbearded, second person to Peter's left, writing his Gospel; Moses, the fourth person

Disputation of the Holy Sacrament, Raphael, 1508–1511, Room of the Signature (Vatican Museums), Rome, Italy

to Jesus' right, with the horns of light on his head and holding the Ten Commandments; and St. Paul, on Jesus' far left, holding the sword of his martyrdom. Others up in the clouds of Heaven surrounding Jesus seem less obvious, where Raphael seems to be making a theological point. For instance, Adam is up there (right next to St. Peter). He's the first sinner, but also the first man to touch God, who we all touch in some way when we receive the Eucharist. Orthodox Christians believe Jesus raised him to Heaven when He descended into Hell in the period between His Crucifixion and Resurrection.

Evelyn and I notice that the Holy Spirit, represented by the dove, does not fly between the Father and Son, as He does in *The Baptism* and as He is normally depicted, but instead flies from Jesus down towards the earth, where Jesus is again present, this time in the Eucharist on the altar. Surrounding the Eucharist on the altar are a variety of theologians and clergy who historically played a role in expounding on the truth of the eucharistic presence, such as St. Ambrose and St. Augustine, as well as others of Raphael's present day, some famous, some everyday laity. Collectively, we below represent the Church Militant, the Body of Christ, discussing with the intent of discerning and teaching the true meaning of the Eucharist and Christ's presence within it. This truth of transubstantiation, the transformation of the Host from a mere wafer of bread to Christ Himself through the sacrifice of the Mass, is being discussed and agreed to by the assembled theologians and clergy.[63]

Disputations have been written about the *Disputation*, particularly about the various people and saints included, and not included, in the image. For our purposes, I want to focus on the Holy Spirit and where He appears. Some scholars have asserted that the dove seems placed in the "wrong spot on the painting." But is He really misplaced? The Holy Spirit is in many ways "the linking verb" of the Faith, the personal Love between the Father and the Son, and the personal Love between the Son and us. Jesus Himself told the apostles, "I will ask the Father, and he will give you another Advocate to be with you always" (John 14:16).

It is the power of the Holy Spirit, working through the ordained priest, that makes possible the total change of the bread and wine into Jesus' Body and Blood. He's the one who makes possible the Eucharist as the Sacrament of Love.

As I meditate on the Holy Spirit flying from Jesus with the Father in Heaven down to the Eucharist with us on earth, I start to see Raphael's point, and it isn't boring at all. Tentatively, I try my explanation on Sr. Francesca.

"The Eucharist is Jesus' sacrifice of Himself. Pure love. The love of God the Father and Jesus the Son for us the sinners. And that love is with us now, in the Mass. It will become our spiritual food."

"So as God's love comes down from Heaven to earth, it is appropriate indeed for us to respond by lifting up our hearts to Him, up there, in the clouds," Evelyn finishes my thought.

"You've got it!" Sister beams. "The philosophers, looking at the world, can only go so far with their reason. They need Divine Revelation to contemplate the full truth about God. That God, who is pure Love, is with us always; He reigns in Heaven and is present with us on earth, in the Eucharist."

That's when it dawns on me that another way to think about the *Disputation,* hanging there across the room from the *School of Athens,* relates back to the virtues themselves. For sure, the great ancient philosophers could discover most of them on their own from observing the world: prudence, self-mastery, integrity. But it is only in Christ, in the Eucharist, that we can discover the virtues that will help us get to Heaven.

It's only in Him that we can find faith, hope, and love. This is the gift we are about to receive in Holy Communion.

And it's perfect.

Holy, Holy, Holy

(*The Sanctus*)

At the end of the Preface, the priest invites us into the great hymn of praise to the Lord, the "Sanctus."

> ***"And so, with Angels and Archangels, with Thrones and Dominions, and with all the hosts and powers of heaven, we sing the hymn of your glory, as without end we acclaim:"*** [64]

"Holy, Holy, Holy
Lord God of Hosts!
Heaven and earth are full of your glory!
Hosanna in the highest!
Blessed is he who comes
in the name of the Lord.
Hosanna in the highest."

The Adoration of the Shepherds, El Greco, 1612–1614, Museo del Prado, Madrid, Spain

Concluding the Preface is a prayer called "The Sanctus," the Latin word for "Holy."[65] These words are partially taken from a vision the prophet Isaiah saw of special angels called seraphim around God's throne. This prayer helps us to glimpse what Isaiah saw, what the angels see, and what is really taking place in the Eucharistic liturgy.[66]

No one could paint us mere humans singing with the Lord's angels more beautifully than El Greco. In some ways, he made a career of it. To see the painting I have in mind, we'll need to head back to Madrid.

A Holy Night

Museo del Prado, Madrid. We are in the Prado and standing before El Greco's last painting, *The Adoration of the Shepherds*. He painted *The Adoration* just before he died in 1614 for his tomb at Santo Domingo in Madrid. The Met has the smaller version of it.

Right away, Evelyn and I spot some key differences that jump at us. But let's set the scene first. It's night. It's dark. A group of humble shepherds, sinners like us, have been called by an angel to witness the birth of Jesus. They've arrived after a short trip from the hill-sides and found Jesus just where they'd been told He would be, outside of what looks like a cave. Mary is there, in the dark with Jesus, just as three shepherds arrive. The only source of light is Jesus Himself; an ethereal, spiritual light is shining out of Him, drawing all toward Him.

The shepherds express awe and wonder as they adore the newly arrived Lord. As they join with the angels above them in praise, their elongated, ethereal forms seem caught somewhere between Heaven and earth. For a moment, Heaven and earth are united, joined in the person of Jesus Himself, shining on them all with His divine light.

Even at this moment of Jesus' dramatic arrival, El Greco reminds us of Christ's mission and His role in the Mass we are now celebrating: the Lamb. Can you see it? It's lying prostrate on its side at the feet of the shepherd on the lower right of the canvas. So we are here now before the altar, joining with the angels before the Lamb of God Himself.

A Closer Look

The Adoration of the Shepherds, El Greco, 1605–1610, The Metropolitan Museum of Art, New York

The Metropolitan's version of the adoration of the shepherds was painted in El Greco's studio in Toledo in preparation for the larger altarpiece which was destined for his tomb and now hangs at the Prado. The earlier version is beautiful in its own right and is instructive for what El Greco added to the composition on his final attempt, painted in his last year of life.

Oh, about those differences between the studio version and the final product. In the final version, completed just before his death, El Greco decided to add a couple more angels to the painting, larger and more spectacular than the three smaller ones at the very top. These last two angels, one in red on the left and one in gold on the right, the colors of the Lord's Passion and of His triumph, are swirling around the tightly compressed scene. They are almost indistinguishable from the shepherds, but for their wings and, well, angelic faces.

Then El Greco made one last change after the extra angels: he added himself.

He's there, kneeling humbly in front before the Lord, sporting the sharply pointed beard that was his trademark. We recognize him from *The Pentecost* we saw earlier during the Introductory Rites. El Greco is joining with us in joyful, pious praise. With his final breaths, he almost seems to be singing with us, "Holy, holy, holy!"

We're ready now for the changing of the bread and wine into the Body and Blood of Christ. Time to drop to our knees, alongside El Greco.

The Invocation of the Holy Spirit

(Epiclesis)

The first prayer after the congregation kneels, just before the transubstantiation of the bread and wine, is the priest's prayer of thanksgiving, followed immediately by a simple but profound invocation of the Holy Spirit.

"Make holy, therefore these gifts, we pray, by sending down your Spirit upon them like the dewfall, so that they may become for us the Body and Blood of our Lord, Jesus Christ." [67]

Now, I don't always focus as much as I should on this invocation. Maybe because it's a prayer to which the congregation does not respond, or maybe because I'm still settling in to kneeling as the priest offers it. And yet the Holy Spirit is so important to the Eucharist that invoking Him occurs throughout the Mass, and especially at this important moment.

That's when the wisdom of Sr. Francesca begins truly to dawn on me. Time for a closer look at the *Disputation*.

As we turn back and focus on the image of the Holy Spirit painted by Raphael, it seems likely the artist had this prayer of invocation very much in his mind. He's painted the Holy Spirit descending from Heaven to the Host being consecrated on the altar below! In fact, those rays of light pouring down on the altar capture my imagination. At the priest's plea that God send His "Spirit upon them like the dewfall!" I envision the Holy Spirit pouring Himself down upon the gifts on the altar as we wait, transfixed, upon the kneelers.

Now, as the church turns completely silent, the priest says the prayer that will transform the bread and wine into the Body and Blood of Christ. The Mass has many high moments, for sure. But if we had to pick one, most Catholics would land here — at the Consecration.

Disputation of the Holy Sacrament (detail), Raphael, 1508–1511, Room of the Signature (Vatican Museums), Rome, Italy

THE CONSECRATION

(The Words of Institution)

The Body of Christ

"On the day he was to suffer, he took bread in his holy and venerable hands, and with eyes raised to heaven to you, O God, his almighty Father, giving you thanks, he said the blessing, broke the bread and gave it to his disciples, saying 'take this, all of you, and eat of it, for this is my body, which will be given up for you.'" [68]

The history of the Mass has been heavily documented by theologians and Catholic scholars in a vast array of literature over the ages. The definitive work on this is still probably Joseph Jungmann's two volume masterpiece *The Mass of the Latin Rite,* published in 1950 but still used by priests and theologians to this day.[69] My personal favorite is Edward Sri's more manageable work, *A Biblical Walk through the Mass.*

As a lay person, I remain transfixed at the moment of consecration by the evangelist St. Luke's two simple verses in the twenty-fourth chapter of his Gospel:

"And it happened that, while he was with them at table, he took bread, said the blessing, broke it, and gave it to them."
—Luke 24:30

This single verse, describing the actions taken by Jesus before the first apostles at the Last Supper and then again in Emmaus, comprises the basic framework of what became the Liturgy of the Eucharist. St. Paul himself highlights again the "words of institution" in his First Letter to the Corinthians, one of the earliest Christian communities:

"For I received from the Lord what I also handed on to you, that the Lord Jesus, on the night he was handed over, took bread, and, after he had given thanks, broke it and said, 'This is my body that is for you. Do this in remembrance of me.' In the same way also the cup, after supper, saying, 'This cup is the new covenant in my blood. Do this, as often as you drink it, in remembrance of me.' For as often as you eat this bread and drink the cup, you proclaim the death of the Lord until he comes."

— 1 Cor. 11:23–26

Msgr. Landry points out the significance — then and now — of the words of Christ. "Obviously these words meant something then, and mean something now. Something very big. Through these words, the simple bread and wine became — become — the Body, Blood, Soul and Divinity of Christ Himself. He is now present, with us: The same Jesus who was in Mary's womb. The same Jesus St. Joseph held in his strong arms. The same Jesus who was pinned to the Cross on Calvary and who rose from the dead. He just looks different under sacramental form."

To get our heads around this moment, let's go back to the beginning — to Emmaus. And at this moment, we'll need an image a little more dramatic than Rembrandt's restrained, intimate version that got us started on this pilgrimage. We'll need Caravaggio.

The National Gallery, London. It's a cloudy and chilly Sunday morning in London, and we've just arrived off the plane from New York. Good time for a wake-up call. What better than Caravaggio's staging of the *Supper at Emmaus*? A quick shower and coffee and we're back at the National Gallery.

The bowl of fruit on the edge of the table literally invites us into the scene, almost asking us to sit down with Jesus and the two disciples. Teetering on the edge of the table, the bowl reminds us how

The Supper at Emmaus, Caravaggio, 1601, The National Gallery, London, England

the souls of the two disciples had been teetering on the edge of darkness before this moment. Until now, they believed that Jesus had abandoned them. They were heading back, into the dark. Perhaps you can identify with this feeling.

For sure, they'd already begun to suspect that Jesus *could* still be alive, at least within their hearts. Walking along the road to Emmaus with this kind stranger, Jesus had been preparing their hearts for this moment of Consecration. And now, at this point of the liturgy, we've arrived at this table in very much the same frame of mind, sensing the presence of God, of Jesus, of the Holy Spirit. Like the two disciples on the road to Emmaus, our hearts are "burning within" us (Luke 24:32). We are ready for the unexpected, even for a miracle.

In this moment captured by the artist, the disciples are not yet "all in." They've been listening, and the man with them is familiar, for sure, but also different. He has a more perfect, resurrected body. To imagine this, Caravaggio paints Jesus without a beard and with a youthful, unblemished face — very little semblance to the tortured man the disciples last saw on Calvary.

Likewise, for us, the Sacred Host up there that the priest is holding sure doesn't look like Jesus.

And then, this wayfarer does something unexpected as the bread is brought to the table. Before He breaks it, He reaches out His right hand to bless the food, and "says the blessing," the words of Consecration. This dramatic gesture is underscored for us by Caravaggio, who uses the same foreshortening technique he used in *The Road to Damascus*, to imagine Jesus' right arm of blessing thrusting right towards us, through the canvas! It is as though we, along with the unnamed disciple on Jesus' right, must duck to avoid it!

As Jesus says the blessing and breaks the bread, we realize He is present, alive, with us.

Cleopas thrusts out his own arms, paralleling Jesus' arm of blessing, in a gesture of joy, excitement, praise, and love all rolled into one.

As Jesus does so, Cleopas remembers the apostles' account of the first Mass, the Last Supper. Then, Jesus gave His Body and Blood in the Eucharist to His first priests, gathered around Him for the meal of a lifetime. Let's go to that moment in the Upper Room that is rattling around Cleopas' head here at Emmaus: the first Mass.

Elevation of the Eucharist

The Last Supper, Juan de Juanes, 1562, Museo del Prado, Madrid, Spain

Museo del Prado, Madrid. The first Mass was celebrated at the Last Supper, and the Last Supper remains one of the most important events of our Faith. Over the centuries, all four of the signature events of that meal in the upper room — the washing of the feet, the foretelling of Judas's betrayal, the institution of the Eucharist, and the communion of the apostles with Jesus — have been the subject of artistic masterpieces. Some, such as da Vinci's *Last Supper,* focus on Jesus' foretelling of Judas's betrayal and Peter's denial. Others focus on communion with Christ and with each other, or on the washing of the feet. And a few focus on the moment of institution that Cleopas and his companion recalled as they sat there in Emmaus with Jesus in the "breaking of the bread."

A Closer Look

The Last Supper, Leonardo da Vinci, 1495–1498, Santa Maria delle Grazie, Milan, Italy

Da Vinci's version of the Last Supper, painted more than one hundred fifty years earlier than Juan de Juanes's version, is perhaps most iconic and was certainly a reference point for the latter artist. Da Vinci's focus was on the drama that ensues immediately after Jesus' announcement that one of the apostles will soon betray Him.

One painting, however, somehow incorporates all these elements, while its primary subject is precisely the moment in Mass to which we've just arrived: the words of institution. We are standing before it now, in the Prado. The painter's name is Juan de Juanes.

We don't know a whole lot about Juan de Juanes; he was certainly less famous than other great painters of his day. Although he never visited Italy, he was clearly influenced by Raphael's precise style, though de Juanes executed in the richer medium of oils on canvas. Importantly, de Juanes started each day with Mass and Communion. He was a committed believer, and his holiness and conviction exude quietly from his canvases. Sometimes he makes me cry.

The Last Supper artfully alludes to all the major events of the Last Supper while keeping its focus on the institution of the Eucharist. A halo-less Judas is departing on the lower right, and the basin with which our Lord had washed the feet of the apostles lies on the floor in the foreground. Yet, amidst all this drama, the focus of *The Last Supper,* and of our eyes as we stand here, is precisely the same focus we now have in the Mass, as we kneel before the altar and the priest holds the Eucharist on high, right after the words of institution.

In the painting, Jesus has just blessed the bread and raised it, saying, "This is my body, which will be given up for you." As He does, the bread itself is transubstantiated into the Real Presence of Christ, and to emphasize this point for us viewers, Juan de Juanes transforms the loaves of bread we see on the table before Christ into the eucharistic Host we are all more accustomed to. Wonderfully, the simple bread has become the Body, Blood, Soul, and Divinity of Jesus.

As Jesus lifts the Eucharist — Himself — towards His Father in Heaven, something beautiful happens. The apostles lift their eyes towards the Eucharist in loving adoration — apart from Judas, whose glance seems to countenance dismissal as he rises to leave the scene. The apostles' prayerful posture here seems spontaneous, rather than deliberate and practiced. Some fold their hands in prayer, some hold their hands over their hearts; all but Judas lean into Christ and the Eucharist He holds aloft. Peter, on the lower left, has almost prostrated himself before Christ, perhaps in agony over Jesus' prediction that Peter would later deny the Lord. As a group, they are, quite simply, in awe.

My eyes turn back again to Judas on the lower right. He's clothed in the color of envy, yellow, and holding his purse of silver. Judas is glancing back at Christ but has already "raised his heel against me [Jesus]" (John 13:18) and is on his way out the door, into the "night" (John 13:30).

This might be a good time to ask a question, as I kneel quietly in my pew and the priest holds aloft the newly consecrated Eucharist: am I looking on spontaneously with awe at the Body of Christ? Or am I checking my watch, with one foot out the door?

The Blood of Christ

Once the priest recites the words of Consecration and the bread is sacramentally transformed into the Body of Christ, the same happens with the wine. Christ says through the priest,

> ***"Take this, all of you, and drink from it,***
> ***For this is the chalice of my Blood,***
> ***The Blood of the new and eternal covenant,***
> ***Which will be poured out for you and for many***
> ***For the forgiveness of sins.***
> ***Do this in memory of me."***[70]

At this point, I ask Msgr. Landry a question some of my non-Catholic friends have asked me: "How do we know the bread and wine are transformed into the Body and Blood of Christ? Is there a simple way to understand it?"

"Well, Steve, simplest is perhaps easiest. We know it becomes the Body and Blood of Christ because Jesus told us so, and He commanded us to do it. To believe in Jesus is to believe in what He said and did. St. Thomas Aquinas once said in the eucharistic hymn *Adoro te devote,* 'I believe whatever the Son of God has said, because nothing is truer than the word of truth.' We believe in the Eucharist because we believe in Jesus. That's why the words of the Consecration are so important: 'Do this in memory of me.'"

And with that, Evelyn and I are off — back on a plane to London, to see one of the greatest images of the Christ's blood pouring into the chalice which is before us now in the Mass: *The Mond Crucifixion.*

The National Gallery, London. If you track the Sotheby's art auctions, you'll find that Crucifixion paintings, in general, are not so popular these days. They're bloody, messy, not pretty. Most modern-day Christians prefer to focus on the "happy side" of the Faith, Jesus' teachings about love, joy, and community.

But here's the rub.

The love He has for us is demonstrated above all by His sacrifice on Calvary. And the Mass itself relives and "commemorates Christ's sacrifice on Calvary."[71] So here we are at that sacrifice. And yes, there's blood involved.

We are standing before one of Raphael's greatest early-career masterpieces, painted in oil as the main panel of an altarpiece in the church of San Domenico in Umbria. As a young painter, Raphael was heavily influenced by two of the older Renaissance masters of his time, Perugino and da Vinci. We can see the latter's influence, for sure, in the gently flowing hair of Mary Magdalen, on her knees beneath the Cross, and the soft atmospheric portrayal of the distant landscape behind them.

Like Raphael's later *Disputation,* it is also organized in mathematically precise symmetry, with the two adorers kneeling at the foot of the Cross, framed behind them by Mary and another woman, possibly "the wife of Clopas" (John 19:25), respectively. Besides the Magdalen, the other adorer, St. Jerome, was not alive in 33 A.D.; he is

The Mond Crucifixion, Raphael, 1502–1503,
The National Gallery, London, England

a "modern" implant into the scene and in some ways stands in for us. Let's put ourselves there, with St. Jerome — on our knees.

Above us, Jesus is dying on the Cross. He is pouring out His life's blood for us, literally. And to remind us of just how precious that blood is, two angels have arrived on the scene, catching every drop of blood pouring out from His side and hands. They are catching the blood not in any ordinary vessel, though. They are using the same chalice the priest is holding up now in front of us. With this little detail, Raphael is doing something like what Juan de Juanes would later do with the Sacred Host raised by Jesus in *The Last Supper*: He is helping us see that that substance in the chalice now before us at Mass is wine no more. It's Christ's Blood, delivered directly from Calvary by the angels of Heaven in the very chalice they used to collect it.

It is the Blood of Christ.

Mystery of Faith

(Memorial Acclamation)

As we kneel in awe before the Real Presence of Christ, like the apostles at the Last Supper and at the Supper at Emmaus, we gasp, almost speechless, at what has just happened. Then we collect ourselves. A sacrifice like this demands a response.

Earlier, in the Liturgy of the Word, we responded to the Gospel proclamation with the Creed, a detailed summary of the Faith we believe. How to respond to the gift of the Eucharist? Maybe we could have prayed the Creed again now, but the Church in her wisdom keeps our response to the central core of our Faith a lot simpler, the central tenet of what it means to be a Catholic. Our "Elevator Speech," if you will.

"The Mystery of Faith is our side of the New Covenant, our response to His self-gift on the Cross, the essence of our renewed commitment to God individually and as a people," Msgr. Landry chimes in. "Even though there are technically three versions of it, all affirm the great mystery that Christ is now present before us in the Eucharist. Each affirms a separate but related element of the great mystery of our Faith, which is how we enter into Jesus' Passion, Death, and Resurrection through the Mass." "And every part of each of the three options has its own image in our minds," Evelyn adds. "For the first mystery, Steve, we have to get back to New York. To the Met."

"We proclaim your death, O Lord . . ."

The Crucifixion, Pietro Lorenzetti, 1340s,
The Metropolitan Museum of Art, New York

The Metropolitan Museum of Art, New York. The only image in Western Art that has been more painted, sculpted, or carved than the Annunciation is the Crucifixion. In Catholic homes and churches all over the world, images of the first part of the proclamation of the mystery of our Faith are readily found. Likewise, most museums include at least one in their collections; the curators of these incredible safe houses of our cultural and religious inheritances all at one point or another acquired this sacred art from donations of private collections, purchases, or from churches selling off their highly valued assets.

Choosing the most poignant, most descriptive version of this first mystery of the Faith is no easy task. But as we talked it through, we kept coming back to this small painting in the early Renaissance galleries of our own Metropolitan Museum of New York. There are elements of it that simply melt us.

Pietro Lorenzetti wasn't the most famous Renaissance artist. In fact, unlike the other Renaissance artists we've visited here, Lorenzetti didn't even make the cut to get into the definitive work on the great artists of the Italian Renaissance, *The Lives of the Artists,* by sixteenth-century painter and architect Giorgio Vasari. Despite Vasari's snub, there is something about Lorenzetti's painting of the Crucifixion at the Met that shakes the soul.

It's one thing to believe "Christ has died." It's quite another to believe that an all-powerful God would be willing to die like this. Lorenzetti, following both Duccio and Giotto, employs both the former's innovation of describing human emotion and the latter's ability to create a three-dimensional, realistic space. And when he brought both traditions together in this image of Calvary, he created a little masterpiece.

For starters, the structure of the image instantly draws our eye to three crucifixions, not just one. It's bad enough that the Romans crucified the God-man, but they also crucified Him as a common criminal, between two thieves. "Just another loser," could have been the sign above His head, instead of "King of the Jews." Just this composition, of Christ hanging there between two bad guys, itself underscores the depth of the sacrifice He made for us. Christ chose not only to die for us, but He also chose to do so in the most gruesome, humiliating way anyone could imagine.

Then there's forgiveness. Lorenzetti references Jesus' famous offer of forgiveness to the two criminals on His left and His right by the way he paints them. Both men are now dead; we can see their recently broken legs, which prevented them from pushing their bodies upward for a last breath. But one has a halo, and his complexion is shining brightly as if still alive — he's in Paradise or Heaven already, having asked Jesus for forgiveness and having just received far more. The other, on Jesus' left, hangs miserably where he died, his body already corrupting and looking, well, dead.

Then there's love.

"What really gets to me," Evelyn muses, "is the gush of water and blood spewing from Jesus as the soldier pierces His side, to be sure He's dead. That powerful, unnatural gush is the artist's way of depicting Christ's abundant, '*agapic*' love for us. He gave everything He had to give. Down to the very last drop of His blood."

Does any of us love like this? Or even anything remotely close to this?

Then — and this is the clincher for why we're here right now in front of this painting, even as we recite the Mystery of Faith — there's our response. Lorenzetti's image portrays several different possibilities as we envision ourselves standing beneath the Cross during Mass.

The first kind of response can be described as "open hostility." This is the response that says, "Christ died, and frankly, He deserved it. Crazy guy! So unnecessary!" The bad thief is probably in this camp, along with some of the soldiers busily breaking bones on the left and right of the scene. None of us harbors this response within us, right?

Hmm. When did we last drag ourselves unwillingly to Sunday Mass, regretful that we were missing the NFL pregame show, political talk shows, or a pleasant Sunday-morning round of golf?

The second kind of response might be termed "casual indifference." This is frankly a more dangerous response, one that all of us from time-to-time lapse into, as our minds drift during the Mass. The two soldiers on the far upper left of the painting seem to fall into this category. "Just another day at the office," they seem to be saying to each other. In the face of all this sacrifice and blood, all they seem to be thinking about is what they are going to have for dinner tonight. And once again, most of us look at those two and thank God, saying, "I'm not one of them." Let's hope we're not.

The third kind of response is the beginning of belief: gratitude. We see it best in the eyes of the soldier who has just pierced Jesus' side and is being drenched right now in the water and blood pouring from it. This centurion's name is believed to have been Longinus, who was believed to have been converted at the foot of the Cross when the blood of Christ healed his eyes. Longinus is considered a saint by tradition within the Church, though he was never formally declared such by the Church.

This scene on Calvary was the beginning of Longinus's journey to Christ, which was rooted in his witness of Jesus' boundless, *agape* love at Calvary. Lorenzetti references his emerging sainthood in that hexagonal halo on his head, which was sometimes used by painters of this era to reference symbolic saints as opposed to fully acknowledged and documented ones. I think of this type of halo as suggesting the possibility of sainthood rather than the certainty of it.

I suspect that the well-dressed man on the horse in the lower right, who also seems to be trying to figure out what is going on here, might be Nicodemus, a wealthy follower of Christ who was present or nearby, according to John's Gospel account. He also wears a hexagonal halo.

And then there is the response of Mary, the mother of Jesus. We see her in the group of women at the foot of the Cross, collapsing into the arms of the "beloved apostle," John. Mary is so passionately in love with Jesus, her Son, that she experiences in a deeper way than anyone else His Passion on the Cross. And as He dies there, she is simply too overwhelmed to carry on.

None of us is Mary, and none of us ever will be. But we can all aspire to loving Him like this, and to feeling His death on the Cross this deeply, when we say, "*We proclaim your death, O Lord.*"

"and profess your Resurrection . . ."

The second part of the proclamation of the mystery of our Faith, the one that every apostle but John suffered a martyr's death defending, follows right behind the first. Without it, there would be no Faith. Jesus would have simply gone down in history as a nice guy with some wonderful ideas, who met an untimely and unfortunate death at the hands of the Romans.

It is the Resurrection that changes that narrative entirely. It is what makes sense out of what to a human mind seems the incredible decision by God to sacrifice His Son on the Cross. It's the point of the entire thing.

Msgr. Landry breaks in. "Jesus died to save us from sin and its consequence, death. To perfect that salvation, Jesus needed to conquer death, to be raised. If our defiance in the Garden stole eternity with God from us and made us mortal, then Christ's Resurrection won back the possibility of eternal life."

Many artists over the centuries have imagined the Resurrection. Some have done so in a deeply theological way, very seriously. Others, formally and symbolically. Both have their merits. Others have done so in kind of pop-culture-inspired cartoonish fashion. To balance off the drama of Lorenzetti's Crucifixion, however, we need something dramatic, vibrant, muscular, triumphant.

We need Peter Paul Rubens.

Cathedral of Our Lady of Antwerp, Antwerp. We are in the Cathedral of Our Lady, a soaring Gothic church that survived a devastating fire in the fifteenth century, two ransackings during the

The Resurrection of Christ, Peter Paul Rubens, 1611–1612, Cathedral of Our Lady of Antwerp, Antwerp, Belgium

religious wars of the sixteenth century, an attack by Napoleon in the eighteenth century, and another by Hitler during World War II. And still, its soaring walls, stained glass, and sacred art remain.

Of the great art at Our Lady, the most prominent are the four paintings by Peter Paul Rubens, commissioned for the Cathedral in 1610. One of those four is the painting we stand before now.

Peter Paul Rubens was to the Catholic southern half of the Netherlands (now Belgium) what Rembrandt was to the north. Both men were world famous in their day, both were devoutly religious, and both did things in the medium of oil painting that had never been done before. But the comparison pretty much ends there.

Where Rembrandt was the consummate loner and introspective artist, Rubens was the man of the world who was as comfortable serving as an Ambassador for the Catholic king of Spain as he was with a brush and easel. Where Rembrandt was at times dark and mysterious, Rubens was flamboyant and triumphant. A Dutch Reformed Protestant, Rembrandt rarely painted nudes; Rubens specialized in painting unclothed or partially clothed human bodies that are brimming with life. When the Bishop of Antwerp wanted a painting of the Resurrection, Rubens was an obvious artist to call upon.

My first reaction gazing upon *The Resurrection of Christ* is just how strong, vibrant, and perfect the resurrected Jesus appears. Horribly beaten and tortured just three days earlier, Jesus now emerges from the tomb stronger than ever. Rubens has painted Him full of life, His athletic body almost jumping out of the tomb that had encased Him. He is raring to go. He's almost doing a "high five" with the angels above Him. He's conquered death, completed His mission.

The drama of the moment is intensified by the reaction of the Roman soldiers, who of course were completely stunned by this sudden turn of events. Having just witnessed Christ's death on the Cross, they must have been beyond shocked when He burst forth from the tomb, bigger than life. Unprepared for this moment, they dive for the ground and darkness, shielding their eyes from the blinding light of the resurrected Christ.

For these soldiers, the resurrected Christ presented personal difficulties, for sure. Their Roman superior would surely be upset with them for "allowing this to happen!"—as if they could have done anything about it. And for the Sanhedrin, the Resurrection of Christ was also a most inconvenient truth. Matthew's Gospel, written at first for Jewish converts to Christianity, tells us that they ended up cutting a deal for gold with "the chief priests" of the Sanhedrin to cover it up (Matt. 28:11–15).

Their plan didn't exactly work.

Soon after, Jesus appeared to Mary Magdalen, then the apostles, then the disciples on the road to Emmaus, and then "one hundred and twenty persons" (Acts 1:15). And soon the word was out. Within three hundred years, millions of people in the known world had become followers. Today, there are an estimated 2.4 billion of us, over half of whom are Catholics.

Nearly all of the apostles and many of the early Christians died martyrs' deaths rather than renounce the Faith, and particularly their faith in this mystery: "*We profess your resurrection.*"

Assenting to this Faith here and now in the Church today is relatively straightforward, particularly for the many of us who have experienced the presence of Christ in our own lives. But here is the essential question: Would we be so brave in proclaiming the second part of this mystery if it meant facing a trip to the Colosseum?

"until you come again."

The third and last part of the mystery is one that, unlike the first two, can't really be "proven" or "disproven." It hasn't happened yet. It's a prediction of what will happen. Not just anyone's prediction, but Jesus'. The Last Judgment is in some ways the subject of the entire Book of Revelation. It is also foretold more directly by Jesus Himself, in Matthew's Gospel:

> *"When the Son of Man comes in his glory, and all the angels with him, he will sit upon his glorious throne, and all the nations will be assembled before him. And he will separate them one from another, as a shepherd separates the sheep from the goats. He will place the sheep on his right and the goats on his left. Then the king will say to those on his right, 'Come, you who are blessed by my Father. Inherit the kingdom prepared for you from the foundation of the world.' "*
>
> —*Matt. 25:31–34*

The coming of Jesus for the Last Judgment is an image that appears in most churches. Several good examples can be found in most of the great museums we've been visiting as well.

But one Last Judgment painting is particularly inspiring, both for its size (forty-five feet high by forty feet wide) and drama. To see it, we need to head back to Rome.

The Last Judgement, Michelangelo, 1535–1541, Sistine Chapel (Vatican Museums), Rome, Italy

Sistine Chapel, Vatican Museums. I have to admit, I've lost track of how many times I've visited with *The Last Judgement* over my lifetime. And yet, every time I visit, I see it differently. That's how it is with mysteries, and with art; as we grow and experience more versions of the same theme, our understanding of them morphs and evolves. They remain relevant wherever we are in our journey towards the light. And this is certainly the case with Michelangelo's *Last Judgement.*

The far wall of the Sistine Chapel, behind the altar where the cardinals of the Church have traditionally celebrated Mass when trying to discern the next pope, was the wall chosen by Popes Clement VII and Paul III for an aging Michelangelo's return project at the Sistine Chapel, nearly twenty-five years after painting its ceiling. Historians wonder why the altar wall was used for this scene, which more normally would be placed on the opposite "exit" wall to remind the laity to stay focused on getting to Heaven.

Liz Lev, one of the foremost experts on the Sistine Chapel, having studied and reflected on it for decades, has a great explanation. She'd taken Evelyn and me to see *The Last Judgement* on a previous visit. Liz believes the motivation for using the altar wall was to remind the cardinals, who in those days would be facing the wall as they said Mass, that "they like the rest of us need to be thinking about eternity" as they are contemplating for whom to vote to lead the Church—about their judgment and the Final Judgment.

With more than three hundred individual characters spread across the enormous wall before us, there are plenty of images to inspire us and, yes, scare the daylights out of us. The images of the damned on the lower right are particularly gruesome, as they are escorted off to Hell by Charon, a mythological figure from classical literature who appears prominently in Dante's *Inferno*. Worse, for me, are the ones above them, still in the air. Some were hoping to sneak into Heaven, but their souls were mortally wounded in their lives on earth, and they can't get in. Some are literally being tossed into Hell by the angels there, others dragged below by the fiends of Hell.

More promising are the souls on Christ's right side, our left as we look at the masterpiece. They are rising back to life from the earth where they've been long buried. As their life force returns to them, there is a moment where I turn around and upward to consider a similar life force entering Adam, on the ceiling above us.

"Steve, stay focused," Evelyn scolds me. "We'll be getting there soon enough." The Sistine Chapel can do that to you. There are so many profound images and ideas to take in, a visitor is literally surrounded by them, left and right, up and down.

Back to *The Last Judgement*. In perfect symmetry with the damnation of the souls on Jesus' left, here on His right we see His angels descending upon the newly restored souls and pulling them up towards Heaven. And we can see Heaven, around and above Jesus.

Sr. Francesca, who is here with us for this latest visit, points out something I'd never noticed before, up there in Heaven, floating around blissfully above the scene of judgment surrounding Christ: the angels. "The angels are holding the *Arma Christi*— the instruments of Christ's Crucifixion. They are symbols of hope, and also joy, because they are the means by which Christ brought about the salvation of mankind."

"It almost seems like they're playing with them, Ev," I whisper to Evelyn.

"Well, Steve," she whispers back, "in some way, they are. In Heaven, those instruments of Christ's suffering have become mere toys for the angels!"

At the center of it all stands the resurrected Jesus, larger than life. Beardless, His divine nature is now fully evident, though He still bears the wounds of His very human Crucifixion. As He twists from right to left up there in Heaven, I recall Cimabue's *Crucifixion,* in which Jesus is twisting in the agony of the Cross.[72] Now, by contrast, Jesus is twisting in the glory of Heaven as He separates the wheat from the chaff in the Final Judgment. In fact, the risen Christ *is* the energy source of the entire composition, which seems to swirl around Him.

Critics at the time, and some since, have complained about all the energy and commotion of Michelangelo's rendition of this scene, predicted both in Matthew's Gospel and in the Book of Revelation. They preferred to see something much tidier, orderly, composed, harmonious. Something more Raphael-esque, if you will.

None of us know what the Last Judgment will truly be like, but Michelangelo's frenetic composition speaks to me. My guess is, even at the gates of Heaven, things might get a little chaotic as all the souls of mankind jostle around awaiting judgment, waiting to hear whether their souls are fit for eternity with God.

Nestled closest to Christ, of course, is His mother, Mary. Forming almost one body with His, she alone appears to be beyond judgment. She was, after all, immaculately conceived. Among those jostling around Jesus are a variety of saints and martyrs, many recognizable especially to the more religiously informed laity of the day. Some are displaying the symbols of their martyrdom, such as St. Bartholomew, holding his flayed skin. Just above him, to his left, stands St. Peter, holding the keys to Heaven. Both secular and religious historians have weighed in over the years as to what the martyrs are hoping to accomplish by displaying the symbols of their martyrdom to Christ. Perhaps, as some say, they are trying to convince Christ that they've earned Heaven. Maybe, as others say, they are advising Christ which souls lack their saintly credentials and need to be sent to Hell. Or maybe they're just manifesting their love for Jesus by showing what they were willing to endure for Him who endured so much for them.

Personally, I agree with the last idea. The saints and martyrs are reminding us that to make it to Heaven, we need Love. The Love we saw in van Dyck's painting of *Charity*. The true Love whose source is God. The love that we practice here on earth — and that we nourish and grow within us by consuming the Eucharist.

You see, God is pure love. And to stand in His presence, we ourselves must be purified in love; we were when God originally created us, as Adam and Eve, but we lost pure love when in our pride we rebelled against Him. We lost it in the Garden of Earthly Delights. That's why Jesus had to come to earth, to teach us what pure love is. It's that love He showed us on the Cross — the love that Lorenzetti painted for us in *The Crucifixion*.

So, we can take Michelangelo's *Last Judgement* literally, if we like. With souls being judged and accountants working out who did what to whom, and who has enough credits to make it into Heaven and who doesn't.

Or we can think of it as an allegory for what it's going to take to get up there, when Christ "will come in glory."

It will take the love of the martyrs — sacrifice, commitment, perseverance — a willingness to sacrifice ourselves fully for others, like Jesus did on Calvary, like Peter did on Vatican Hill, and like St. Bartholomew did when they skinned him alive.

It's going to take pure love, and God's grace.

And when we've spent a lifetime practicing this kind of love, our resurrected soul will meet the test; it will be able to be in the presence of God. That's the "test" we'll need to pass — the test of love.

One last image to contemplate. The man sitting on a cloud, reminiscent of the posture of Auguste Rodin's *The Thinker*. He's being dragged down to Hell by two devils, who've got him in their grip. He is all alone; no one can help him. He is in a state of complete, eternal anguish.

Le Penseur (*The Thinker*), Auguste Rodin, 1904, Musée Rodin, Paris, France

We don't know for sure what he's thinking, but between the visits over the years to the Sistine Chapel, and hundreds of visits in New York to Rodin's ode to him in *The Thinker,* I'm going to take a stab at this. Could it be he's finally realized, too late, what it takes to get to Heaven, and that he simply doesn't have an ounce of it in him? That he's spent his whole life loving himself, and no one else, and certainly not Jesus?

Could it be that he's realized, too late, that he doesn't have love?

Love is what we will need imprinted on our souls through a lifetime of practice when the last part of the Mystery of Faith happens: When Christ "will come again in glory."

Good time to ask, "What virtue, or vice, did I 'practice' this week?" Will it help me be ready when Jesus "comes again?"

The Offering

(Anamnesis)

"Therefore, O Lord, we celebrate the memorial of the saving Passion of your Son, his wondrous Resurrection and Ascension into heaven, and as we look forward to his second coming, we offer you in thanksgiving this holy and living sacrifice."[73]

Immediately following the Mystery of Faith, the priest begins a prayer called "the Offering," where the priest reviews the offerings we are making to God as part of the Wedding Feast of the Lamb.

The greatest of these offerings is Christ Himself, "the holy and living sacrifice." And there is perhaps no painting that portrays this moment in the Mass better than one that many of us have never seen, in person or in an art book. I too would not have known about it had not my friend Dony McManus, the modern liturgical artist we visited with in chapter 8, insisted I see it on a recent trip to Florence.

"Steve, go see Pontormo's *The Deposition from the Cross* in the Chiesa di Santa Felicita. It changed my life as an artist."

The Holy and Living Sacrifice

Chiesa di Santa Felicita, Florence. The Chiesa di Santa Felicita is not on many tour routes through Florence. One of more than one hundred churches in this relatively small city, it is tucked away

The Deposition from the Cross, Jacopo Pontormo, 1525–1528, Chiesa di Santa Felicita, Florence, Italy

along a small street on the less popular, southern bank of the Arno River, not far from the Ponte Vecchio. It is a little church, and off to a side chapel near the entrance, it holds a masterpiece painted by the Italian Mannerist painter, Jacopo Pontormo.

Unlike Lorenzetti, Pontormo actually made it into Vasari's *Lives of the Artists,* though the latter seems to have included him reluctantly, saying he was "a man without a firm and steady mind and who always went about indulging in fanciful ideas."[74] It's quite possible Vasari was referring to *The Deposition of the Cross,* which is alarmingly different from the high Renaissance paintings that Vasari so admired.

Painting just after that period, during an unsettled decade that included the sack of Rome in 1527, Pontormo and others were searching for a new form for their art, one that was more dynamic and provocative. That brought him to *The Deposition* at the Chiesa di Santa Felicita.

We're standing in front of it now, gasping, as we consider what form of "holy and living sacrifice" the priest is now praying about.

As we enter the scene, Christ's dead body is sliding off Mary's lap, suddenly and perhaps a bit reluctantly released into the arms of a young man, perhaps an angel (is that a bright red cloak he's wearing, or wings?). The angel in turn is sliding him onto the shoulders of another young man, who himself seems about to slide further out of the canvas, towards us. We guess the second man is the apostle John, who is often portrayed as in this scene. John stands in here for all the apostles and, more deeply, for the newly established Church itself. He has just been chartered by Jesus to care for Mary. And Mary in turn has been told that John, symbolizing the Church, is now her son.

Between Mary and Jesus, a mysterious void has appeared, the void through which Jesus' body has just passed. The High Renaissance artists of just a decade earlier would never have considered such a void in the center of the canvas; their tightly controlled images rather focused the viewers' eye directly towards a tightly compacted center where the main subject lay. So scholars have long since debated what Pontormo's mysterious void stands for. Maybe for the feeling of grief and emptiness Mary feels at this moment in her heart? Maybe the void that all the apostles were feeling at this moment, the hole that Jesus' death has created in all their hearts?

Once our eyes adjust to all the bright colors bursting off the Pontormo's fresco, we begin to notice the ethereal qualities of the people in the painting. They remind us of Pontormo's famous Mannerist successor, El Greco. While the people in the painting have realistic depth and solidity, at the same time they appear to be almost outside of their own elongated bodies. They seem to float on the canvas. Mary is floating backward in grief, as Jesus leaves her arms. Jesus slides toward the shoulders of John, helped along by a little angel half his size. John bears the weight of Jesus on his shoulders while his feet are barely even touching the ground; the only sign of strain is perhaps the tone of his face and back, which are turning bright pink. The whole heavenly impression is enhanced by the almost psychedelic colors that Pontormo employs, shining within a divine light. The colors remind me a little of those wonderful, heavenly-lit rainbow wings of Fra Angelico's angel of *The Annunciation*, just a short walk away in San Marco. (Don't worry, we'll be visiting *The Annunciation* in due course!)

As Jesus slips out of the arms of Mary, and across the shoulders of John, all the movement and energy in *The Deposition* lead us to look down, to where the body of Jesus might be heading next. And there, just below the feet of John, is something that has been there from the day Pontormo painted *The Deposition*.

The altar — he's heading for the altar.

A Closer Look

The reference point for an image of the Pietà, in Pontormo's day and ever since, remains Michelangelo's masterpiece in stone for a side altar at St. Peter's. Like most others prior to Pontormo's painting, the tightly compacted center of the painting is filled by the dead body of Christ pressed against his mother's chest.

Pietà, Michelangelo, 1498–1499, St. Peter's Basilica, Rome, Italy

Suddenly, we notice the Cross, or lack thereof. We search the canvas; no sign of it. Odd, all paintings of the deposition, until now, had always included the Cross from which Christ is being deposed. But Pontormo left it out.

The Cross is no longer present. It's already gone.

We're not actually on Calvary. Somehow, we're in Heaven, or maybe somewhere in between Heaven and earth. Jesus, the "holy and living sacrifice," is floating down, from Mary, our Mother, across the back of John, the Church, to the altar below, where we are about to receive Him in Communion.

Then, as we peer through the grill and imagine ourselves on our knees before the altar, I understand the void. Soon, in the Mass, the priest on the altar will hold up Jesus in the Eucharist for us to behold. And when he does, the suspended Eucharist will be precisely on the plane from our eyes to the void in the *Deposition*.

The Eucharist, Christ, will fill the void.

And when that happens, we ourselves, at least for a moment, will float with Him up to Heaven.

I can't wait!

Calling Upon The Holy Spirit

(Second Epiclesis)

"Look, we pray, upon the oblation of your Church, and, recognizing the sacrificial Victim by whose death you willed to reconcile us to yourself, grant that we, who are nourished by the Body and Blood of your Son and filled with his Holy Spirit, may become one body, one spirit in Christ." [75]

One Body in Christ

Van Gogh Museum, Amsterdam. Evelyn and I are here at the Van Gogh Museum and standing before a painting we've neither seen before nor even ever heard of: van Gogh's *Pietà*, inspired by a similar, though very different, painting by Delacroix. *Pietà* was painted from a lithograph print, one of many that van Gogh's devoted brother, Theo, sent him during his confinement at the hospital in Saint-Rémy. Early in his stay there, van Gogh was confined to his cell and had no access to the landscapes of Provence that he employed to inspire many of his greatest works. So Theo sent him lithographs that he could use as models to practice his painting.

There is one similarity of Delacroix's and van Gogh's composition to Pontormo's *Deposition*, which we just visited, that instantly strikes us: the loving way in which Mary, despite all of her grief, releases the body of Christ to us, on the altar below. (We presume

Pietà (after Delacroix), Vincent van Gogh, 1889,
Van Gogh Museum, Amsterdam, Netherlands

that Delacroix's original was also intended as an altarpiece.) Mary does so with pain and agony, yet also with great love and devotion. Mary is here fulfilling her own mission, to deliver Christ to the Church. She at this moment has in fact become the mother of Jesus' Church.

Then, we turn to the limp body of Jesus, who has just given His all for Mary, for the Church, for us. He is bruised and battered, completely spent, worn out. Or is He? His eyes seem more closed in the rest of sleep than in death.

As we study the face of Jesus more, it hits us. This face is not Jesus'! It's van Gogh's! The red hair, the trimmed beard that draws to a sharp point beneath his chin. Van Gogh has painted himself as Jesus, at the foot of the Cross, at the entrance to the tomb, on the altar before us now.

We don't know, of course, what van Gogh was thinking here. Just months before his tragic death by suicide, his mind was probably not thinking normally, if at all, as he hurriedly sketched out *Pietà*. In fact, maybe he wasn't even "thinking." Maybe he was just painting.

As discussed in chapter 7, van Gogh seemed to have had a special relationship with God. In fact, before painting, he'd tried his hand at becoming a Methodist minister, but that somehow didn't work out. Just before he turned to painting as his vocation, he wrote in a letter to his brother Theo, that "one man will love Rembrandt, genuinely, and so that man will surely know that there is a God."[76] Some believe that van Gogh's search for God led him to paint in order to try to find him.[77]

So, here's a thought. Did van Gogh find Jesus in the Cross? In his own suffering at this time at Saint-Rémy?

We'll never know. But here at this moment of the Mass, as the priest prays that "we become one body, one spirit in Christ," van Gogh's image of himself as Christ in the Pietà is something to contemplate. As we enter into communion with Christ and with each other through the Eucharist, we're not just entering into communion with all the "good stuff": the trip to Heaven, the joy of discipleship. We're also entering into communion with Him on the Cross, in His suffering.

And yes, in His Death. And in Him, we are one with all those for whom He died.

Am I ready for this? Am I prepared to become one with Him? And with those He loves? Even unto death?

Prayer of Intercessions

"May he make of us an eternal offering to you, so that we may obtain an inheritance with your elect, especially with the most blessed Virgin Mary, Mother of God, with blessed Joseph, her Spouse, with your blessed Apostles and glorious Martyrs (with Saint N.: the Saint of the day or Patron Saint) and with all the Saints, on whose constant intercession in your presence we rely for unfailing help. . . ."[78]

As the priest completes the Eucharistic Prayer, he begins a roll call of sorts of the members of the universal Church. With the sacrifice of Christ present on the altar, he is making intercession for the Church and all her members. He begins with the pope, then the local bishop, then all the other bishops and clergy, and then all the members of the Church, living and dead. It's the moment in the Mass in which the whole Church is called upon. We are not alone! We are all together now, somewhere between Heaven and earth.

I can think of no better image to express this idea of the Universal Church than the inside of a great gothic cathedral at midday, when the shimmering light of the soaring walls of the stained glass windows bathe the participants in the Mass as they pray. The very idea of building these soaring walls of light and glass was, in the twelfth century, a seemingly impossible task. Without steel to support the walls, how could a structure one hundred sixty feet high stand up if its walls were mostly glass?

The medieval architects solved this problem with a combination of flying stone buttresses and iron rods and chains, which collectively relieved the stress of the walls by transporting their weight to secondary pillars in the lower walls of the churches. This caused a lot of trouble and expense, and some of the great gothic cathedrals of this age for this reason famously took centuries to complete. But in the minds of the Church, giving all of us a little slice of Heaven was worth it.

The heart of gothic cathedral-building in the Middle Ages was France, and the heart of France was Paris. Unfortunately, most of the original medieval stained-glass windows of the churches in Paris were lost over the centuries to fire or age, or worse, to the deliberate destruction of the Reign of Terror in the early 1790s. But one church there still has the soaring stained glass windows as they originally were conceived, thanks to a near perfect restoration in the mid-nineteenth century after the fall of Napoleon. It was the chapel church of the King of France himself. Today, it is the most spectacular example of what it would have been like in the Middle Ages as the priest appealed for prayers to the Universal Church, fully present here with Christ on the altar, somewhere between Heaven and earth.

The church's name is Sainte-Chapelle. To see it, we'll need to get back to Paris.

Gathering the Church and All the Saints

Sainte-Chapelle, Paris. Evelyn and I have arrived at Sainte-Chapelle with our good friend and first spiritual guide, Fr. John Connor, L.C. We're on a little pilgrimage of several churches or former churches in Paris; Sainte-Chapelle is one of the latter, having been decommissioned by the French State during the Revolution and never again used for its original purpose. Although the church was heavily vandalized during the Reign of Terror, almost two-thirds of its original glass panels survived, sometimes in piles of fragments around the grounds. In the mid-nineteenth century, one of the most extensive and detailed renovations ever attempted restored the glass walls to their original medieval glory. And although the church has been declared a "museum" by the French state, Evelyn and I, with Fr. John, can't help but stand silent within its soaring walls and begin to pray.

Books have been written about the design and layout of these walls. Like Orvieto and many other medieval churches, almost the entire Faith is up there in that glass. And at one time, the chapel housed a relic of the crown of thorns itself. But as we stand here silently praying with Fr. John, none of that seems to matter. We put

Sainte-Chapelle, ca. 1238, Paris, France

the archaeological guidebook provided by France's scientists away for a moment, and we just breathe it all in. I'll let you do the same.

All around us, shimmering images of Jesus, the apostles, the prophets, and the saints illumine the chapel. We are immersed in what feels like a divine light — the light of God.

Sainte-Chapelle is, indeed, a little slice of Heaven.

THE PRAYER OF PRAISE

(The Doxology)

"Through him, and with him, and in him,
O God, almighty Father,
in the unity of the Holy Spirit,
All glory and honor is yours,
for ever and ever."

At the very closing of the Eucharistic Prayer, the priest prays the words that acknowledge that all of us are joined together through and with Jesus. He is the linking verb, the beginning, the middle, and the end — the *alpha* and the *omega*. The prayer is called the Great Doxology.

During the Middle Ages, churches used the image of Christ the Vine, and the members of the Church as His branches, to illustrate for us what "through Him, with Him, and in Him" actually means. The most famous of these images is in Rome.

Apse Mosaic of the Tree of Life, 12th–13th century, Basilica of San Clemente, Rome, Italy

San Clemente, Rome. Nearly every time we come to Rome, Evelyn and I find ourselves at San Clemente. I'm not entirely sure why we come so often to this quiet church, a little off the beaten path. Sometimes it's for the archeological interest that the church has three churches built on top of one another, the first dating back to the early Christian era when the Christians celebrated Masses secretly in private homes, and when St. Clement — confirmed by St. Peter himself — was pope. Sometimes we visit to see in its cellar vaults the ruins of the original pagan worship space that the original church was built on. And always, it's for the image we are standing in front of now: *The Tree of Life*.

We don't know for sure when San Clemente's apse was decorated in the mosaic we call the *Tree of Life,* though most historians date it to shortly after the uppermost "third" church was built, late in the twelfth century. Although there are a few other "trees of life" elsewhere, San Clemente's is the most iconic and studied. There is so much detail going on within the teeming image of life portrayed here, it could take an entire book to break down. Don't worry. I'm not going to do that!

As we sit and pray within this ancient basilica, the dominating element is always the image on the apse, right behind and above the altar of sacrifice. The central component from which the entire composition evolves is the Cross. Its dark wood stands out clearly against the glittering gold backdrop of the apse. Christ is there on the Cross, but more abstractly than realistically. The image more resembles the beautiful medieval Cross we saw at the Abbey of Conques when we first entered the church than the more realistic and gruesome version painted one hundred years later by Cimabue at Santa Croce.

Here, the Crucifixion is symbolic, and not devastatingly real. Christ stands in front of the Cross, flanked by Mary His mother and John the Baptist and protected above by His Father, whose hands appear emerging from Heaven as He sends the Holy Spirit, in the form of a dove, to Jesus. Jesus appears to be holding Himself to the Cross as He stands before it, rather than hanging from it. His outstretched arms welcome us into the scene as much as serving to portray His actual Crucifixion. This is a scene of Christ's victory over the Cross, not His torturous death.

And as if to emphasize this key point, a larger-than-life image of Jesus reigning in Heaven has been placed above the scene. The image is calm, loving, serene. This Jesus does not appear judgmental or scary. What a difference from Michelangelo's *Last Judgement* across town at the Sistine Chapel!

All this beautiful imagery would have been normal enough in this era, and even now. But what makes the apse at San Clemente so very special is where Jesus and His Cross are standing. We've seen this place before, sort of.

It's a garden, a renewed and reawakened Garden of Eden — remade by the New Covenant, sealed with the Body and Blood of Christ who now is with us on the altar. And the Cross is the trunk of a tree that flows throughout the rest of the image — The Tree of Life. This is the vine that Jesus told us about in John 15, during His Last Supper discourse. It is the Church itself, which He instituted that night:

> *"I am the vine, you are the branches. Whoever remains in me and I in him will bear much fruit, because without me you can do nothing. Anyone who does not remain in me will be thrown out like a branch and wither; people will gather them and throw them into a fire and they will be burned. If you remain in me and my words remain in you, ask for whatever you want and it will be done for you. By this is my Father glorified, that you bear much fruit and become my disciples. As the Father loves me, so I also love you. Remain in my love."*
>
> *— John 15:5–9*

The garden, and the Church it represents, is being watered by four rivers, flowing out of the foot of the Cross. These are thought to represent "the four rivers of Eden,"[79] now flowing from Jesus. His is "the water … that will become in … us a spring of water welling up to eternal life" (John 4:14). Along the banks of the river, we can see beautiful little details suggesting the abundance of life flowing from its water of eternal life — four little stags drink their fill; a fisherman fishes; a shepherd herds his sheep to its banks for a drink. All these images within the mosaic are referencing biblical themes that collectively represent the Church incarnate. The four stags, for instance, probably stand for the four evangelists.

Within the abundant branches of the vine flowing out of the Cross, we can find the entire Church in some way represented. The four Gospel writers are most prominent, seated there amidst the first level of branches. As the lively tree grows and expands to fill the whole apse, all sorts of life appear in its branches: birds, animals, and yes, us. The place is teeming with life! — clergy, princes, and yes, even us.

At the base of the entire structure are twelve sheep. Those represent the apostles, the foundation of the Church. And all of them have their eyes focused attentively on Jesus in the center. He appears here as the Lamb, whom we saw earlier in El Greco's *Adoration* at Jesus' birth. Now He appears directly above the altar as the Lamb of God, an iconic image for Christ dating back to Roman times. We'll be seeing more of the Lamb of God in all His glory soon enough.

As we sit and pray at San Clemente, we keep coming back to the prayer that the priest is now praying here at Mass, the Prayer of Praise, or the Doxology. Let's listen to it together. For Jesus is truly the source of all that is good.

"Through him, and with him, and in him,
O God, almighty Father,
in the unity of the Holy Spirit,
all glory and honor is yours,
for ever and ever."

Amen to that!

Which brings us to "the Great Amen."

THE GREAT AMEN

By my count, we pray "Amen" approximately twelve times during the course of any given Mass. Of these, the "Amen" that completes the Liturgy of the Eucharist is given a special prominence. If a choir is present, we often sing it.

In singing out "Amen" at this moment, we are proclaiming our agreement with and faith in the eucharistic miracle, and in the eucharistic presence of Christ who is now before us on the altar. As Dr. Sri tells us, " 'Amen' transliterates a Hebrew word that affirms the validity of what has been said and was often used in liturgical settings [by the Jews at Jesus' time]." The choir in this case stands in for "the angels and saints in heaven," who surround us now and join with us in affirming the mystery of the eucharistic presence.[80] So, let's join with the angels and sing, "Amen!"

Here's one of my favorite angels from another museum we've been visiting, the Uffizi. It's painted by Rosso Fiorentino. The angel's lute seems bigger than she is. Maybe that's appropriate for "the Great Amen." Can any song be bigger than this?

"Amen! Amen! Amen!"

Angel Playing the Lute, Rosso Fiorentino, 1521, Uffizi Gallery, Florence, Italy

– 11 –

Communion

WITH CHRIST FULLY present on the altar, surrounded by all the angels and saints, we now enter the climactic moment of the holy Mass: Communion. This is where we will come directly into physical contact with God Himself, when we will consume the Eucharist. Because all of us in a state of grace at Mass will likely receive Him, we also commune with each other in the process. We become, as St. Paul urged us, "one body . . . one spirit . . . in Christ" (1 Cor. 12:12–13).

Before we receive Him into us, though, there are a few final things we must do. The first is to pray the prayer He taught us, the Our Father — a prayer given to us by Jesus Himself that all of us know. The deepest theological prayer of our Faith, whole books have been written about it by the Church's greatest theologians.[81] We're going to try to summarize their insights with one painting. Appropriately, it is probably the single most Catholic painting in the history of art.

THE OUR FATHER

"At the Savior's command, and formed by divine teaching, we dare to say . . ."

There are many iconic images of God the Father throughout Christian art. Usually, He is somewhat removed from the action, rising aloofly above His Son, who is busy in the world, saving us. There is one unique image that portrays Him as He truly is, not as a symbol, not as an icon, but as the real deal. *Our* Father. And to see that image, we need to get back to Rome to the Sistine Chapel.

Creation of Adam, Michelangelo, ca. 1511, Sistine Chapel Ceiling (Vatican Museums), Rome, Italy

Sistine Chapel, Rome. The year is 1511. The already-famous Renaissance artist, Michelangelo, has recently completed the first half of the Sistine Ceiling, begun in 1508. Painting by night and in secret, with his revolutionary creation covered from below by a scaffolding, he is painting the Genesis story in reverse of how it will be viewed. He's started at the entrance of the church with the last panel, the fall of man via *The Flood*, which we visited earlier in one of the Old Testament readings. Now, the artist is starting the back half, which will include the *Creation of Adam* at the center of the ceiling, followed by three panels describing the Creation of the world.

In a room nearby, his rival Raphael is working furiously to complete his own masterpiece, *Loggias*. Raphael has finished the first and most important room, the papal office known as the Room of the Signature. The pope and a few other dignitaries have already had a "sneak peek" at the first half of the ceiling, and all are in awe. Michelangelo, the sculptor, has reinvented painting. His images, painted sixty-five feet above ground, are monumental, full of life, energy, and drama. They almost appear like three-dimensional sculptures hanging off the ceiling. But Michelangelo isn't finished yet.[82]

His own view was that in the first half of the ceiling there were still too many figures to see each clearly, particularly in the first panel of *The Flood*. So, for the climactic image of God creating Adam, he decided to go large. The result became perhaps the most iconic image in the history of art.

Nearly nineteen feet wide and nine feet high, the gigantic image contains only two central figures, Adam and God, along with a parcel of nine mysterious smaller beings surrounding God the Father. Adam takes up half the canvas. He is lying languidly on the ground, seeming to rise from a deep sleep. His body is perfectly sculpted, some say from the image of an idealized Greek statue called the Apollo Belvedere. Michelangelo would probably say he copied it from God.

God's image, which does look remarkably like an older image of Adam, is on the other side of the panel. He is flying energetically towards Adam, stretching out His hand to him. As His finger touches Adam's, or I should say "almost touches" Adam's, a spark of energy seems to jump across, instilling a living soul into the sleepy being who becomes the first man on earth. The image of God's divine finger extended towards Adam's human finger, made in God's likeness, has become a symbol for all humanity of what makes us human, of what separates us from the rest of creation. The spark that lifts us up towards the transcendent.

That spark is love — the love of "Our Father."

Somehow, the way God looks so caringly towards Adam, so proud of His achievement in creating him, so loving of him as He touches his finger, resonates in my heart as I say the words "Our Father." This is not the harsh, vengeful God of the Old Testament, though the story is from there. No, this is a God of pure love.

Then there's the mystery of those beings within God's cloak. Are they angels, or perhaps uncreated souls, or, more ambiguously, *putti*? And particularly there is the question surrounding that image of the young woman nearest Him, encircled by His left arm. Art historians love to debate who she and the others are. Everyone seems to have a theory, some based in theology, others in science. We're here today with the indomitable Sr. Francesca, who has studied the ceiling for years. So, I ask her.

Like any good nun, she doesn't hesitate. "Steve, my goodness, it's Eve. Period!"

And as we take a closer look, we see her point. It's in the very gentle way that God wraps His arm around Eve — not yet created but already in His mind — even as He seems to focus all His energy on creating Adam, and all the while He carries the rest of the crowd of souls or angels on His broad back. As if to emphasize this point, the entire form of God's cape, which envelops the grouping, itself is in the shape of the cross section of a brain.

"This was no accident, Steve," Sister adds. "Michelangelo was known to dissect cadavers to better understand how to sculpt and paint the human body. He thought about this for a while. Very few 'accidents' with Michelangelo!"

And then there's the small boy on the Father's right shoulder. "Who is that, Sister?"

"Why, that has to be Jesus Himself. After all, Michelangelo knew and believed that Jesus was "consubstantial with the Father" and that "through him all things were made." Michelangelo is making the point that Jesus was present at Adam's creation."

As we stand beneath this masterpiece of Western Art, I can't help but feel like I've experienced this scene before. Then I remember *Charity*, the image of multi-tasking, all-giving Love! It's the image of the busy mother tending her huddle of young children that we visited while reading 1 Corinthians 13. Although the visages are different, the attitudes are the same. It's the attitude of *caritas, agape,* the love of God. Only the Father doesn't need to look upwards to Heaven for inspiration; He is Heaven.

Perhaps as Michelangelo painted his climactic image of God on the Sistine Ceiling, he was inspired by "the prayer our Savior gave us," the Our Father. And as we approach the climactic moment of Communion with God in the Mass, we are suddenly overwhelmed by one big thought.

God is love. And He loves us like a father would: all giving, firm but tender, just but merciful, mindful of our future, with His loving eyes always on us.

This is the Father that Jesus taught us to pray to.

Let's pray together now:

"Our Father, who art in heaven.
Hallowed be thy name.
Thy kingdom come.
Thy will be done,
On earth as it is in heaven.
Give us this day our daily bread,
And forgive us our trespasses,
As we forgive those who trespass against us,
And lead us not into temptation,
But deliver us from evil.
Amen."

SIGN OF PEACE

Immediately following the Our Father, the priest concludes the prayer with a petition to God to

"Deliver us from every evil, and graciously grant peace in our days."

Then he begins the prayer of peace:

"Lord Jesus Christ,
who said to your apostles,
'Peace I leave you. My peace I give you.
Look not on our sins,
but on the faith of your Church,
and graciously grant her peace and unity
in accordance with your will. Amen."

Now, he turns to all of us and offers us that very peace, in Jesus' name.

"The peace of the Lord be with you always."

To see what happens next, we'll need to go to the Upper Room itself, in Jerusalem. For a visual, we'll visit one of our favorite paintings of the apostle Thomas in the Upper Room, by Guercino, in London's National Gallery.

Peace Comes to Thomas

Upper Room, Jerusalem. Evelyn and I visited what by tradition is believed to be the "Upper Room" in Jerusalem on a pilgrimage with Fr. John Connor many years ago. It is located on the second floor of what would have been the property of a wealthy Jewish follower of

The Incredulity of St. Thomas, Giovanni Barbieri Guercino, 1621, The National Gallery, London, England

Jesus, squeezed into a narrow street in Old Jerusalem. Up here, we can imagine how the secluded room of this substantial home, probably protected at that time by a private guard, must have been a place of refuge for the terrified apostles in the early days after Jesus' gruesome execution. And yet, it is meaningful to us as well: These days, we're all in some ways hiding in our own "upper rooms" from a culture that is indifferent at best, hostile often, and murderous at times. And in some ways, we're all gathered now in a kind of upper room of sorts, at Mass. Maybe we're not terrified, but many of us are at least running scared. A little like Thomas and the others in the Upper Room when the resurrected Jesus suddenly appeared to them.

This was a return visit by Jesus. Thomas, who'd been out on an errand the first time, had missed Jesus' first post-Resurrection appearance to the disciples and, famously, doubted that Jesus had actually risen — notwithstanding what the others proclaimed. His faith, despite all he'd seen and heard over three years, and despite his close relationship with the other apostles, was not as strong as it needed to be. Maybe a little like ours.

We've been through a lot at Mass today. We've heard the Lord's words, we've been with Him on Calvary, we've seen Him arrive as the Bread of Life. And yet, we're still not sure.

"Peace be with you," are Jesus' first words as He bursts suddenly onto the scene. And to help Thomas along, He invites him to put his hand into the wound in His side. This is the moment that Guercino imagines for us here.

Thomas presses his hand into Jesus' side, and as he does so, the flesh softly compresses, not as a ghost's would, but as a living person's body would. Somewhat like the reaction of Cleopas as Rembrandt imagined him at Emmaus the week before, Thomas clutches his robe in a gesture of suppressed joy and enthusiasm. As he does so, Jesus gazes tenderly towards Thomas and contemplates what's in his heart.

This is the same Thomas He had called to be His apostle, who He'd sent out with the others to "cure the sick, raise the dead" (Matt. 10:8). Jesus believed in Thomas then, and He believes in him now. Despite Thomas's lack of faith, Jesus loves him like a son. And He's only too happy to have him back.

For all our lack of faith, Jesus loves us, too.

"My Lord and My God," is all Thomas needs to say at this moment. His Lord, our Lord, is alive and with us in the Upper Room.

And with this, all of Thomas's worries and concerns about what's waiting for him "out there," outside the Church, now drain away. He is at peace, the kind of peace that reaches deep into the roots of your soul — an unshakable peace, the peace of faith.

And at this moment, with Thomas, our instant response is to turn with joy to the disciples around us and share this newfound peace with them. We become one community in faith.

With joy in our hearts and a confident joy rising from within to our faces, we turn to our fellow apostles in the Upper Room.

"Peace be with you."

The Breaking of the Bread

(Lamb of God)

We are at peace, with God and each other. Jesus is present, alive. Now we are ready to receive Him into our bodies, and our souls. As the priest and we make final preparations for this moment, the priest breaks the Sacred Host, as Jesus did at the Last Supper and at the supper at Emmaus—and as Jesus' body was broken on the Cross. Then, we begin the Agnus Dei prayer,

"Lamb of God, you take away the sins of the world, have mercy on us.

Lamb of God, you take away the sins of the world, have mercy on us.

Lamb of God, you take away the sins of the world, grant us peace."

From the earliest days of the Church, the evolving structure of the Mass was heavily influenced by the apostle John's account of the "Wedding Supper of the Lamb" in the Book of Revelation, a feast described there as "the wedding day of the Lamb" (Rev. 19:7). In Hebrew tradition, eating a lamb was a key component of the wedding ritual[83]; we witnessed this visually in Veronese's *The Wedding at Cana* (see chapter 1). The early Christians applied this tradition within the Mass, which celebrates the marriage of Christ to us, the Church.

At the same time, another Hebrew tradition, the sacrifice of an unblemished lamb to honor God and seal His covenant with us, was repurposed by Christ Himself as a way to explain the mystery of the Eucharist, Christ's self-sacrifice on Calvary, and His New Covenant.[84] John, this time in his Gospel, also presented the Eucharist as a sacrificial offering of the Lamb of God (see John 1:29). So these two Jewish acts of worship, the marriage supper of the lamb and the sacrifice of the lamb, are both referenced in the eucharistic liturgy. Theologians have written whole books about these two intertwined themes, very dense, high-level stuff, difficult for some of us to comprehend.

Fear not. Our friends the artists have, as usual, developed a way to break through the theological cobwebs with images. Two talented and devout brothers from the southern Netherlands, in the early fifteenth century, created a revolutionary masterpiece on this very topic. It awed everyone who saw it at its unveiling in 1432 and it has awed millions since. To see it, we'll need to take a few train connections to a relatively small town in what is now Belgium. At the time, it was a thriving trade center.

We need to go to Ghent.

Ghent, Belgium. "Whoa!" We have finally arrived at the newly restored Ghent altarpiece, set in the Chapel of the Sacrament of Ghent's St. Bavo's Cathedral. Reaching it entails a three-hour, three-stop trek from Amsterdam, and many people have heard of it yet not seen it.

I had long studied about this storied, "first ever" Renaissance oil painting that had survived thirteen attempts to destroy or steal it over its five-hundred-year history. The Protestant Iconoclasts, Napoleon, and Hitler — none of whom believed in the Eucharist — all went to great lengths to possess it, burn it, or blow it up. Yet the panel that some call the "greatest painting ever created" has miraculously survived to this day.[85] And, despite all that I had read and studied for this moment, I was completely unprepared for what I saw as I turned the corner and suddenly stood before it.

All I could think was, "Behold, the Lamb of God!"

The altarpiece, conceived and probably begun by Hubert van Eyck and completed after his death by his now-more-famous brother Jan, was designed to sit behind the altar of a prominent chapel in the medieval St. Bavo's Cathedral. Nearly eighteen feet wide and twelve feet high, it took more than a decade to create. The artists used what was then a new medium of painting, oil, which allowed for more detail and richness in the composition. The

The Adoration of the Mystic Lamb (Ghent Altarpiece), Hubert and Jan van Eyck, 1432, St. Bavo's Cathedral, Ghent, Belgium

van Eyck brothers used every advantage that oil painting gave them to crown the moment in the Mass at which we've just arrived: the presentation of the Lamb of God. We can see Him there, on the altarpiece's central panel. Everyone is looking right at Him.

The Adoration of the Mystic Lamb (Ghent Altarpiece, detail of central panel), Hubert and Jan van Eyck, 1432, St. Bavo's Cathedral, Ghent, Belgium

The Lamb stands steadfastly on the high altar, unconcerned about the various attempts throughout history to unseat Him. From His side, He is calmly spewing His life's blood into the chalice from which we will all soon drink. Water is flowing from the altar beneath Him into the fountain of eternal life; these are the same waters we saw flowing from the Tree of Life at San Clemente during the Doxology prayer.

The Lamb is surrounded most immediately by His Father's angels, gathered around the altar, celebrating joyously His victory on the Cross. Grouped around Him in the verdant green pastures of Heaven on earth are groups of people who collectively represent the Church now present: (clockwise from the lower right) the apostles and clergy, the Jewish prophets, the male saints, and the female saints. Beyond, on the outer panels, there are knights and princes on the left two panels and we pilgrims on the right panels. Above are the Holy Spirit, God the Father, Mary and John the Baptist. And, yes, Adam and Eve. Even the original sinners are invited to the supper!

All present are basking in the divine light of Heaven, shining down from the Holy Spirit who is hovering above the Lamb. All are bathed in the light of the divine. Even the very jewels of the angels are shimmering in it, reflecting the stained-glass windows around us![86]

As beautiful as the overall effect of the Ghent Altarpiece is, the detail is even more stunning. Even as he attempted to display the abundance of life on earth that God created for us — botanists tell us that seventy-five species of fauna are portrayed in the central panel — van Eyck managed to add realistic botanical symbols of eternity (the evergreen tree) and purity (the lily). Texts from the open books that several figures in the painting are holding have been deciphered. One, in Mary's hands, reads "*De visio Dei*" ("About the vision of God" or seeing God face to face).[87]

Some of the faces we see in the crowds appear to be portraits of present-day people who might be at Mass with us today. As in Veronese's *The Wedding at Cana* (see chapter 1), all strata of society are present, past and future: martyrs, saints, clergy, hermits, pilgrims, nobles, knights, and we, the everyday laity. Some of the churches on the horizon are familiar to anyone who has traveled around the major cities of the lowlands region even to this day, such as what appears to be the bell tower of Utrecht Cathedral in the distance, to the upper left above the Lamb of God. The skyline in the upper right may be contemporary Jerusalem, the ancient city of God. The view out the window of Mary during her Annunciation, on the back of the altarpiece, has been identified as possibly being a picture of Ghent as it stood in the fifteenth century.

The Lamb is here, now. In the present.

Then, with the magnifying lens of my camera, I get close enough to the center panel to come face to face with the eyes of the Lamb of God.

Not what I expected.

Certainly not the unaware gaze of a simple lamb, nor the look of a reprimanding Father.

The Adoration of the Mystic Lamb (Ghent Altarpiece, detail of central panel), Hubert and Jan van Eyck, 1432, St. Bavo's Cathedral, Ghent, Belgium

No. What I see instead is the loving, compassionate gaze of the Good Shepherd. That face seems so happy that I am here. In love with me, despite all of my faults. So joyful to save me from myself, pleading that I come to the Feast. Even as He calmly and firmly stands there, pouring out His blood into the chalice.

He is pouring Himself out for you, and for me.

Here at Mass, the priest now raises the Eucharist and proclaims,

"Behold, the Lamb of God."

At this moment, we can only respond:

"Lord, I am not worthy that you should enter under my roof, but only say the word and my soul shall be healed. . . ."

Feeling unworthy to receive and consume Jesus, even when we are in a state of grace, is natural. In fact, it's completely true, when you think about it. How can any of us mere mortals be "worthy" enough to receive our Lord, sacramentally within us? The answer, of course, is that we are not. And guess what, He loves us so much, He comes anyway. He *makes us* worthy to receive Him.

The saint who has been preparing us to receive Jesus since the beginning of Mass has been Mary Magdalen, the great sinner converted by Jesus into one of His greatest saints. Let's turn to her now. She's down there on the floor, under the altar, kissing Jesus' feet.

"Not Worthy to Receive You"

Santa Croce, Florence. We are back in Santa Croce, surrounded by some of the great masterpieces of the Florentine Renaissance. Like Cimabue's *Crucifixion,* Gaddi's fourteenth-century works for the Church have been weathered by time and were badly damaged in the 1966 flood. Yet they still resonate with much of their original power and physical presence. Painting in the "new style" introduced by Giotto 50 years prior, Gaddi's realistic images are weighty and sculpted, set in a three-dimensional space that gives the impression we are there with the apostles, in the scene. The bright colors, particularly when we stand within the fresco-covered walls of Santa Croce, radiate a liveliness that awakens our senses.

Like most frescoes, Gaddi's remain where they were first plastered into the walls of the Santa Croce complex. To see the panel of Mary Magdalen anointing Christ's feet, we'll need to walk through the

The Last Supper and the Tree of Life, Taddeo Gaddi, ca. 1345–1350, Basilica di Santa Croce, Florence, Italy

church to the former dining room of the monks, called the refectory. It's there that Gaddi painted *The Last Supper* composition, with the Tree of Life (influenced probably by the image we've already seen at San Clemente). As we pray "I am not worthy to receive you," we're here to reflect on a small side panel of the great fresco. Let's focus in on that.

Today's Gospel scholars are not all in agreement on the identity of the woman who anointed Jesus' feet at dinner. There are two different occasions when Jesus' feet were anointed by a woman while He was at dinner with the disciples. One is recorded in Luke's Gospel (see Luke 7:36–50) and occurred midway in Christ's ministry; the second is detailed in John's (see John 12:1–8) and occurred a week before the Passover meal that became the Last Supper. The two stories were often conflated, and sometimes confused with Jesus' own washing of the apostles' feet at the Last Supper.

Gaddi here is most likely describing the second story, where "Mary," the sister of Martha of Bethany, anoints the feet of Jesus with precious oils and dries them with her hair. Although Mary of Bethany is confused here and elsewhere as Mary of Magdala, whether the

Mary Magdalen Anointing the Feet of Jesus (*Tree of Life* side panel), Taddeo Gaddi, ca. 1345–1350 , Basilica di Santa Croce, Florence, Italy

woman who did this was really Mary Magdalen or Mary of Bethany doesn't matter. In some ways, she is one of us — a forgiven sinner. So, let's imagine we are there, at that dinner, as Gaddi describes the story.

It is late in Jesus' ministry, and He's been hinting to the apostles that His Passion and death are near. Most of the men choose to ignore Him, but Mary has a feeling that something terrible is about to happen. Mary had been on the wrong track, to say the least, possessed by seven demons (see Mark 16:9). Her life was a mess and heading to disaster. She believed she was uncurable, unforgivable — until she met Jesus.

No one is unforgivable in the eyes of God.

When Jesus forgave her, when He reminded her that she remains a beloved child of God, her life changed. We saw her the night of her first meeting in La Tour's masterpiece, *The Repentant Magdalen* (see chapter 1). Despair became hope, loneliness became joy, hate became love. Mary was transformed from sinner to saint. She became a devout follower of Jesus. Now, in grief for what Jesus has intimated is to come, Mary crawls on the floor beneath the dining table and washes the feet of Jesus. Only slaves did this kind of thing; the feet of travelers in Jesus' time were generally dirty, and Jewish tradition would have avoided physical contact with impure things, especially at dinner. But Mary not only washes the feet of Jesus. She also drys them with her own hair, then anoints them with some of the most precious oil she could find.

We assume this was not Mary's "first confession," though it may have been. Luke's version for sure alludes to this. Either way, at this moment of the meal, as all are about to break bread with Jesus, Mary hesitates. She feels unworthy, undeserving of something so special as a shared meal with the Lord. And so, she crawls to Jesus' feet, seeking assurance that she is really forgiven. She is most certainly praying a supplication like the words of another sinner, the Roman centurion, recorded earlier in the same seventh chapter of Luke: "Lord . . . I am not worthy to have you enter under my roof. . . . but say the word and let my servant . . . be healed" (Luke 7:6–7).

Then Jesus does something very special, incredibly reassuring — for Mary, and for us.

Jesus reaches across the table, forgives Mary, and reassures her that yes, she is a beloved daughter of God.

With that, Mary — and we — have the healing we need. She's ready to receive Him under her roof — here at Mass, Heaven on earth.

Before we leave Santa Croce, my eye catches the man at the head of the table, on Jesus' right. He's well dressed, and in a position of honor, at the head of table. "That's the guy I want to be!" I think for a moment, "not poor Mary crawling on her belly beneath the table." Then I notice a small detail. He doesn't have a halo.

And Jesus isn't reaching across the table to him. He's reaching for Mary.

Hmmm.

Have I ever had that attitude at Mass? That not only was I not a sinner this week, but rather, a saint? That I "deserve" to receive Jesus in the Eucharist?

When I start thinking like that, I try to remember Santa Croce and its lessons. None of us deserve Jesus. Still, He will reach across the table for us anyway. We just have to ask Him, with the humility of Mary Magdalen. Then we, like her, will get our halo too.

Communion Hymn

As we begin to come towards the altar for Communion, the liturgy calls for a Communion antiphon or hymn. The latter is normally a gentle, "quiet" hymn that enhances the reverence of the moment. The Church has several for this very special moment, and one of its longtime favorites is the Latin hymn *Panis Angelicus,* written by St. Thomas Aquinas for the Feast of Corpus Christi in the thirteenth century. If you don't know the tune, don't worry — the angels from the Ghent Altarpiece will lead us. They are in the upper left panel, above *The Adoration of the Lamb.*

"Panis Angelicus"

Panis angelicus
fit panis hominum,
Dat panis caelicus
figuris terminum.
O res mirabilis! manducat Dominum
Pauper, servus et humilis.

Holy and living bread,
Wondrous food, from heaven sent,
God's sacrifice, behold —
The mysteries hidden here.
Sign and reality,
As we eat, the Lord we see,
With humble hearts, adore
Fairest Jesus, his heart so pure.[88]

Singing Angels (Ghent Altarpiece), Hubert and Jan van Eyck, 1432, St. Bavo's Cathedral, Ghent, Belgium

Angel Playing the Organ (Ghent Altarpiece), Hubert and Jan van Eyck, 1432, St. Bavo's Cathedral, Ghent, Belgium

RECEIVING COMMUNION

As we approach the altar for the grace and privilege of consuming the Body and Blood of Christ, we do so humbly and reverently. We know, that on our own, we are not worthy, and can never be worthy, of this. But, reassured that we are indeed beloved sons and daughters of Jesus, and conscious that we are in sacramental, moral, and doctrinal communion with Him, we also know He wants this for us, and for Himself. So, to honor Him, we come.

The actual distribution of the Eucharist parallels the Consecration of the Host earlier in the Mass. The beautiful images we used there could serve for what is happening now: Juan de Juanes's image of Jesus holding up the Eucharist to the gathered apostles at the Last Supper and Raphael's painting of Jesus pouring out His blood into the chalice on Calvary. Yet, there is another that focuses almost entirely on the moment we now find ourselves in at the Mass, the distribution of Holy Communion. It hangs on the walls of a church in Rome, just a three-minute walk from the Pantheon.

Get ready. The Lord Himself is up there, distributing the Eucharist at the front of the line.

Santa Maria sopra Minerva, Rome. Rome is one of those blessed cities where you can find a beautiful Catholic church on nearly every third block, and most of them still have the rich artwork created for the faithful on the solemn occasion of their visits to Mass. Santa Maria sopra Minerva is one of those. It's located in the old district near the Pantheon, built on the ruins of an old Roman temple to the goddess Minerva. From the outside, its simple façade does not prepare us for the luminous Gothic spectacle within. The soaring vaults, shimmering mosaics, and magical stained-glass windows project, well, Heaven. Just where we want to be when receiving Communion. Let's go ahead to the side chapel where Federico Barocci's *Communion of the Apostles* hangs.

Federico Barocci's long career in Rome spanned the Counter-Reformation period of the late-sixteenth and early-seventeenth centuries. Like Juan de Juanes, he was a devout Catholic. He was also a member of the lay order of Capuchin friars. His religious devotion infuses his art with a sublime beauty. And in the case of the image we stand before now, he had help from the pope; Pope Clement VIII commissioned this painting from him and is said to have been heavily involved in the composition.[89]

Interior (restored mid-nineteenth century), 1280–1370,
Santa Maria sopra Minerva, Rome, Italy

The scene Barocci is imagining for us here is the Last Supper, the first Mass, as Jesus distributes the Eucharist. Full of motion and energy, *Communion of the Apostles* resembles the enthusiastic bustling of the assembled people of God that is now happening around us here, at Mass.

The room is dark but for the heavenly light that emanates from Jesus. The Lord appears confident, loving, peaceful. A group of figures jostle about Jesus as He distributes the Eucharist. Below, two young altar boys clear the basin beneath the table where Jesus has washed the feet of the apostles, forgiving them of their sins and preparing them to commune with Him. Mary Magdalen, dressed

Communion of the Apostles, Federico Barocci, 1603–1608, Santa Maria sopra Minerva, Rome, Italy

in her customary red cloak, is still on her knees, finishing up from having just anointed Jesus' feet. Peter, dressed in gold as the leader of the apostles, is first to receive and is on his knees as Jesus literally gives him a piece of Himself. As he does so, Jesus' light shines brightly, reflecting brilliantly off Peter's bright golden cloak. The other apostles swirl in a line behind Peter, awaiting their turn. The ones closest to Peter and Jesus appear focused and in awe at what is happening. Others, deeper back in the line, still seem a little distracted. Perhaps that's me, or you.

Off to Jesus' left, our eye catches the man dressed in orange, a color used to symbolize blind ambition; he is an apostle with his own agenda, not Jesus'. Worse, he's looking down, away from Jesus and the light, into the darkness — no halo. This must be Judas. He's already turned his back to the Lord, slithering away from Him, into the night.

A Closer Look

The figure of Judas in *Communion of the Apostles* is a very close copy of the figure that Raphael used to paint Michelangelo into the *School of Athens,* which was at our backs as we viewed the *Disputation* at the Room of the Signature. Scholars debate whether this little quotation by Barocci was a salute or a rebuke to his Renaissance forbear, but either way, in the context of Barocci's *Communion,* the man is clearly meant to portray the fallen Apostle Judas.

School of Athens (detail), Raphael, 1508–1511, Room of the Signature (Vatican Museums), Rome, Italy

There are times at Mass where I have not been in the state of grace I would need to be to receive Communion and so had to stay seated at this moment. I've got to tell you, it doesn't feel great. I feel left out, alone, unworthy — a traitor, of sorts. But even then, I always look up to the Eucharist, and I plead with the Lord to help me back on the road. I commit to reconciling with Him in Confession, as Peter did, as Mary Magdalen did.

And as Judas did not.

It's sad for me to think of being in Judas's state.

"His problem wasn't his sin, Steve," Msgr. Donald Sakano assures me. Msgr. Sakano is a joyful and confident fellow missionary friend from our mission days in SoHo around the Basilica of St. Patrick's Old Cathedral, where he was pastor at the time. From a lifetime of hearing Confessions and dispensing the Lord's mercy, Monsignor understands the sacrament as well as anyone. "We all fall at some point. Judas's problem was he believed he was unforgivable. He was afraid to seek the Lord's forgiveness. He didn't just skip a chance for Communion this one time. He did so permanently. It was this permanent denial of Jesus' offer of mercy that wounded Judas's soul so mortally."

We are all called to be Peter and Mary Magdalen. In fact, we all need to be them. And the only way to get there is to do what they did. Stay in the fight. Get up when you get knocked down. Seek His grace in Reconciliation, with the humility of Mary Magdalen and the perseverance in faith of Peter.

And receive Jesus in Communion.

And then, you are neither Peter, nor the Magdalen, nor Judas.

You are Christ.

"The Body of Christ."

"Amen"

In the instant before we receive our Lord in the Eucharist, we say "Amen."

Although the "Amen" at the end of the Eucharistic Prayers is often referred to by theologians as "the Great Amen," in many ways for us it is this "Amen," which we declare as we receive Jesus into us, that might be the greatest of them all. As Msgr. Landry reminds me, "It's this 'Amen' as we receive Jesus that testifies our faith that Jesus is truly present in the Eucharist — Body, Blood, Soul, and Divinity."

"Another way to think about this, Steve," Msgr. Landry adds, "is that we are assenting here not just to consuming the Eucharist, but *to the Eucharist consuming us*; to Jesus making us more like Him."[90]

Evelyn nods. "And if we assent to that, Monsignor, doesn't that mean we're assenting to discipleship? To a transformation from 'pilgrims' to 'evangelists'?"

"That's it!" I conclude. "We're consenting to the whole deal. To the joys along with the sufferings. To whatever it takes to grow the Kingdom. We are entering into a covenantal — not transactional — relationship with Jesus."

"This amen," Evelyn adds, "is our assent to His will for us — cross and all."

And that brings us to our Mother, Mary. After Jesus' "Amen" in the Garden of Gethsemane, there has been no more perfect "Amen," or "Fiat" ("Let it be done to me") in history than Mary's during her Annunciation. So having her accompany us now, at this moment, seems appropriate.

The Annunciation is probably the single most popular image in Catholic churches and, today, in many museums. The Met alone, for instance, has more than twenty Annunciation images, more than any other single subject in the museum. My rough guess is that the total number of original Annunciation images in the world runs in the tens of thousands; if you count reprints, the number would have to be counted at well over a billion.

Among all these Annunciation images, the one almost universally recognized as the most impactful throughout art history is a masterpiece by a humble monk, painted on the walls of a monastery. We've been with him before, at the Convent of San Marco. His name is Fra Angelico.

To see his masterpiece, we'll need to hop the train from Rome back to Florence.

The Annunciation, Fra Angelico, ca. 1442–1443, Convent of San Marco, Florence, Italy

Convent of San Marco, Florence. For our "Amen" as we receive the Lord in Communion, Evelyn and I are here in the Convent of San Marco, where Fra Angelico painted perhaps the most famous and influential Annunciation painting of all time. This image we are standing before, frescoed into the wall as you come up the stairs to the monks' quarters, revolutionized how artists ever since have painted the Annunciation. Among other things, Fra Angelico's *The Annunciation* brought the Annunciation back to earth. Fitting, perhaps, as we contemplate our own "Amen" here in Mass, as we receive the Eucharist.

Prior to Fra Angelico's San Marco image, the Annunciation was typically painted while Mary was at prayer within her room, and often in a two-dimensional setting that was more symbolic than real. At San Marco, Fra Angelico set the Annunciation in the patio of a walled, outdoor garden. The architectural perspective he employed, using mathematics to create a three-dimensional space, creates the illusion of depth and emphasizes the physical reality of this moment as God literally comes out of the heavens to earth. The cloister architecture, similar to the cloisters of San Marco where the Annunciation is frescoed into the wall, suggests that the scene is not just happening somewhere on earth, but potentially right here in San Marco. Or maybe even here, in our own church, at the head of the Communion line.

The garden setting also emphasized Mary's purity from original sin, as a garden in the fifteenth century stood for the purity of creation, before the corrosive effects of sin had entered the world. It is a reference to the original virginal garden, the Garden of Eden, from which we witnessed Adam and Eve's banishment in the first sample Old Testament reading; they pursued their own will, not God's. The pillar, separating Mary and the angel, was Fra Angelico's technique to emphasize that Mary's virginal conception of Jesus was by the Holy Spirit; she was untouched by even the angel. This pillar would hereafter be used by other Renaissance artists for the same purpose.

In short, Mary is the New Eve, the beginning of the "do-over" that becomes the New Covenant we are celebrating here today.

As we receive our Lord in Communion, and as we recommit to the New Covenant, none of us can ever be in the spiritual condition, without original sin, that our Mother Mary was at the moment of the Annunciation. Still, the need to be in a state of grace as we receive our Lord in Communion is real. It's not just "one of those old-fashioned rules of the Church." We are about to host our Lord Himself within us. A spiritual echo, if you will, of the Annunciation.

Am I spiritually ready for this moment?

As we stand here in the monastery contemplating Mary, we consider the humble and quiet way that she bows before the will of God. The scene is so intimate, so restrained. Despite the quiet bustle of others around us, you can hear a pin drop as we stand here, reflecting in awe. The only noise seems to be coming from those fluttering, multi-colored wings of Heaven on the angel. But for those, the colors around us are muted, the atmosphere, still.

As is the church, as we stand before Jesus.

As quiet and subdued as the scene is, we sense that something very profound is happening. A kinetic energy pulses. Trumpets are blaring in my heart, even though none appear in the cloister.

Do I feel this restrained energy as I stand before the priest, offering me Jesus Himself?

Mary is alone, with the angel. Although Mary casts a shadow, the angel does not. Rather, he projects the divine light of God, which now envelops her. The two are separated by the pillar, yet seem connected in a very deep, spiritual way. They are connected by the divine light. Their eyes lock.

As we watch, Mary bows to the angel's message, bearing the will of God for her. Then, as Jesus is conceived within her, the angel bows before Mary and the baby Jesus now in her womb.

As the priest holds the Eucharist before me, do I bow as reverently?

The angel's message is not an easy one. Mary is to become the virgin mother of a child who will challenge not just the political authorities that rule Judea, but the religious authorities as well. And what a mess this will make of her marriage to Joseph — though betrothed and, in a Jewish context, contractually married, what if he divorces her over it? And even if he doesn't, escaping the combined forces of Herod and Caesar will be terrifying for a young unwed girl who'd barely ever even left the little town of Nazareth. Egypt? Where is that?

Still, Mary offers no counterpoints — no side agreements, footnotes, or fine print.[91]

Reflecting on Mary's wholehearted consent, am I ready to give my own assent to Jesus and accept the gift as offered? Or am I preparing my list of counterpoints, as if entering a transaction, a contract? Am I ready to enter the covenant relationship with Jesus that is on offer here, along with the crosses that relationship will entail?

Then, Mary bows. She humbly gives her fiat. Her "Yes." Her "Amen."

"May it be done to me according to your word."
(Luke 1:38)

Quietly. No trumpets.

And with that simple yes, the Lord and Savior comes into the world.

Now, it's our turn to receive Him. And to let Him help us illumine the world, whatever it takes.

It's time for us to give our consent to the whole deal. Our "all in" moment. Our,

"Amen."

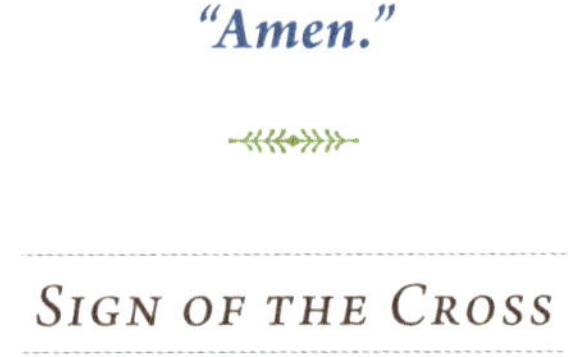

SIGN OF THE CROSS

We Cross Ourselves in Awe and Silence

As we receive Christ in the Eucharist, many Catholics make another Sign of the Cross. We're in such awe, we don't know what else to do. And we know that what we just said "yes" to will take supernatural help. So we invoke the Trinity. And make the Sign of the Cross.

We've seen a lot of crosses already, but I want to take you to one that I only discovered on this special pilgrimage to the Eucharist. It's already become one of my favorites. It's back in Rome, at the Basilica di San Lorenzo in Lucina.

Basilica di San Lorenzo in Lucina, Rome. I first found Reni's *Crucifixion* by accident, engaged in the most prosaic of tasks. I'd just arrived in Rome and realized I needed a shirt; so I marched off through the winding side streets of the Colonna district and found something appropriate. As I chatted about art and God with Eva, a cheerful salesperson there, she insisted I visit the nearby Basilica di San Lorenzo in Lucina. I'd passed by its nondescript façade on many occasions, but I had never paused for a look inside. When she mentioned Guido Reni, I was sold. Evelyn and I are big Reni fans from our pilgrimages to the Met.

As I open the church door, all is quiet and dark inside. A lone worshiper kneels, praying. Then, I look at the altar. Just above, I see it. Guido Reni's painting of Christ on the Cross. Oh, my!

The Crucifixion, Guido Reni, 1640, Basilica di San Lorenzo in Lucina, Rome, Italy

This is not just another Crucifixion painting. It's a Crucifixion and a Resurrection painting rolled into one. And so very appropriate as we've just received the crucified and risen Jesus in the Eucharist. Three hundred years later, Salvador Dali would carry this idea to an even more pronounced expression. We'll be visiting Dali's crucifix later, but let's pray for a moment here.

Although Christ is hanging on a Cross, Reni has painted Him vibrantly; He is very much alive, not dead. This effect of life is enhanced by the way Jesus' waist garment is flying in the wind, evoking images of the Resurrection. The blinding light reflecting off Jesus' body has the effect of almost shadowing out the Cross itself; from the distance of the pews, it almost seems that Jesus is floating in the air, resurrecting.

He is bigger than the very Cross that He has defeated.

Then, I look for His wounds and can barely see them. It seems Jesus is almost not even nailed to the Cross. As He looks upward to His Father, He seems to be holding Himself on the Cross, in an act of pure, all-willing love — for me, and for you.

So, we receive Him into us.

"In the name of the Father, and the Son, and the Holy Spirit."

"Jesus said to them, "Amen, amen, I say to you, unless you eat the flesh of the Son of Man and drink his blood, you do not have life within you. Whoever eats my flesh and drinks my blood has eternal life, and I will raise him on the last day. For my flesh is true food, and my blood is true drink. Whoever eats my flesh and drinks my blood remains in me and I in him. Just as the living Father sent me and I have life because of the Father, so also the one who feeds on me will have life because of me."

—John 6:53–57

– 12 –

Reflections Following Communion

AFTER DISTRIBUTING HOLY Communion and cleaning the sacred vessels used for Mass, the priest will sit down, to give all of us a few moments to contemplate what just happened: "a miracle of love."[92] This is no time for our heart and mind to begin wandering! Jesus has just given His all for us; "imagine how he must feel to give Himself so closely to us and then to be ignored."[93] So, if you find yourself getting restless at this point in the Mass, try to use it just to be alone with Jesus and have a short conversation. Make this one of your favorite times in the Mass. Complete silence, alone with the Lord. Just you, and Him. This moment, in some ways, is the entire reason you are here.

SECOND COMMUNION HYMN

Often, for this silent meditation time, the choir will sing a second Communion hymn. This one captures the unified spirit of the congregation at this special time. We are indeed one body in Christ. Just imagine one of those music-playing angels from the Ghent Altarpiece leading us.

Angel Playing the Organ (Ghent Altarpiece detail), Hubert and Jan van Eyck, 1420–1432, St. Bavo's Cathedral, Ghent, Belgium

"Thou, Who at Thy First Eucharist Did Pray"

Lord, who at Thy first Eucharist did pray
That all Thy Church might be forever one,
Grant us at ev'ry Eucharist to say
With longing heart and soul, "Thy will be done."
O may we all one bread, one body be,
Through this blest Sacrament of Unity.

For all thy Church, O Lord, we intercede;
Make Thou our sad divisions soon to cease;
Draw us the nearer each, to each we plead,
By drawing all to Thee, O Prince of Peace;
Thus may we all one bread, one body be,
Through this blest Sacrament of Unity.[94]

Reflection Following Communion (Sample 1)

"As Special as the First Time"

First Holy Communion, Pablo Picasso, 1896,
Picasso Museum, Barcelona, Spain

Picasso Museum, Barcelona. When Evelyn and I found this painting by Picasso at the Picasso Museum in Madrid, we were stunned. Neither of us was aware that Picasso had painted an image so realistic. Also, we knew him as his adult self, an apparent non-believer, so we never suspected he'd painted so religious a scene as a First Holy Communion. He painted it as a precocious fifteen-year-old, still studying painting under the strict tutelage of the art teachers at a formal Barcelona school of art called La Llotja. His father, a strong Catholic, is said to have been heavily involved in supervising the creation of this very formal image. According to the museum's guide, the young girl in the painting is thought to be the artist's younger sister Lola. Lola and Pablo became especially close after their younger sister died of diphtheria the year before. The sponsors behind Lola were close friends of Picasso's father.

At first, we struggle to get over the idea that this painting came from the brush of the same artist as the creator of *Demoiselles d'Avignon*, and other works by which he relished in transforming images of the Divine into images of the profane.[95] We take some comfort in the fact that Picasso kept this painting in his private collection until shortly before his death in 1973. Maybe it was just a sentimental attachment to his first major work, or to his sister Lola. Or maybe this image stirred something more in his soul. We don't know.

With that thought, our own souls are stirred as we ourselves remember that very special moment when we received our First Holy Communion. All the preparation, all the singing practice, all the relatives who came to witness it, the celebration feast that followed! The young girl's translucent white dress, so delicately painted by the young Picasso, seems almost to glow with the grace of this moment. I can't help remembering the little blue suit my mom bought for me, which seemed so special, especially knowing the tight budget the family lived on in those days. Both the customary blue suit for the boys and white gown for the girls references in some way how this occasion of our First Communion is a marriage to Christ, the first time He becomes "one flesh" with us. Picasso's brush picks up the seriousness of the moment in the attentive faces of the two sponsors standing behind his little sister. And certainly, in the posture of Lola herself.

As she awaits the arrival of the priest, she is undisturbed by the last-minute preparations of the altar boy in front of her. Little Lola is focused, so preciously and so devoutly reciting her prayer readings, wanting to be sure she receives Jesus perfectly—just right.

As we contemplate the Communion with Jesus we've just experienced, this would be a good time to reflect on the excitement and seriousness of our First Holy Communion. Did we, and do we, receive Christ in this same way today? Or have we fallen into a state of such familiarity that we've forgotten just how special this is?

Reflection Following Communion (Sample 2)

"As Special as the Last Time"

Another way to contemplate Communion is to imagine not our first time, but our last time. What will it be like to receive Communion for the last time, on our death bed? How seriously will that moment be? Fortunately, another Spanish painter, one who heavily influenced Picasso, painted this very subject. And to see it, we just need to hop a short flight up to Madrid.

Museo del Prado, Madrid. We're standing before an early Velásquez masterpiece about the meeting of two well-known Christian hermits in the Egyptian desert: the aged St. Paul the Hermit and his younger successor, St. Anthony the Abbot. Shortly before Paul died, Anthony searched for and found him at his hermitage. While they were praying together, a raven from Heaven carried to them a loaf of bread, which they blessed, broke, and shared. Although the tradition around this meeting does not call it a Mass or Communion per se, there are several hints in Velásquez's painting that suggest that is precisely what the artist was contemplating. The bread is in the form

Saints Anthony Abott and Paul the Hermit, Diego Velásquez, 1635, Museo del Prado, Madrid, Spain

of a Host. The Host is being carried in the mouth of a raven, a bird thought in these times to be a messenger from Heaven and potentially a harbinger of pending death. The two saints are prayerfully kneeling like Picasso's Lola, waiting to receive.

On the lower left behind St. Anthony, there's a second image of the two saints. It's a painting within the painting. Here, St. Anthony reverently buries the now-dead St. Paul. Anthony is helped by two lions, who, according to tradition, helped the saint dig the hermit's grave.

The burial scene in the distance suggests this is St. Paul's "Last Communion." As we contemplate the mystery of the Communion we've just experienced, none of us knows if this, too, is our "Last Communion."

If it is, are we approaching it as prayerfully and solemnly as St. Paul is doing? Are our eyes looking up towards Heaven? Can we see Jesus coming down in the Eucharist, being borne by one of His messengers from Heaven?

And is the whole Church around us suddenly as light and luminescent as the landscape before us?

Another way to reflect on Communion, rather than Heaven coming down to us, is our being pulled by Communion right into Heaven. There's a spectacular image of this possibility back in Florence.

Reflection Following Communion (Sample 3)

"Transported to Heaven"

Ascension of St. John the Evangelist, Giotto, ca. 1315, Peruzzi Chapel (Santa Croce), Florence, Italy

Chiesa di Santa Croce, Florence. We are back in Santa Croce amidst Giotto's famous frescoes that changed the course of Western Art. We're in the Peruzzi Chapel, contemplating a scene at the base of the left wall called the *Ascension of the Evangelist.* Like many of the frescoes in Santa Croce, overpainting and then the 1966 flood have taken their toll, but through the haze, Giotto's seven-hundred-year-old images still have great solidity and life to them.

The scene follows the Christian tradition that John, the youngest apostle and identified as "the one Jesus loved," has now finally died of old age, perhaps on the Greek island of Patmos or Ephesus. John is the only apostle believed not to have died a martyr's death.[96] In fact, John lived long enough to write his Gospel of Christ's life, three letters to the early Church, and the Book of Revelation. Much of Revelation was incorporated into the Mass liturgy in which we are now participating.[97]

John has just died, and mourners are grouped on the left and right of a large patio of what appears to be a cloister. The dark blue nighttime sky is glowing. From above, Christ Himself has flown in from Heaven, reaching through an opening in the roof.

He has come back for John.

Jesus is literally raising him up from the grave and hoisting him to Heaven. As he does so, the whole dark room is lit up with a heavenly light, and John floats effortlessly out of his grave into the waiting arms of Christ.

"I guarded them, and none of them was lost except the son of destruction" (John 17:12).

What really gets to me about this image is how the eyes of Christ and John lock so lovingly on each other. For each, it's as if no one else is there, and nothing else matters. Their eyes bond them as one. Giotto underscores this communion of the two with those rays of heavenly light, which emanate from Christ and seem to fully surround and bathe the apostle.

As we kneel here having just received Communion, can we feel Jesus' heavenly light bathing us, and lifting us up to Heaven?

Giotto's image of heavenly rays bathing a saint in communion with Jesus bring our minds back to one of our most treasured images from the churches in Rome, one we almost always visit in our pilgrimages there. It's an image of a saint literally lifted off the ground in the spiritual ecstasy of communion with God. Let's go back to Rome to see it.

Reflection Following Communion (Sample 4)

"Spiritual Ecstasy"

Chiesa di Santa Maria della Vittoria, Rome. Whenever we visit with St. Teresa here, there is always a gaggle of tourists snapping photos of Bernini's masterpiece, which floats above a side altar on the left aisle of the church. Modern scholars and many tourists, perhaps unaware of St. Teresa and her story, might look at Bernini's image and see a physical expression of love. Nothing could be farther from the truth. As my friend Liz Lev explains: *St. Teresa* is an image of divine love, pure and simple. "Later centuries have grown so tragically lost in the immediacy of bodily pleasure that viewers have come to lack the capacity even to imagine divine love."[98]

St. Teresa of Ávila was what the Church would call a mystic, whose prayer life had taken her to heights of intimacy with Jesus that most of us won't fully experience until we, God willing, reach Heaven. Her sense of communion with Him is something for all of us to contemplate in this quiet moment in Mass, because it is also happening to us, now. In her autobiography called *El Libro de mi Vida* in Spanish or *The Life of St. Teresa* in English, she left us with an idea of what Communion should be:

The Ecstasy of St. Teresa, Gian Lorenzo Bernini, 1652,
Chiesa di Santa Maria della Vittoria, Rome, Italy

"Sometimes [Jesus] comes with such great majesty that no one could doubt but that it is the Lord Himself. Especially after receiving Communion — for we know that He is present since our faith tells us this — He reveals Himself so much the Lord of this dwelling that it seems the soul is completely dissolved; and it sees itself consumed in Christ."[99]

Later in her spiritual journey, something even more dramatic occurred. She was mystically pierced by "a spear of gold" borne by an angel of the Lord, and when he drew it out, she said, it "left me all on fire with a great love of God. The pain was so great that it made me moan, and yet so surpassing was the sweetness of this excessive pain, that I could not wish to be rid of it.... *The pain is not bodily, but spiritual*."[100]

Sometimes after receiving Communion, my mind drifts off to my busy "To Do" list that is awaiting me shortly as the Mass draws to an end. Yet even then, Jesus is stirring my soul, to remind me of my reflection here, with Bernini's *The Ecstasy of St. Teresa*. This is what Communion with God is meant to be. This is what it will be continuously if I get to Heaven.

I am consuming the Eucharist. I am consuming Jesus. And more importantly, Jesus is consuming me.

Reflection Following Communion (Sample 5)

"One Body in Christ"

"As a body is one though it has many parts, and all the parts of the body, though many, are one body, so also Christ."

— *1 Cor. 12:12*

Convent of San Marco, Cell 35, Florence. As we reflect following Communion, we've come back to San Marco one last time, to Cell 35. This is one of the cells reserved for the more senior monks, where Fra Angelico painted scenes designed for this very purpose: spiritual reflection. In this case, we have one of the most beautiful

Communion of the Apostles, Fra Angelico, 1439–1443, Convent of San Marco (Cell 35), Florence, Italy

reflections on Communion ever created, before or since. It's a reflection on the First Communion of the apostles.

In some ways, we've seen this composition earlier: in the Prado with Juan de Juanes for the "words of institution" and more recently, in Santa Maria sopra Minerva with Barocci, for the moment in which we received Communion amidst the bustle of communicants around us in the Mass. (See chapters 10 and 11, respectively.) Both of these paintings, executed in later centuries, owe something to Fra Angelico's depiction we stand before now. Yet, somehow, the "angelic friar's" version remains unique.

"What I love so much about this image," Evelyn explains, "is how intimate it is, and how connected all the apostles seem to be with one another as they receive. Even as they each approach Jesus in the Eucharist with their individual attitudes and personalities, they somehow also seem to be in the process of literally becoming one body, in Christ."

One of the magnificent aspects of the monk cells in San Marco is the limited and not always uniform space on the walls that Fra Angelico had available to paint. To solve the technical challenges presented, he often improvised in a spectacular way. In this fresco, for instance, lacking the space to show the apostles in the usual theatrical format of a single long horizontal table, he instead squeezed in all of them by using an L-shaped table. Then he placed four on their knees across on the right. Crammed together in this intimate, quiet setting, the apostles become part of one circle, with Christ at the center.

Fra Angelico adds other elements that extend the layers of meaning for the monks, and for us. First, there's Judas. He's there among the four apostles on their knees, but his halo is not the same as the others. Rather than shining brightly, it's gone dark. Mentally, he's already gone out into the darkness. As I reflect here in Mass about what just happened, am I still here? Or is my mind already back in "the world," on my next event after Mass? Or worse, am I already physically outside, having rushed from the Communion line straight to my car in the parking lot?

Has my shiny halo already started to darken up?

Next, there's Mary. Fra Angelico has painted her into the image, even though there is no record in the Gospel accounts of her having been present. Of course, we don't know one way or the other whether Mary was present. Was she simply not acknowledged by the Gospel writers? All four of them omitted her. In Fra Angelico's time, for sure, Catholics believed Mary was not present. So why did he include her?

Fra Angelico helps us meditate on this by the stool, or I should say, the lack of a stool. Unlike the four apostles on the right, whose four stools sit empty from where they'd left them as they advanced to receive Communion, Mary has no stool. She is also disproportionately smaller than she should be if she were physically present. Mary is in the scene spiritually, not physically. Mustn't it be that spiritually, Mary *was* there, and is there now, in Mass with us, receiving the Body and Blood of her Son? After all, as we receive the

Body of our Lord, as we enter into communion with Him, we also enter into communion with all other members of the Church who are in communion with Him. First of these is Mary.

Then, there's the empty seat at the table, hidden behind Jesus' head as He distributes Communion. We know that was probably the seat He'd been using, but we can also imagine it as our seat, right there at the scene — right here, at Mass.

As we place ourselves there at the table, nestled in amongst the apostles, so close to Christ, a thought occurs. We can't see ourselves because, in the painting, the body of Christ occludes us. We are hidden behind His body.

Or in some ways, we've become His Body, along with the others in that intimate little room.

We have become One Body in Christ.

Reflection Following Communion (Sample 6)

"I Love You So Much"

The presence of Mary at the Last Supper as imagined by Fra Angelico suggests a sixth reflection in these final moments while the priest or deacon is carefully cleaning the sacred vessels. There's a wonderful way to think about Mary's relationship in communion with Christ back in New York, at our own Metropolitan Museum of Art. It's presented somewhat surprisingly in their newly redesigned and reconfigured European Painting galleries.

The Metropolitan Museum of Art, New York. Shortly after the European galleries reopened after the long-delayed "Skylights project," Evelyn and I rushed up there one Sunday afternoon to see our favorite paintings. Some of them had been in storage for five years, others moved to temporary spaces in other areas of the museum. When we found Duccio's *Madonna and Child* back where it

Madonna and Child,
Duccio di Buoninsegna,
ca. 1290–1300, The Metropolitan
Museum of Art, New York

The Virgin Adoring the Host,
Jean-August-Dominique
Ingres, 1852, The Metropolitan
Museum of Art, New York

belonged, in the fourteenth-century Florentine gallery, we were greeted by a very pleasant surprise: the Met had paired alongside it an equally intimate nineteenth-century Ingres image of Mary adoring Christ in the Eucharist. Wow!

On the left, Duccio single-handedly begins a new movement in European art to paint human emotion and the intimacy of human relationships, "To paint the soul of man."[101] Mary gazes lovingly upon her dear Son, Jesus, so very precious to her. She is deeply in love with the young boy, whom she knows has both a difficult and triumphant path before Him. Then Jesus does something special: He loves her back. His eyes reach out toward hers, and their gazes meet.

As Jesus reaches up to her face with His little hand, curling her hair in His fingers, He's telling her, "Thank you Mom, for all you're doing for me. It's all going to be okay. I love you so much." In this little painting, barely nine by six inches, Duccio helps us imagine what a quiet, intimate moment with our Lord can be like — and the bond that can happen between a human soul and God's at moments like these.

Beside the Duccio, the Met has now placed a kind of nineteenth-century equivalent of Mary in Adoration of our Lord, by the French realist painter Jean-Auguste-Dominique Ingres. We once again have a relatively small painting, intended for private devotion, barely larger than the Duccio. Yet again, though there are two saints attending her in the background, Mary is alone with Jesus. This time, Jesus is present not as a young boy, but as a eucharistic Host on the altar — the way we are experiencing Him right now.

Still, Mary's gaze seems to be the same: love, gratitude, faith. Her eyes appear to lock with Jesus'. She sees His familiar eyes, there in the Eucharist.

And in the quiet of the moment, we can hear Jesus say to her, and to us, "It's all going to be okay. I love you so much." We can almost see those familiar eyes of Jesus in the *Lamb of God* at Ghent.

As I kneel here in the quiet church, with the choir singing the last bars of "One Bread, One Body," I'm suddenly there with Mary, adoring the Lord before me, and within me. And as I put myself there with her, I hear His voice:

"I love you so much."

Before we leave Communion, let's imagine going back to the Uffizi Gallery for one last painting about the delight of this moment with Jesus, the sheer joy of it. The painting we have in mind is not the Uffizi's most famous, but it might be its most joyful. To accompany it, let's sing this familiar Christmas carol about the joy of Jesus coming into our lives at Bethlehem. We don't usually do three Communion hymns at Mass — and yet it occasionally happens when we're especially full of joy!

"What Child Is This?"

What Child is this, who, laid to rest,
on Mary's lap, is sleeping?
Whom angels greet with anthems sweet,
while shepherds watch are keeping?

Refrain:
This, this is Christ the King,
Whom shepherds guard and angels sing:
Haste, haste to bring Him laud,
the Babe the Son of Mary!

Why lies He in such mean estate,
where ox and ass are feeding?
Good Christian, fear: for sinners here the
silent Word is pleading. (Refrain)

So bring Him incense, gold, and myrrh.
Come, peasant, king to own Him;
The King of kings salvation brings; let
loving hearts enthrone Him. (Refrain)

"I Am Full of Joy"

How a "Dutch Golden Age" artist from Utrecht ended up with a painting at the Uffizi is not entirely clear. Probably, *Adoration* was purchased by one of the Medici clan not long after it was first painted. Van Honthorst studied in Rome and was heavily influenced by Caravaggio and his studies of light and darkness. The Italians called him "Gherardo delle Notti," or "Gerard of the Nights." His painting of the Adoration is squeezed into the Uffizi's less-frequented third floor galleries with others from the Netherlands.

Adoration of the Child, Gerrit van Honthorst, ca. 1619–1620, Uffizi Gallery, Florence, Italy

The scene van Honthorst imagines for us here is a quiet moment with the Holy Family, shortly after Jesus' birth. The dark background suggests it is night. The only light is that radiating from Jesus, and that light is so bright it shimmers and bounces off the delighted faces of everyone present. Mary, so young, is wrapping Jesus "in swaddling clothes" and placing Him "in a manger" (Luke 2:12). An older Joseph and two innocent angels look on, their entire faces radiating with joy. Mary herself can't help but smile as she looks down on her beautiful, newborn Son. She and Joseph know there will be trials ahead, but none of that matters in this moment. They have Jesus with them, lighting the darkness.

Sometimes, after I've received Communion, I try to imagine myself in this scene. My mind then usually takes me back to the birth of my two sons, Richard and Michael. Evelyn, like Mary, had done all the heavy lifting, and she had the same quiet, joyful face on. I had Joseph's — so proud, so absolutely delighted in the little miracle before me.

How much more delighted am I now, here with Jesus within and before me?

-⋘⋄⋙-

All of us have good days and bad days. On our best days, I like to think we're "in the zone," with Mary as Duccio and Ingres and van Honthorst imagined her, contemplating Jesus and His love for us. Other days, the world outside continues to distract, even at a high moment in the Mass as we're in right now. Often, when I'm in the zone at least, I only reluctantly rise from my knees as the priest approaches the lectern and starts leafing through the Missal to find today's closing prayer. But in the zone or not, we must get to our feet.

The Concluding Rites are about to begin.

Part IV

CONCLUDING RITES

"So they set out at once and returned to Jerusalem where they found gathered together the eleven and those with them who were saying, 'The Lord has truly been raised and has appeared to Simon!' Then the two recounted what had taken place on the way and how he was made known to them in the breaking of the bread."

—Luke 24:33–35

– 13 –

Sent Forth

Prayer After Communion

"Peace be with you. As the Father has sent me, so I send you."
—John 20:21

The last prayer of the Communion Rite is like the Collect; it is a special one for today's liturgy.

As the Mass begins, we invoke the Holy Spirit to guide and inspire the entire celebration. Now, as the Mass ends, we do the same. But even as we do so, getting ready to go back "out there," something is tugging at our hearts. We're in our happy place. We don't want to leave Jesus, still present within us and, in eucharistic form, now present in the tabernacle. But leave we must; our call is to get back out there and bring Him to the world.

For centuries, the Church had a traditional image that brings to mind this moment, called "*Noli me tangere*." These are the words of Christ recorded in the Gospel of John as He meets Mary of Magdala on Easter morning:

> *But Mary stayed outside the tomb weeping. And as she wept, she bent over into the tomb and saw two angels in white sitting there, one at the head and one at the feet*

where the body of Jesus had been. And they said to her, "Woman, why are you weeping?" She said to them, "They have taken my Lord, and I don't know where they laid him." When she had said this, she turned around and saw Jesus there, but did not know it was Jesus. Jesus said to her, "Woman, why are you weeping? Whom are you looking for?" She thought it was the gardener and said to him, "Sir, if you carried him away, tell me where you laid him, and I will take him." Jesus said to her, "Mary!" She turned and said to him in Hebrew, "Rabbouni," which means Teacher. Jesus said to her, "Stop holding on to me [Noli me tangere], for I have not yet ascended to the Father. But go to my brothers and tell them, 'I am going to my Father and your Father, to my God and your God.'" Mary of Magdala went and announced to the disciples, "I have seen the Lord," and what he told her.

—John 20:11–18

One of the most poignant images of this Easter morning meeting of Mary Magdalen with Jesus is in Florence, no surprise! It's in the Uffizi.

Uffizi Gallery, Florence. Andrea del Sarto was a colleague of Renaissance greats Michelangelo and Raphael. Art historians view him as an artist who began with great promise but never lived up to his potential. *Noli Me Tangere* was one of his early works and has been moved around Florence multiple times over the years; it's now housed permanently at the Uffizi. The softly painted figures of Christ and Mary Magdalen, along with the atmospheric landscape fading into the distance, evidence da Vinci's influence on him. The slightly elongated and stylized image of Christ mark the early beginnings of shift a towards Mannerism

The Risen Christ Appearing to St. Mary Magdalene, or *Noli me Tangere*, Andrea del Sarto, 1509–1510, Uffizi Gallery, Florence, Italy

that would bloom later via del Sarto's pupil, Jacopo Pontormo, in his magnificent *Deposition* that we've already visited during the Eucharistic Prayer (chapter 10).

Like many Renaissance paintings of the day, *Noli me Tangere* is chock full of symbols, several of which we are now familiar with. The garden where Mary meets Jesus, drawn from John's Gospel account, also references the New Eden that Jesus has initiated with His recent Passion and death. The palm tree is the tree of martyrdom. The small well near the palm's base refers to Jesus' meeting at the well with the Samaritan woman, who also was sometimes conflated with Mary of Magdala. Mary's red dress references both her former life of sin, along with Christ's sacrifice on the Cross that saved her; her blue dress matches Jesus' blue cloak, the cloak of eternal life that now joins them. He will soon ascend to Heaven, and He will bring Mary to Him there when her time has come.

Standing quietly here with Evelyn before del Sarto's *Noli me Tangere,* having sorted out the symbolism, I allow myself to be drawn into the quiet, intimate scene at dawn in that garden outside the tomb. I am imagining the moment we are now in at the Mass, and something moves me. A tear wells up inside. I see myself in the garden, as Mary who's run to the tomb, distraught that my Lord and my God is missing. I see a man who looks like a gardener, and I don't recognize Him. Then, He simply invokes my name.

"Steve!"[102]

With that, I recognize His voice. I know He's alive. He's with me.

I'm here in the Mass, still on my knees contemplating His love for me, His mercy towards me.

I reach out to touch Him, to embrace Him. As He hugs me back, He has a simple message.

This is the "Do not be afraid" moment.

"Noli me tangere."

"Get up, Steve, and get on with your mission. You have a job to do. Carry my message to that world out there that is fallen, confused. That has lost love. It's time to go!"

"And don't be afraid! I will always be with you. Have faith."

Then I get up off my knees. I am transformed from listener to evangelist, from disciple to apostle. From lover of Jesus to lover of all. I run out from that garden to tell the world:

"I have seen the Lord!" (John 20:18).

Final Blessing

As we stand, preparing for the Final Blessing, the priest will often say a prayer of blessing designed for that day's liturgy, as a last message for us to carry as we go forth. It will normally reference back to one of the messages from that day's Liturgy of the Word. Then we all make the Sign of the Cross, just as we did when the Mass began.

Through the course of Mass, we've been showered with words and images of God the Father, God the Son, and God the Holy Spirit, sometimes together and sometimes in their respective Persons. For this final blessing, Evelyn and I wanted to use a Crucifixion image that incorporated all three Persons at once. Often, such as in the mosaic of the Vine that we visited at San Clemente, God the Father is incorporated in the form of His providential hands, emerging from the heavens. More rarely, all three are shown all at once, in full. To see one of these images, we need to get into the vaults of the Met. Or at least, take an imaginary trip into the vaults. Very few ever actually get down there.

"May Almighty God Bless You, the Father, and the Son, and the Holy Spirit"

Vaults of The Metropolitan Museum of Art, New York. The curators of the Met started relatively late in their efforts to collect art, at least in comparison with the other great museums of the world we've been visiting. But what they lacked in time they made up for in enthusiasm and almost messianic zeal since the museum's founding in 1870. By its own estimates, the Met today possesses more than 1.5 million works of art. Most of them are actually in their storage vaults and are only rotated occasionally into their viewing galleries. One such image is Agnolo Gaddi's late-fourteenth-century *The Trinity.* To see it currently, we will have to make an imaginary journey into the very heart of the Met's vaults.

The Trinity, Agnolo Gaddi, ca. 1390–1396,
The Metropolitan Museum of Art, New York

Gaddi painted during Florence's "International Gothic" era, so elements of Byzantine-style symbolism and Giotto-inspired realism appear side by side. The gold backdrop of *The Trinity* tells us we are in Heaven, as we've been throughout the Mass. God the Father, painted in the Gothic, symbolic style, solemnly presides over the scene. He is bigger than life! The Holy Spirit, in the symbol of a dove, is above Jesus, between Father and Son. Jesus is still on the Cross. Here Gaddi has painted Jesus with more solid, Renaissance-style three dimensionality, to remind us that this Crucifixion really happened, here, on earth. As Jesus hangs from the Cross, His blood pours out for us. It spills down the Cross and over the skull, conquering death.

What is special for me about Gaddi's image is the intimate connection he draws amongst the three Persons of the Holy Trinity. They are not just all part of the painting; they are literally connected within the painting! God the Father is not just looking down from Heaven toward Jesus, He's somehow there with Him, solemnly presenting His sacrificed Son to us. And the Holy Spirit is not just hovering above the Cross. He's just landed on it! He shares in the sacrifice, too.

So, the Father, the Son, and the Holy Spirit — three Persons, one God — now with us, and in us, and we, in them.

The Sending Forth

"Go forth, the Mass is ended."

As we bless ourselves in the name of our Trinitarian God, the deacon, if one is present, and, if not, the priest celebrant, speaks. An ordained evangelist, he directs the laity to go forth, carrying the Word to the world outside. Although the prayer here is just a few words, often simply "Go forth, the Mass is ended" (other times, "Go and announce the Gospel of the Lord" or "Go in peace, glorifying the Lord by your life"), it is in some ways the entire point of the Mass.

The United States Conference of Catholic Bishops (USCCB) explains the "Sending Forth" this way:

"The word 'Mass' comes from the Latin word, 'Missa.' At one time, the people were dismissed with the words *'Ite, missa est'* (literally meaning 'Go, you (the Church) have been sent.' The word *'missa'* is related to the word 'missio,' the root of the English word 'mission.' The liturgy does not simply come to an end. Those assembled are sent forth to bring the fruits of the Eucharist to the world."[103]

As the deacon exhorts us to mission, many of us assent at this moment somewhat unconsciously. Filled as we have been with love of the Lord, now present within us, the idea of carrying this stuff outside still seems a bit of a stretch. It might be embarrassing, or difficult — or even … dangerous.

If you're thinking this, don't worry. You're in good company. By Church tradition, the apostle Peter felt the same way, at least until he met Jesus again, on the Appian Way.

Annibale Carracci painted this very scene. To see it, we'll need one last trip back to London, but first, let's stop at the Appian Way, leading outside of Rome.

Where Are You Going?

Outside the Porta San Sebastiano, Appian Way, outskirts of Rome. By tradition, this is the spot on the Appian Way where Peter, who often acted before he thought, met Christ on earth one last time. Nero had begun his persecution of the Christians, and Peter was on the menu. Urged by the local Christians to flee the city so as to continue to lead the Church, Peter was hightailing it out of Rome. Then, he ran into Jesus.

"Quo Vadis?" Peter asked Jesus. "Where are you going?"

"I'm heading back to Rome to get crucified again. I'm going to stand in for you, since you're going the wrong way."

Like a splash of cold water, that gentle rebuke woke Peter up. He at once headed back to Rome to face his cross.

The National Gallery, London. We're standing now before one of Annibale Carracci's great paintings, *Quo Vadis?* Carracci painted it

Domine, Quo Vadis?, Annibale Carracci, 1601–1602,
The National Gallery, London, England

at the beginning of the seventeenth century, trying to recapture the naturalism and magnificence of Michelangelo and Raphael, but with the same energy and spirit that the Mannerist painters who followed them brought to the canvas.

Deliberately less dramatic and theatrical than Caravaggio, the Carracci family helped create a toned-down Italian Baroque style that flowered in the work of Guido Reni, with whom we've already visited. Here, in *Quo Vadis,* he utilizes all these elements to create for us the collision of spiritual centrifugal forces that happened out there on that lonely road outside Rome more than two millennia ago.

Peter is already outside the walls, safely evading Nero's persecution. Then, he bumps into Jesus.

Well, he doesn't exactly "bump" into Jesus. More like, gets run over by Him. Peter's right foot is still propelling himself forward, but his left is suddenly planted solidly. He's come to a screeching halt; we can almost see him skidding on the famous stone pavement of the Appian Way. His face betrays his utter amazement at seeing Christ at this critical moment.

Peter's suddenly halted movement helps us imagine that his mind and heart must have also suddenly hit a wall. He seems to be quickly jumping to his senses. Safe for the moment, outside the walls of Rome, he has probably begun to reflect on what he's done. And like many of us after a wrong turn, it's not sitting well with him. The old emotions of the first time he denied Christ during a different spiritual crisis, many years earlier, have already begun to settle in.

"What was I thinking?" he's asking himself. "This is the cross Jesus asked me to carry. It's the cross I promised to carry, that I swore to Him I was up for. Yet here I am, slinking off like a coward."

How often have any of us had a moment like this? How many of us are about to have another one, when we head out of the front door of this church, just after all our promises to Him during our reflection after Communion?

Then Jesus shows up.

As Carracci imagines the scene, he doesn't just "show up." He bounds into the scene, bigger than life, walking—no, jogging—straight into the fire from which Peter (and we ourselves) are running to escape. Jesus appears athletic, strong, unblemished. His crown of thorns, loosely placed on His head, has been repurposed as His heavenly crown.

And He's got a cross on His back, carrying it lightly, like a piece of balsam wood, with one hand. That way, He can use His right hand to point us in the right direction, away from "safety" (which is already feeling less safe than we thought), toward the fire — toward Rome.

Jesus' feet are bounding forward, with even greater velocity and power than Peter's are running away. Aside from the crown of thorns, the cross, and a loincloth, Jesus is unclothed and unarmed.

Then, Peter looks up and sees the face of Christ. He expects to see a look of disapproval, disgust at Peter's weakness. Instead, he sees the same eyes we saw in the eyes of the Lamb painted by van Eyck, and the eyes we saw of the newly risen Lord as He appeared to Guercino's *Doubting Thomas* (chapter 11).

Love, compassion, support, communion — the weapons that would conquer an empire.

"I'm with you on this last journey, Steve. I'm with you. We can do this, together."

And all we can think of at this moment are four words:

"Thanks be to God."

– 14 –

And as We Go

Closing Hymn

As we prepare our things to leave the church, the choir — the angels — break out in song. Their joy is contagious as they lead us out! We can hardly keep from singing!

Musician Angels (from the Fresco Paintings of the Basilica dei Santi Apostoli), Melozzo da Forlì, ca. 1480, Pinacoteca (Vatican Museums), Rome, Italy

"How Can I Keep from Singing?"

My life flows on in endless song
above earth's lamentation.
I hear the real though far-off hymn
that hails a new creation.

Refrain:
No storm can shake my inmost calm,
while to that rock I'm clinging,

Since Christ is Lord of heaven and earth,
how can I keep from singing?

Through all the tumult and the strife,
I hear that music ringing.
It sounds and echoes in my soul,
how can I keep from singing? (refrain)

What, though my joys and comforts die,
the Lord, my Savior, liveth.
What though the darkness gather 'round?
Songs in the night He giveth. (refrain)

The peace of Christ makes fresh my heart,
a fountain ever springing.
All things are mine since I am His;
how can I keep from singing? (refrain)[104]

In many congregations, right after the priest has processed out of the church, someone from the laity will break into the Prayer to St. Michael. It's no longer an official part of the Mass liturgy — it was before 1970 — though it is often prayed by Catholics for divine protection as they take on their mission out in the world, as they prepare for spiritual battle.

For an image of the great archangel Michael, leading the battle of light over darkness, we'll need to make a trip to Vienna. Don't worry, it will be worth it.

Prayer To St. Michael

The Fall of the Rebel Angels, Luca Giordano, 1666,
Kunsthistorisches Museum, Vienna, Austria

Kunsthistorisches Museum, Vienna. During the seventeenth century, the Habsburg Empire was centered in Vienna, with ties via a second branch of the family to imperial Spain and Naples. So it was not unusual for an Italian painter from Naples painting in far-off Vienna to be heavily influenced by Spanish art from Spain. This may explain how Giordano's monumental masterpiece of the Spanish baroque found its way here. It is perhaps the most famous and heavily quoted image of the great battle of light and darkness, referenced in Revelation 12:

> *"Then war broke out in heaven; Michael and his angels battled against the dragon. The dragon and its angels fought back, but they did not prevail and there was no longer any place for them in heaven. The huge dragon, the ancient serpent, who is called the Devil and Satan, who deceived the whole world, was thrown down to earth, and its angels were thrown down with it. Then I heard a loud voice in heaven say: 'Now have salvation and power come, and the kingdom of our God and the authority of his Anointed. For the accuser of our brothers is cast out, who accuses them before our God day and night. They conquered him by the blood of the Lamb.'"*
>
> *— Rev. 12:7–11*

One of the most striking elements of *The Fall* is just how different the painting appears in its upper half and its lower half; it's almost as if a different artist painted it. Above, all is light and bright, as the archangel effortlessly strikes down Lucifer and his minions below him. Michael has flown out of the clouds above him where the light of Heaven shines. That's the place we're trying to get to.

Below Michael, all is darkness. The rebels twist and turn in their descent to Hell, the fiery light of which we can see reflecting off their bodies as they transform before us from angels to devils. Although their sinewy muscles imply at least human strength, they seem no match for Michael's heavenly power. Many will roam from Hell to earth, seeking the ruin of souls, but for them, Heaven is no more.

Although Michael is clearly outnumbered, he's already well on his way to dispensing with the devils. With his foot, he presses the last of his opponents downward, out of Heaven. Michael is imagined by Giordano as young, vigorous, full of life and even joy. The fine brushstrokes and bright colors, the athletic body, all remind us of that wonderfully alive image of Jesus in *Quo Vadis* that we just visited.

So, as we leave the church, let's call on St. Michael. He's been assigned by God to protect us, so we know he'll answer the call.

Let's pray together:

St. Michael the Archangel,
Defend us in battle,
Be our protection against the
wickedness and snares of the devil.
May God rebuke him, we humbly pray.
And do thou, O prince of heavenly hosts,
By the power of God,
Cast into Hell Satan, and all the evil spirits
Who prowl about the world seeking
the ruin of souls. Amen.

One Last Sign

The last thing most Catholics do as they leave the church is, you guessed it, make the Sign of the Cross with our hand dipped in holy water. Having just been in Mass, we know more than ever what that sign means. It's a symbol of the place of Jesus' suffering and death in our life. And it's also the sign of His great triumph over sin and death, for us.

When we make the sign with holy water, it's even more offensive to Satan and his minions. We last saw the holy water pouring out of the altar of the Lamb on the Ghent Altarpiece. That water, blessed by the sacrifice of Christ through one of Christ's priests, is kryptonite to Satan's troops. The devils whom we just saw defeated by the archangel Michael deeply fear the Sign of the Cross; and combined with holy water, it's nearly as bad as the arrival of St. Michael himself. The Sign of the Cross stands for everything evil hates: humility, obedience, faith, hope, and love.

For our last Sign of the Cross, we wanted an image that conveys all these aspects. We traded ideas back and forth, argued about them, talked them through. But we kept coming back to a Crucifixion painting by Salvador Dali. One of his Crucifixions, *Christ on the Hypercube*, hangs at the Met and appeared as the last image in *The Pilgrimage to the Museum*.[105] The other, which the artist painted based on a sixteenth-century vision that was had by St. John of the Cross, and following his own surrealistic dream of Christ crucified, is perhaps even more spectacular. But its location is a bit more remote. To see it, we'll have to hop a puddle jumper from London to Glasgow, Scotland.

Kelvingrove Art Gallery and Museum, Scotland. Evelyn and I are here at the Kelvingrove to see the painting now before us. Although controversial from its initial unveiling, even to this day, it's risen above the theological and artistic debates of its time, and since. Among the religious and art world "laity," it's been dubbed "Scotland's favorite painting." So, for sure, we expected fireworks when we got here. Still, we were not prepared for this.

Christ of St. John of the Cross, Salvador Dali, 1951, Kelvingrove Art Gallery and Museum, Glasgow, Scotland

Looming above us, nearly nine feet high and almost four feet wide, *Christ of St. John of the Cross* transfixes. Unlike any Crucifixion painted before or after, we are looking at Christ from above, from the perspective of the eyes of God the Father Himself. We can almost imagine ourselves as Eve in that image of the *Creation of Adam* on the Sistine Ceiling; the Father has us up there with Him, cradled in His big fatherly arm, watching the scene of Christ's sacrifice unfold below.

One of the initially disarming aspects of *Christ of St. John* is the darkness above. That darkness was one of several "problems" that made Dali's *Christ of St. John* so controversial when it first appeared. Unlike Giordano's *The Fall,* which we just visited in Vienna, and unlike every other image of Heaven we've seen, Dali has painted Heaven above as pitch black, at least in this moment. Dali never fully explained this, but I think the darkness in Heaven is a sign that God the Father is in mourning, for the sacrifice of His son. Maybe God is even crying, for a moment.

In the name of the Father ...

As we look down with God the Father from Heaven, we see Christ's strong body hanging from the Cross. Well, not exactly "hanging." Although He appears to be hanging, as we look closer, we can't find any nails holding Him on. In fact, we don't see any sign at all of the wounds or blows inflicted on Christ in His Passion. Rather, as he did in the *Hypercube,* Dali portrays the spiritual reality of Christ's sacrifice here, rather than the bloody, physical one. Christ is *holding* Himself unto the Cross, in an act of complete and total self-giving. He's holding Himself to the Cross with his love.[106]

and of the Son ...

We look for the Holy Spirit and don't initially see Him. Like the Father, He's invisible. Then, we realize we *do* see Him. We see Him in that very loving way Jesus holds Himself to that Cross. That *agapeic* love is the love of Anthony van Dyck's *Charity*. It's the Love of the Holy Spirit. And then we notice something we didn't initially see. The Cross, with Christ on it, is not actually on the ground anymore. It is rising, through the opening in the clouds, towards Heaven. It is being lifted there by the Holy Spirit, by love, back to the Father.

and of the Holy Spirit.

This is not just a painting of the Crucifixion. It's a painting of Christ's victory of the Cross, of the Resurrection and, then, His Ascension. Christ is alive. He's ascending into Heaven.

As our eyes descend lower towards the earth, we can see the landscape below clearly, bathed in a bright light. This light must be the divine light of Heaven, which God the Father has poured out, to the very last photon, onto the earth. Not unlike the sacrifice of His Son's very last ounce of blood.

Down there, in the bright shimmering light that has poured out of Heaven, we see an iridescent blue lake. There's an open boat in it. That boat must be for us — for you, and for me. It would seem to be the Barque of Peter, the boat of the fishermen. The boat we'll need to fulfill the priest's last command, to go forth on mission, to be fishers of men. And we'll be doing so with and through the Trinity. He's there in the scene, giving every ray of light He has, to light our way.

"As he was walking by the Sea of Galilee, he saw two brothers, Simon who is called Peter, and his brother Andrew, casting a net into the sea; they were fishermen. He said to them, 'Come after me, and I will make you fishers of men.' At once they left their nets and followed him."

— Matt. 4:18–20

Amen.

Epilogue

Back Out There

Somewhere back out there. One of the greatest struggles for many Catholics is the parking lot after Mass. Following the uplifting prayers and music of the Mass, and the sheer spiritual intensity of receiving Christ into our bodies and hearts, we are sometimes unprepared for the mundane task of navigating our car through a crowded parking lot. Having just resolved to carry Christ into the world, we quickly find ourselves distracted by the whirlwind around us. We fall, again.

Additionally, as much as we feel ourselves transformed by the graces we've just received, we are sometimes disappointed to find the world seems completely unchanged by our experience at the Mass.

There's still hunger, loneliness, and despair.

There's still temptation to slip out of the Garden into sin.

And there are still false prophets calling to us, trying to lead us away from Christ.

As I put the finishing touches on *Visions,* it has finally occurred to me that the Mass, and the images we've been reflecting on to deepen our journey into it, is a gift from God for "out there." One prayer at a time, the Mass has armed us with everything we need to bring Christ into the world. We just need to recall the many little miracles that happen there, and the images we have in our minds of them:

The power to listen, as Mary listened to the angel.

To answer His voice, calling us out of the darkness, as He called St. Matthew and the others.

To look to His light in the storm, and to let Him lead us out of it, as He did for the apostles in that storm on Lake Galilee.

To remember we are His beloved sons and daughters, whom He lovingly created in His image; that He is Our Father.

To let ourselves be loved, as He loved Mary Magdalen, despite the sins of her past.

To remember that He is very much alive, bursting from the tomb; and that He is with us, and within us — the Eucharist, the Lamb of God.

To conform our will to His in prayer, even when His answer is to drink from the cup of sacrifice.

To love like Him, *especially* when it hurts to do so.

To invoke the Father, Son, and Holy Spirit as we make the Sign of the Cross, unafraid.

And never to forget that He is with us always, on our own road to Emmaus, on our journey to the Light.

The Supper at Emmaus, Rembrandt, 1648, Louvre Museum, Paris, France

Acknowledgements

TAKING ON A project of this breadth and magnitude, on a topic this profound, was at the same time incredibly fulfilling and physically challenging. So, as I begin my "thank- you list," I must start first and foremost with my dear bride, soulmate, and co-author, Evelyn. Evelyn has been with me on every step of this journey, from discerning the path we were being called to pursue, through the many pilgrim trips we took together to the United States and Europe, to the drafting of our initial reflections and the nightly discussions that ensued, to the editing process that transforms a manuscript into a book. *Visions* would simply have been impossible to produce without her.

I'd also like to express my deep gratitude to Msgr. Roger Landry. Msgr. Landry is an incredibly busy man with many responsibilities and projects on his plate. Still, he did not hesitate to say "yes" when I asked him to take on the co-authorship role for *Visions* and to assure me of its theological correctness. His gentle but firm priestly voice was invaluable throughout development of the manuscript, elevating it to a higher level.

As the discerning reader already knows, many others contributed to *Visions* and enriched the narrative. "Sr. Francesca" — our spiritual art friend in Rome — was a persistent voice of truth and beauty when Evelyn and I made repeated visits to the Vatican Museums. Her special tours of these museums enriched our spiritual understanding of its art, and we tried to incorporate her insights into several of the works we included here. Likewise, Liz Lev has led Evelyn and me through the art of Rome and Naples on multiple occasions over the years. Her insights, enthusiasm, and eye for the Divine in art are very special.

The voices of many of my priest friends are incorporated in these reflections, so intertwined now with my own that it is hard to distinguish them. Msgr. Donald Sakano, who first involved Evelyn and me in what became the street evangelization mission in New York City, described in *The Missionary of Wall Street*, is a lifelong friend and confidant. His initial edits of the text were the first steps toward theological correctness, upon which Msgr. Landry later built. Likewise, Fr. Shawn Aaron, my longtime spiritual guide and occasional spiritual director, was involved at the earliest stages and made a number of helpful additions.

Another voice in *Visions* is Dony McManus, the devout and energetic Catholic artist who is reimagining art for the contemporary world. I met Dony a few years ago over a burger at Shake Shack, and somehow we've clicked. His insights and thoughts about religious art have enriched and deepened my own journey.

Among the other fellow pilgrims we recruited along the way, Carlos and Maria Angeles Sanzos stand out. Lifelong friends from Spain, they did not hesitate when they heard we were heading to Madrid. Their guidance and advice at the Prado made our visits there particularly poignant. Other pilgrims included Don and Cathy Dion, with our mutual friend Fr. Brian Cummings; their insights on the art of Florence, Orvieto, and Rome helped us to see truths we hadn't. Don, his daughter Caroline, and his systems expert Gene Belotti, have also been invaluable members of the market development team for *Visions* and were early editors of the manuscript. My younger son, Michael, was in some ways with me from the beginning, on that mission to Guadalajara described in the prologue; he also helped with the research on the cathedrals in the background of the Ghent altarpiece. His brother Richard also supported us throughout, with his understanding and patience through our travels around Europe and the United States.

Another valuable member of the *Visions* team was the persistent and always-organized Mary Soressi. Mary is my longtime assistant at Federated Hermes, and she is particularly gifted at finding the most efficient paths through my long days of work on Wall Street alongside my "evangelization business." On any given day, she juggles effortlessly my calendar, replete with internal investment meetings on two continents, talks with clients, my evangelization activities, and media connections. Mary manages it all without ever losing her joyful demeanor or pleasant disposition. When I agreed to pursue the development of *Visions,* it was to Mary I turned to find the time on my schedule to make it happen. I have even learned to forgive her for deleting a year's worth of golf outings, weekends, and vacation time in the process!

I need of course to thank the staff of Sophia Press, my partners in this journey from its inception. Charlie McKinney, the president, exudes a special energy and verve for inspiring souls to find God through the written word, and he is contagious. He inspires not just me, but his entire wonderful staff. Mollee Rublee and Sarah Lemieux have also been on this project from its inception, and their enthusiasm is similarly easy to pick up. Michael Lichens was an enormous help in doing the initial research to discern what art scholars had already written about the works we intended to use; the background research and bibliography for *Visions* was improved enormously by his input and hard work.

Of course, I need to thank my primary editor at Sophia for *Visions,* Heidi Saxton. Heidi has a keen eye for how to tell a story, and her input and suggestions were always insightful. Heidi was never afraid to offer constructive suggestions, and virtually all of them led to improvements in the text. She is a seasoned and consummate professional and is always willing to pick up the phone and talk. She made *Visions* better. Thank you, Heidi!

Finally, I want to thank all the people Evelyn and I met along the journey, from museum guards to information desk personnel to, yes, store clerks! I still remember the chat I had one day with the pleasant woman outfitting me with shirts in Rome who first suggested we visit Reni's *Crucifixion* at Chiesa di San Lorenzo in Lucina.

"My goodness, Eva, how do you know so much about art?" I asked her.

"Well, I'm Roman. What would you expect?"

Art is like that. It speaks to all of us, whatever our background, whatever our training. It's a path to the Divine.

We just have to open our eyes and look up to the Light.

Appendix A

Art Reflections Organized by Parts of the Mass

Before Mass

The Supper at Emmaus, Rembrandt (Rembrandt van Rijn), Louvre Museum, Paris, 9, 313

Winter, Houdon, Jean Antoine, The Metropolitan Museum of Art, New York, 17

The Garden of Earthly Delights, Bosch, Hieronymus, Museo del Prado, Madrid, 20, 76

The Preaching of the Antichrist, Signorelli, Luca, San Brizio Chapel (Orvieto Cathedral), Orvieto, 22

The Good Shepherd, Unknown, Museo Pio Cristiano (Vatican Museums), Rome, 25

The Repentant Magdalen, de La Tour, Georges, National Gallery of Art, Washington, D.C., 29

The Penitent Magdalen, de La Tour, Georges, The Metropolitan Museum of Art, New York, 30

The Wedding at Cana, Veronese, Paolo, Louvre Museum, Paris, 32

Christ Crucified, Velásquez, Diego, Museo del Prado, Madrid, 35

Introductory Rites

Façade, Orvieto Cathedral, Unknown, Orvieto Cathedral, Orvieto, 38, 152, 153, 154, 155, 156, 157, 158, 159

The Crucifixion Medallion, Abbey Church at Conques, Abbey of Conques, The Metropolitan Museum of Art, New York, 43

St. Jerome in the Desert, Pinturicchio, Bernardino, Walters Museum of Art, Baltimore, 45

Preparation for the Liturgy of the Word

First Reading

Psalm

Second Reading

Conversion on the Way to Damascus, Caravaggio (Michelangelo Merisi), Cerasi Chapel (Santa Maria del Popolo), Rome, 104

Charity, Reni, Guido, The Metropolitan Museum of Art, New York, 110

Charity, van Dyck, Anthony, The National Gallery, London, 108

Gospel Proclamation

Musician Angels (from the Fresco Paintings of the Basilica dei Santi Apostoli), da Forlì, Melozzo, Pinacoteca (Vatican Museums), Rome, 49, 113, 170, 301

St. Dominic Adoring the Cross, Fra Angelico (Guido di Pietro), Convent of San Marco, Florence, 114

The Calling of St. Matthew, Caravaggio (Michelangelo Merisi), Chiesa di San Luigi dei Francesi, Rome, 118

Sermon on the Mount, Brueghel the Elder, Jan, J. Paul Getty Museum, Los Angeles, 122

The Good Samaritan, van Gogh, Vincent, Kröller-Müller Museum, Otterlo, 127

The Dogmatic Sarcophagus, Unknown, Pio Cristiano (Vatican Museums), Rome, 130, 132

Eucharistic Fish and Loaves, Unknown, Catacomb of Callistus, Rome, 131

Christ Healing the Paralytic at the Pool of Bethesda, Murillo, Bartolomé Esteban, The National Gallery, London, 135

The Storm on the Sea of Galilee, Rembrandt (Rembrandt van Rijn), current whereabouts unknown, Unknown, 138

The Agony in the Garden, Mantegna, Andrea, The National Gallery, London, 143

Responding to the Word

The Road to Emmaus, Zund, Robert, Kunstmuseum, St. Gallen, 148

Baptismal Font of Orvieto Cathedral, Various, Orvieto Cathedral, Orvieto, 160

The Resurrection of the Flesh, Signorelli, Luca, Orvieto Cathedral, Orvieto, 161

The Elect in Paradise, Signorelli, Luca, Orvieto Cathedral, Orvieto, 162

Pentecost — The Birth of the Church, MacManus, Dony, The Chapel of PRABB (Campus Bio-Medico), Rome, 165

PREPARING TO ENTER THE SACRED MYSTERY

SACRIFICE AND TRIUMPH

Pietà (after Delacroix), van Gogh, Vincent, Van Gogh Art Museum, Amsterdam, 225

Sainte-Chapelle, Various, Sainte-Chapelle, Paris, 229

Apse Mosaic of the Tree of Life, Various, Basilica of San Clemente, Rome, 230

Angel Playing the Lute, Fiorentino, Rosso, Uffizi Gallery, Florence, 234

Communion

Creation of Adam, Michelangelo (Michelangelo di Lodovico Buonarroti Simoni), Sistine Chapel Ceiling (Vatican Museums), Rome, 236

The Incredulity of St. Thomas, Guercino, Giovanni Barbieri, The National Gallery, London, 241

The Adoration of the Mystic Lamb (Ghent Altarpiece), van Eyck, Hubert & Jan, St. Bavo's Cathedral, Ghent, 245, 246, 248, 254, 268

The Last Supper and the Tree of Life, Gaddi, Taddeo, Basilica di Santa Croce, Florence, 250, 251

Interior (restored mid-nineteenth century), Various, Santa Maria sopra Minerva, Rome, 256

Communion of the Apostles, Barocci, Federico, Santa Maria sopra Minerva, Rome, 257

The Annunciation, Fra Angelico (Guido di Pietro), Convent of San Marco, Florence, 261

The Crucifixion, Reni, Guido, Basilica di San Lorenzo in Lucina, Rome, 265

Reflections following Communion

First Holy Communion, Picasso, Pablo, Picasso Museum, Barcelona, 269

Saints Anthony Abott and Paul the Hermit, Velázquez, Diego, Museo del Prado, Madrid, 272

Ascension of St. John the Evangelist, Giotto (Giotto di Bondone), Peruzzi Chapel (Santa Croce), Florence, 273

The Ecstasy of St. Teresa, Bernini, Gian Lorenzo, Chiesa di Santa Maria della Vittoria, Rome, 276

Communion of the Apostles, Fra Angelico (Guido di Pietro), Convent of San Marco (Cell 35), Florence, 278

Madonna and Child, di Buoninsegna, Duccio, The Metropolitan Museum of Art, New York, 281

SENDING FORTH

CLOSING

Appendix B

Art Reflections Organized by City

Ghent

Glasgow

London

Los Angeles

J. Paul Getty Museum, *Sermon on the Mount,* Brueghel the Elder, Jan, 122

Madrid

Museo del Prado, *The Garden of Earthly Delights,* Bosch, Hieronymus, 20, 76

Museo del Prado, *Christ Crucified,* Velásquez, Diego, 35

Museo del Prado, *Pentecost,* El Greco (Domenikos Theotokopoulos), 55

Museo del Prado, *The Adoration of the Shepherds,* El Greco (Domenikos Theotokopoulos), 190

Museo del Prado, *The Last Supper,* de Juanes, Juan, 199

Museo del Prado, *Saints Anthony Abbot and Paul the Hermit,* Velázquez, Diego, 272

Milan

Santa Maria delle Grazie, *The Last Supper,* da Vinci, Leonardo, 200

New York

The Metropolitan Museum of Art, *Winter,* Houdon, Jean Antoine, 17

The Metropolitan Museum of Art, *The Penitent Magdalen,* de La Tour, Georges, 30

The Metropolitan Museum of Art, *The Crucifixion Medallion,* Abbey Church at Conques, Abbey of Conques, 43

The Metropolitan Museum of Art, *The Annunication,* Sassetta (Stefano di Giovanni), 72

The Metropolitan Museum of Art, *The Toilet of Bathsheba,* Rembrandt (Rembrandt van Rijn), 97

The Metropolitan Museum of Art, *Charity,* Reni, Guido, 110

The Metropolitan Museum of Art, *The Adoration of the Shepherds,* El Greco (Domenikos Theotokopoulos), 192

The Metropolitan Museum of Art, *The Crucifixion,* Lorenzetti, Pietro, 206

The Metropolitan Museum of Art, *Madonna and Child,* di Buoninsegna, Duccio, 281

The Metropolitan Museum of Art, *The Virgin Adoring the Host,* Ingres, Jean Auguste Dominique, 281

The Metropolitan Museum of Art, *The Trinity,* Gaddi, Agnolo, 294

Orvieto

Otterlo

Paris

Rome

Chiesa di San Luigi dei Francesi, *The Calling of St. Matthew,* Caravaggio (Michelangelo Merisi), 118

Pio Cristiano (Vatican Museums), *The Dogmatic Sarcophagus,* Unknown, 130, 132

Catacomb of Callistus, *Eucharistic Fish and Loaves,* Unknown, 131

The Chapel of PRABB (Campus Bio-Medico), *Pentecost — The Birth of the Church,* MacManus, Dony, 165

Room of the Signature (Vatican Museums), *School of Athens,* Raphael (Raffaello Sanzio da Urbino), 186, 258

Room of the Signature (Vatican Museums), *Disputation of the Holy Sacrament,* Raphael, Raffaello Sanzio da Urbino, 187, 195

Sistine Chapel (Vatican Museums), *The Last Judgement,* Michelangelo (Michelangelo di Lodovico Buonarroti Simoni), 214

St. Peter's Basilica, *Pietà,* Michelangelo (Michelangelo di Lodovico Buonarroti Simoni), 223

Basilica of San Clemente, *Apse Mosaic of the Tree of Life,* Various, 230

Sistine Chapel Ceiling (Vatican Museums), *Creation of Adam,* Michelangelo (Michelangelo di Lodovico Buonarroti Simoni), 236

Santa Maria sopra Minerva, *Interior* (restored mid-nineteenth century), Various, 256

Santa Maria sopra Minerva, *Communion of the Apostles,* Barocci, Federico, 257

Basilica di San Lorenzo in Lucina, *The Crucifixion,* Reni, Guido, 265

Chiesa di Santa Maria della Vittoria, *The Ecstasy of St. Teresa,* Bernini, Gian Lorenzo, 276

St. Gallen

Kunstmuseum, *The Road to Emmaus,* Zund, Robert, 148

St. Petersburg

Hermitage Museum, *The Return of the Prodigal Son,* Rembrandt (Rembrandt van Rijn), 62

Strasbourg

Musée des Beaux-Arts de Strasbourg, *Return of the Prodigal Son,* Drölling, Michel-Martin, 63

Bibliography

Art History and Museums

Angelini, Alessandro. *Piero Della Francesca*. Scala Press, 2023.

Auth, Stephen. *Pilgrimage to the Museum*. Sophia Institute Press, 2022.

Boyle, Leonard. *A short guide to St. Clement's, Rome*. Collegio San Clemente, 1989.

Campbell, Thomas P. *The Metropolitan Museum of Art: Director's Tour*. Scala Arts Publishers Inc., 2014.

"Chiesa di Sant'Ignazio di Loyola," Rome, Ristampa Aggiornata, 2011.

Cohen, Meredith. "An Indulgence for the Visitor: The Public at the Sainte-Chapelle of Paris." *Speculum* 83, no. 4 (2008): 840–83. http://www.jstor.org/stable/20466372.

Davis, Robert C., and Beth Lindsmith. *Lives of the Renaissance*. Thames & Hudson, 2019.

Di Cagno, Gabriella. *Florence: The Cathedral, the Baptistery, and the Campanile*. Mandragora, 1999.

Fahy, Everett. "Florentine Paintings in the Metropolitan Museum: An Exhibition and a Catalogue." *The Metropolitan Museum of Art Bulletin* 29, no. 10 (1971): 431–43. https://doi.org/10.2307/3258561.

Finaldi, Gabrielle. *The National Gallery: Masterpieces of Painting*. National Gallery Company Ltd., 2020.

Foster, Elisa. "Church and Reliquary of Sainte-Foy, France." *Smart History*, August 8, 2015. https://smarthistory.org/church-and-reliquary-of-sainte%e2%80%90foy-france/.

Frazer, Margaret English; Kurt Weitzmann; and The Metropolitan Museum of Art. *Age of Spirituality: Late Antique and Early Christian Art, Third to Seventh Century*. The Museum, 1977.

Gerry, Kathryn B. "Panels from a Window Showing the Life and Martyrdom of St. Vincent of Saragossa." Treasures of Heaven. https://projects.mcah.columbia.edu/treasuresofheaven/relics/Panels-from-a-Window-Showing-the-Life-and-Martyrdom-of-St-Vincent-ofSaragossa.php.

Todescato, Don Gianni. *Brief Guide of Sant'Agnese in Agone*. Lozzi Roma, 2009.

Grebe, Anja. *The Vatican: All the Paintings*. Black Dog & Leventhal, 2013.

Hand, John Oliver. *National Gallery of Art: Master Paintings from the Collection*. Harry N. Abrams, 2004.

Janson, H.W. *History of Art*. Prentice Hall, 2015.

Kane, Eileen. *San Clemente: The Saint Catherine Chapel*. Collegio San Clemente, 2000.

King, Ross, and Anja Grebe. *Florence: The Paintings & Frescoes, 1250–1743*. Black Dog & Leventhal, 2015.

Letta, Elisabetta Marchetti, *Pontormo Rosso Fiorentino: Library of Great Painters*, Riverside Book Co., 1994.

Lev, Elizabeth. *How Catholic Art Saved the Faith*. Sophia Institute Press, 2018.

Linares, Marina. *Prado (Museum Collections)*. Koenemann, 2019.

Long, John. "The Shroud of Turin's Earlier History: Part One — To Edessa." Associates for Biblical Research, March 14, 2013. https://biblearchaeology.org/the-shroud-of-turin-list//2284-the-shroud-of-turins-earlier-history-part-one-to-edessa.

McIver, Katherine A. "Banqueting at the Lord's Table in Sixteenth-Century Venice." *Gastronomica* 8, no. 3 (2008): 8–11. https://doi.org/10.1525/gfc.2008.8.3.8.

Meehan, Bernard. *The Book of Kells: An Illustrated Introduction to the Manuscript in Trinity College Dublin*. Thames & Hudson, 2015.

Michelleti, Emma. *Santa Croce*. Becocci Editore, 1985.

Palffy, Georgina and Sam Atkinson. *The Art Book*. Penguin Random House, 2017.

Pijbes, Wim and Taco Dibbits. *Rijksmuseum in Detail*. Rijksmuseum, 2017.

Fasola, Umberto Maria B. *The Catacombs of Domitilla and the Basilica of the Martyrs Nereus and Achilleus*. Pontificia Commissione di Archeologia Sacra, 2011.

Rose, Elizabeth A. "The Meaning of the Reliefs on the Second Pier of the Orvieto Façade." *The Art Bulletin* 14, no. 3 (1932): 258–76. https://doi.org/10.2307/3050828.

Remensnyder, Amy G. "Legendary Treasure at Conques: Reliquaries and Imaginative Memory." *Speculum* 71, no. 4 (1996): 884–906. https://doi.org/10.2307/2865723.

Scudieri, Magnolia. *San Marco: Complete Guide to the Museum and Church.* Scala — Becocci, 1996.

Scudieri, Magnolia. *The Frescoes by Angelico at San Marco.* Giunti Editore, 2004.

Shepard, Mary. "The Relics Window of St. Vincent of Saragossa at Saint-Germain-de Pres." Gesta 37, no. 2 (1998). https://www.journals.uchicago.edu/doi/10.2307/76268.

Spencer, John R. "Spatial Imagery of the Annunciation in Fifteenth Century Florence." *The Art Bulletin* 37, no. 4 (1955): 273–80. https://doi.org/10.2307/3047619.

Stauble, Claudia and Julie Kiefer. *The Paintings That Revolutionized Art.* Prestel, 2015.

Tabraham, Chris. *Glasgow Cathedral: Official Souvenir Guide.* Historic Scotland, 2022.

Taylor, Alice. "The Problem of Labels: Three Marble Shepherds in Nineteenth-Century Rome." *Memoirs of the American Academy in Rome. Supplementary Volumes* 1 (2002): 47–59. https://doi.org/10.2307/4238445.

Thompson, Nancy M. "The Franciscans and the True Cross: The Decoration of the Cappella Maggiore of Santa Croce in Florence." *Gesta* 43, no. 1 (2004): 61–79. https://doi.org/10.2307/25067092.

Torriti, Piero. *Orvieto: History and Masterpieces.* Bonechi Edizioni il Turismo, 2014.

Tribe, Shawn. "Exploring the Subterranean Basilica and Christian Art of the Roman Catacombs of Domitilla." *Liturgical Arts Journal,* October 23, 2023. https://www.liturgicalartsjournal.com/2023/10/exploring-subterranean-basilica-and.html.

Waldman, Louis Alexander "New Light on the Capponi Chapel in S. Felicita." *The Art Bulletin* 84, no. 2 (2002): 293–314. https://doi.org/10.2307/3177270.

Weiss, Daniel H. "Architectural Symbolism and the Decoration of the Ste.-Chapelle." *The Art Bulletin* 77, no. 2 (1995): 308–20. https://doi.org/10.2307/3046103.

Wilson, Elaine L. *Transcending Time: The Magnetism of Mary Magdalene*. CreateSpace Independent Publishing Platform, 2016.

Wilson, Ralph F. "Early Christian Symbols of the Ancient Church from the Catacombs." *Jesus Walk Bible Study Series*. Accessed August 15, 2024. https://www.jesuswalk.com/christian-symbols/.

Artists

Fra Angelico

Ahl, Diane Cole. "Fra Angelico: A New Chronology for the 1430s." *Zeitschrift Für Kunstgeschichte* 44, no. 2 (1981): 133–58. https://doi.org/10.2307/1482082.

Delistraty, Cody. "Fra Angelico's Divine Emotion." *The Paris Review* (blog), August 19, 2019. https://www.theparisreview.org/blog/2019/08/19/fra-angelicos-divine-emotion/.

Fisher, Anthony. "A New Interpretation of Fra Angelico: Part II." *New Blackfriars* 75, no. 883 (1994): 290–302. http://www.jstor.org/stable/43249612.

Gerbron, Cyril. "The Story of Fra Angelico: Reflections in Mirrors." *Mitteilungen Des Kunsthistorischen Institutes in Florenz* 57, no. 3 (2015): 292–319. http://www.jstor.org/stable/43738210.

Hood, William. "Saint Dominic's Manners of Praying: Gestures in Fra Angelico's Cell Frescoes at S. Marco." *The Art Bulletin* 68, no. 2 (1986): 195–206. https://doi.org/10.2307/3050930.

Nygren, Barnaby. "Fra Angelico's San Marco Altarpiece and the Metaphors of Perspective." *Source: Notes in the History of Art* 22, no. 1 (2002): 25–32. http://www.jstor.org/stable/23206819.

Anonymous

Banker, James R. "The Program for the Sassetta Altarpiece in the Church of S. Francesco in Borgo S. Sepolcro." *I Tatti Studies in the Italian Renaissance* 4 (1991): 11–58. https://doi.org/10.2307/4603669.

Caldwell, Zelda. "Three of the Oldest Images of Jesus Portray Him as the 'Good Shepherd.'" *Aleteia*, May 12, 2019. https://aleteia.org/2019/05/12/three-of-the-oldest-images-of-jesus-portrays-him-as-the-good-shepherd/.

Clemens, Theo. "Searching for the Good Shepherd." *Nederlands Archief Voor Kerkgeschiedenis / Dutch Review of Church History* 83 (2003): 11–54. http://www.jstor.org/stable/24012935.

Huskinson, Janet. "Some Pagan Mythological Figures and Their Significance in Early Christian Art." *Papers of the British School at Rome* 42 (1974): 68–97. http://www.jstor.org/stable/40310729.

Lamberton, Clark D. "The Development of Christian Symbolism as Illustrated in Roman Catacomb Painting." *American Journal of Archaeology* 15, no. 4 (1911): 507–22. https://doi.org/10.2307/497187.

Ramsey, Boniface. "A Note on the Disappearance of the Good Shepherd from Early Christian Art." *The Harvard Theological Review* 76, no. 3 (1983): 375–78. http://www.jstor.org/stable/1509531.

Bosch

Bilger, Ryan. "To Save a Soul? Analyzing Hieronymus Bosch's Death and the Miser." *Student Publications*, 661 (2018). https://cupola.gettysburg.edu/student_scholarship/661.

Calas, Elena. "Bosch's Garden of Delights: A Theological Rebus." *Art Journal* 29, no. 2 (1969): 184–99. https://doi.org/10.2307/775227.

Gibson, Walter S. "The Garden of Earthly Delights by Hieronymus Bosch: The Iconography of the Central Panel." *Nederlands Kunsthistorisch Jaarboek (NKJ) / Netherlands Yearbook for History of Art* 24 (1973): 1–26. http://www.jstor.org/stable/24706821.

Glum, Peter. "Divine Judgment in Bosch's Garden of Earthly Delights." *The Art Bulletin* 58, no. 1 (1976): 45–54. https://doi.org/10.2307/3049463.

Meldrum, Linus. "Inspired Through Art: Death and the Miser by Hieronymus Bosch, c. 1490." *Catechetical Review* 6.3 (September 2020). https://review.catechetics.com/inspired-through-art-death-and-miser-hieronymus-bosch-c-1490.

Mittman, Asa Simon. "Spotlight — Hieronymus Bosch, The Garden of Earthly Delights." *Smart History*, March 5, 2024. https://smarthistory.org/garden-bosch/.

Morganstern, Anne M. "The Pawns in Bosch's 'Death and the Miser.'" *Studies in the History of Art* 12 (1982): 33–41. http://www.jstor.org/stable/42617947.

Silver, Larry. "God in the Details: Bosch and Judgment(s)." *The Art Bulletin* 83, no. 4 (2001): 626–50. https://doi.org/10.2307/3177226.

Sullivan, Margaret A. "The Timely Art of Hieronymus Bosch: The Left Panel of 'The Garden of Earthly Delights.'" *Oud Holland* 127, no. 4 (2014): 165–94. http://www.jstor.org/stable/24766228.

Vinken, Pierre, and Lucy Schlüter. "The Foreground of Bosch's 'Death and the Miser.'" *Oud Holland* 114, no. 2/4 (2000): 69–78. http://www.jstor.org/stable/42712016.

CARAVAGGIO

Ahlquist, Dale. "Two Different Views of the Story of Emmaus." *Faith & Culture,* February 6, 2019. https://www.faithandculture.com/home/2019/2/6/two-different-views-of-the-story-of-emmaus.

Bell, Janis C. "Light and Color in Caravaggio's 'Supper at Emmaus.'" *Artibus et Historiae* 16, no. 31 (1995): 139–70. https://doi.org/10.2307/1483502.

Graham-Dixon, Andrew. *Caravaggio: A Life Sacred and Profane.* W.W. Norton & Company, 2012.

Harris, Beth and Steven Zucker. "Caravaggio, *The Conversion of St. Paul* (or *The Conversion of Saul*)." *Smart History,* April 24, 2017. https://smarthistory.org/caravaggio-saul/.

Hass, Angela. "Caravaggio's Calling of St Matthew Reconsidered." *Journal of the Warburg and Courtauld Institutes* 51 (1988): 245–50. https://doi.org/10.2307/751282.

Meyers, Jeffrey. "Thom Gunn and Caravaggio's *Conversion of St. Paul.*" *Style* 44, no. 4 (2010): 586–90. http://www.jstor.org/stable/10.5325/style.44.4.586.

Pericolo, Lorenzo. "Visualizing Appearance and Disappearance: On Caravaggio's London 'Supper at Emmaus.'" *The Art Bulletin* 89, no. 3 (2007): 519–39. http://www.jstor.org/stable/25067339.

Pfatteicher, Philip H. "Caravaggio's Conception of Time in His Two Versions of the 'Supper at Emmaus.'" *Source: Notes in the History of Art* 7, no. 1 (1987): 9–13. http://www.jstor.org/stable/23202269.

Racco, Tiffany. "Darkness in a Positive Light: Negative Theology in Caravaggio's 'Conversion of Saint Paul.'" *Artibus et Historiae* 37, no. 73 (2016): 285–98. http://www.jstor.org/stable/44082065.

Thomas, Troy. "An Augustinian Interpretation of Caravaggio's 'Calling of St. Matthew.'" *Studies in Iconography* 27 (2006): 157–91. http://www.jstor.org/stable/23923696.

Thomas, Troy. "Expressive Aspects of Caravaggio's First Inspiration of Saint Matthew." *The Art Bulletin* 67, no. 4 (1985): 636–52. https://doi.org/10.2307/3050848.

Tuschka, Alexandra. "Caravaggio — The Conversion of Saint Paul." *The Art Inspector*. Accessed July 21, 2025. https://www.the-artinspector.com/post/caravaggio-the-conversion-of-pauli.

Vodret, Rossella. *Caravaggio: The Complete Works*. Silvana Editoriale, 2010.

Giovanni Cimabue

Brink, Joel. "Carpentry and Symmetry in Cimabue's Santa Croce Crucifix." *The Burlington Magazine* 120, no. 907 (1978): 645–640. http://www.jstor.org/stable/879354.

Messina, Isaac. "A New Approach to the Restoration of Cimabue's Santa Croce Crucifix." *Renée Crown University Honors Thesis Projects* (2014). https://surface.syr.edu/honors_capstone/747/.

Spencer, John R. "Cimabue." *Encyclopedia Britannica*. Updated April 18, 2024. https://www.britannica.com/biography/Cimabue.

Leonardo da Vinci

Reinke, Kira. "The Story of Leonardo Da Vinci's Unfinished Saint Jerome Painting." *Barnebys Magazine*, July 31, 2023. https://www.barnebys.com/blog/the-story-of-leonardo-da-vincis-unfinished-saint-jerome-painting.

Dali

Cevasco, George A. "Dali's Christianized Surrealism." *Studies: An Irish Quarterly Review* 45, no. 180 (1956): 437–42. http://www.jstor.org/stable/30098833.

Frisch, Patricia. "An Alternative Paradigm to the Oppression of Nuclear War: Salvador Dali's Painting of Christ of St. John of the Cross." *CrossCurrents* 64, no. 1 (2014): 111–15. http://www.jstor.org/stable/24462365.

Macdonald, Fiona. "The Painter Who Entered the Fourth Dimension." BBC, May 11, 2016. https://www/bbc.com/culture/article/20160511-the-painter-who-entered-the-fourth-dimension.

Nnadozie, Fr. Emmanuel. "A Reflection on Salvador Dali's 'Christ of St. John of the Cross,'" *Apostolate of the Little Flower* 86, no. 1. https://littleflowerbasilica.org/blog/a-reflection-on-salvador-dalischrist-of-st-johnof-the-cross.

Donatello

Dunkelman, Martha Levine. "Donatello's Mary Magdalen: A Model of Courage and Survival." *Woman's Art Journal* 26, no. 2 (2005): 10–13. https://doi.org/10.2307/3598092.

Jara, Soledad Castillo. "Donatello's Mary Magdalene: Penitence and Salvation." *Daily Art Magazine,* March 17, 2024. https://www.dailyartmagazine.com/donatellos-mary-magdalene/.

Duccio

Christiansen, Keith. "Duccio and the Origins of Western Painting." *The Metropolitan Museum of Art Bulletin* 66, no. 1 (2008): 1–61. http://www.jstor.org/stable/25434148.

Santicola, Garan. "An Inconspicuous Miracle." *Catholic New York,* December 15, 2021. https://www.cny.org/stories/an-inconspicuous-miracle,23170.

Agnolo Gaddi

Boskovits, Miklós. "Some Early Works of Agnolo Gaddi." *The Burlington Magazine* 110, no. 781 (1968): 209–15. http://www.jstor.org/stable/875586.

Giotto

Codell, Julie F. "Giotto's Peruzzi Chapel Frescoes: Wealth, Patronage and the Earthly City." *Renaissance Quarterly* 41, no. 4 (1988): 583–613. https://doi.org/10.2307/2861883.

El Greco

Gómez, Leticia Ruiz. *El Greco's Pentecost in a New Context.* Meadows Museum, 2010.

Scholz-Hansel, Michael. *El Greco: Domenikos Theotokpoulos, 1541–1614.* Taschen America, 2004.

Sullivan, Edward J. "El Greco of Toledo." *Art Journal* 42, no. 3 (1982): 239–42. https://doi.org/10.2307/776587.

Jean Antoine Houdon

Hecht, Johanna. "Jean Antoine Houdon (1741–1828)." In *Heilbrunn Timeline of Art History.* The Metropolitan Museum of Art, October 2008. https://www.metmuseum.org/toah/hd/jahd/hd_jahd.htm.

Phillips, John Goldsmith. "Monsieur Houdon's Frileuse." *The Metropolitan Museum of Art Bulletin* 22, no. 1 (1963): 29–36. https://doi.org/10.2307/3258209.

Ugolino Di Prete Ilario

James, Sara Nair. "The Exceptional Role of St. Joseph in Ugolino Di Prete Ilario's Life of the Virgin at Orvieto." *Gesta* 55, no. 1 (2016): 79–104. https://www.jstor.org/stable/26556479.

Georges de La Tour

Sims, Marc. "Art Explained: The Repentant Magdalene." September 20, 2022. https://marcjsims.com/2022/09/19/art-explained-the-repentant-magdalene.

Andrea Mantegna

Dewil, Rene. "The Agony in the Garden." *The Art of Painting,* January 2007. https://www.theartofpainting.be/AOP-Agony_in_the_Garden.htm.

"The Genius of Andrea Mantegna." *The Metropolitan Museum of Art Bulletin* 67, no. 2 (2009): 4–64. http://www.jstor.org/stable/40588545.

Masaccio

Coolidge, John. "Further Observations on Masaccio's Trinity." *The Art Bulletin* 48, no. 3/4 (1966): 382–84. https://doi.org/10.2307/3048393.

Masolino da Panicale

Art in Tuscany. "Masolino da Panicale." Accessed July 30, 2024. http://www.travelingintuscany.com/art/masolinodapanicale.htm.

Melozzo da Forli

Amore, Katia. "Italian Art: Melozzo da Forlì's 'Musician Angel.'" *Italy Magazine,* November 23, 2014. https://www.italymagazine.com/featured-story/italian-art-melozzo-da-forlis-musician-angel.

Michelangelo

Barolsky, Paul. "The Genius of Michelangelo's 'Creation of Adam' and the Blindness of Art History." *Source: Notes in the History of Art* 33, no. 1 (2013): 21–24. http://www.jstor.org/stable/23595750.

Barolsky, Paul. "Michelangelo's 'Creation of Adam' and the Aesthetics of Theology." *Source: Notes in the History of Art* 20, no. 4 (2001): 9–11. http://www.jstor.org/stable/23206731.

Cartwright, Mark. "Michelangelo's Sistine Chapel Ceiling." *World History Encyclopedia,* September 16, 2020. https://www.worldhistory.org/article/1607/michelangelos-sistine-chapel-ceiling/.

Levine, Saul. "Michelangelo's 'David': The Continuing Mythology." *Source: Notes in the History of Art* 4, no. 4 (1985): 15–20. http://www.jstor.org/stable/23202289.

Levine, Saul. "Michelangelo's Marble 'David' and the Lost Bronze 'David': The Drawings." *Artibus et Historiae* 5, no. 9 (1984): 91–120. https://doi.org/10.2307/1483171.

Rzepińska, Maria. "The Divine Wisdom of Michelangelo in 'The Creation of Adam.'" *Artibus et Historiae* 15, no. 29 (1994): 181–87. https://doi.org/10.2307/1483492.

Steinberg, Leo. "Who's Who in Michelangelo's Creation of Adam: A Chronology of the Picture's Reluctant Self-Revelation." *The Art Bulletin* 74, no. 4 (1992): 552–66. https://doi.org/10.2307/3045910.

O'Keefe

Friedman, Samantha. *Georgia O'Keefe: To See Takes Time.* The Museum of Modern Art, 2023.

Pinturicchio

The Artistic Adventures of Mankind, "Pinturicchio's Saint Jerome in the Desert," *Word Press* (blog), February 2, 2021. https://arsartisticadventureofmankind.wordpress.com/tag/pinturicchios-saint-jerome-in-the-desert/.

Pontormo

Steinberg, Leo. "Pontormo's Capponi Chapel." *The Art Bulletin* 56, no. 3 (1974): 385–99. https://doi.org/10.2307/3049264.

Wasserman, Jack. "Pontormo in the Capponi Chapel in Santa Felicita in Florence." *Mitteilungen des Kunsthistorischen Institutes in Florenz* 53, no. 1 (2009): 35–72. http://www.jstor.org/stable/40961896.

Raphael

Gutman, Harry B., and Philotheus Boehner. "Raphael's Disputa." *Franciscan Studies* 2, no. 1 (1942): 35–48. http://www.jstor.org/stable/23801580.

Rembrandt

Arguimbau, Peter Layne. *Rembrandt's Lost Secret.* Palmetto Publishing, 2023.

Bramsen, Henrik. "The Classicism of Rembrandt's 'Bathsheba.'" *The Burlington Magazine* 92, no. 566 (1950): 128–31. http://www.jstor.org/stable/870290.

Brown, Christopher. "Rembrandt and the Face of Jesus: Paris, Philadelphia and Detroit." *The Burlington Magazine* 154, no. 1310 (2012): 375–76. http://www.jstor.org/stable/23232759.

Meldrum, Linus. "Inspired Through Art: The Supper at Emmaus by Rembrandt Van Rijn, c. 1628." *Catechetical Review* 1.3 (July 2015). https://review.catechetics.com/inspired-through-art-supper-emmaus-rembrandt-van-rijn-c-1628#:~.

Nouwen, Henri J. M. *The Return of the Prodigal Son*. Doubleday, 1992.

Oakley, Howard. "Work in Progress: Rembrandt's Bathsheba." The Eclectic Light Company, 2019.

Rousseau, Theodore. "Rembrandt." *The Metropolitan Museum of Art Bulletin* 11, no. 3 (1952): 81–92. https://doi.org/10.2307/3258296.

Van De Wetering, E. "Rembrandt — The Supper at Emmaus." In *A Corpus of Rembrandt Paintings V*, 465-478. Springer, 2011. https://doi.org/10.1007/978-1-4020-5786-1_19.

Vcherashnyaia, Anna. "Three women in Rembrandt's life: a goddess, a mistress, and a maid." Art Smarts, 2017.

Walsh, John. "Observations on Rembrandt's 'Christ in the Storm on the Sea of Galilee.'" *Source: Notes in the History of Art* 5, no. 1 (1985): 44–52. http://www.jstor.org/stable/23202263.

Andrea del Sarto

Cody, Steven J. "Andrea del Sarto's *Noli me Tangere*: Sight, Touch, and an Echo of St. Augustine." *Arion: A Journal of the Humanities and the Classics* 26, no. 2 (2018): 37–68. https://doi.org/10.1353/arn.2018.0020.

Sassetta (Stefano di Giovanni di Consolo)

Carli, Enzo. "Sassetta's Borgo San Sepolcro Altarpiece." *The Burlington Magazine* 93, no. 578 (1951): 145–52. http://www.jstor.org/stable/870453.

Luca Signorelli

James, Sara Nair. "Penance and Redemption: The Role of the Roman Liturgy in Luca Signorelli's Frescoes at Orvieto." *Artibus et Historiae*, Vol. 22, No. 44 (2001): 119–147. https://doi.org/10.2307/1483716.

Mancini, Francesco Federico. "Luca Signorelli, the Frescoes in the Chapel of San Brizio in Orvieto Cathedral." *Finestre sull'Arte,* May 8, 2021. https://

www.finestresullarte.info/en/works-and-artists/luca-signorelli-the-frescoes-in-the-chapel-of-san-brizio-in-orvieto-cathedral.

Riess, Jonathan B. *The Renaissance Antichrist: Luca Signorelli's Orvieto Frescoes.* Princeton University Press, 1995.

Titian

Gurney, Tom. "Pentecost." *TheHistoryofArt.Org,* June 19, 2020. https://www.thehistoryofart.org/titian/pentecost/.

Jan van Eyck

BBC. "Ghent Altarpiece: Lamb's 'alarmingly humanoid' face surprises art world." January 22, 2020. https://www.bbc.com/news/world-europe-51205614.

Homa, Ramsay. "Jan van Eyck and the Ghent Altar-Piece." *The Burlington Magazine* 116, no. 855 (1974): 326–29. http://www.jstor.org/stable/877698.

Praet, Danny and Maximiliaan P.J. Martens. *The Ghent Altarpiece: Art, History, Science and Religion.* Hannibal Books, 2019.

Velden, Hugo van der. "The Quatrain of 'The Ghent Altarpiece.'" *Simiolus: Netherlands Quarterly for the History of Art* 35, no. 1/2 (2011): 5–40. http://www.jstor.org/stable/41407890.

Vincent van Gogh

Edwards, Cliff. *Van Gogh and God: A Creative Spiritual Quest.* Loyola Press, 2002.

Van Gogh, Vincent. "Letter to Theo van Gogh." Written July 1880 in Cuesmes. July 1880." Translated by Johanna van Gogh-Bonger, edited by Robert Harrison. *WebExhibits,* no. 133.https://www.webexhibits.org/vangogh/letter/8/133.htm.

Diego Velázquez

Lahuerta, Juan José. "The Crucifixions of Velázquez and Zurbarán." *RES: Anthropology and Aesthetics,* no. 65/66 (2014): 259–74. http://www.jstor.org/stable/24871255.

Lopez-Rey, Jose. *Velázquez: The Complete Works.* Taschen America, 2020.

Paolo Veronese

Hanson, Kate H. "The Language of the Banquet: Reconsidering Paolo Veronese's Wedding at Cana." *Invisible Culture: An Electronic Journal for*

Visual Culture 14 (Winter 2010). January 1, 2010. https://www.rochester.edu/in_visible_culture/Issue_14/hanson/index.html

Theology and the Liturgy

Aquilina, Mike, *The Fathers of the Church*. Our Sunday Visitor, 2006.

Aquinas, Thomas. *Aquinas's Shorter Summa*. Translated by Cyril Vollert, S.J. Sophia Institute Press, 2002.

Auth, Stephen. *The Missionary of Wall Street*. Sophia Institute Press, 2019.

Barron, Bishop Robert. *This Is My Body: A Call to Eucharistic Revival*. Word on Fire, 2023.

Cardinalli, AnnaMaria. *Music and Meaning in the Mass*. Sophia Institute Press, 2020.

Catechism of the Catholic Church: Modifications from the Editio Typica. United States Conference of Catholic Bishops — Libreria Editrice Vaticana, 2011.

The Catholic Travel Guide. "Orvieto, Italy: The Eucharistic Miracle of Bolsena and the Cathedral of Orvieto." *The Catholic Travel Guide*. Accessed September 16, 2024. https://thecatholictravelguide.com/destinations/italy/orvieto-italy-eucharistic-miracle-bolsena-cathedral-orvieto/.

Dolan, Cardinal Timothy M. *To Whom Shall We Go?* Our Sunday Visitor, 2008.

Dolan, Archbishop Timothy M. *Doers of the Word: Putting Your Faith into Practice*. Our Sunday Visitor, 2009.

Flynn, Vinny. *Seven Secrets of the Eucharist*. Mercy Press, 1986.

Pope Francis, *Evangelii Gaudium* (The Joy of the Gospel), November 24, 2013 www.vatican.va/content/francesco/en/apost_exhortations/documents/papa-francesco_esortazione-ap_20131124_evangelii-gaudium.html.

Guardini, Romano. *The Spirit of the Liturgy*. Translated by Ada Lane. Sheed & Ward, 1930.

Hahn, Scott. *The Lamb's Supper: The Mass as Heaven on Earth*. Image, 2009.

Hahn, Scott. *Signs of Life: 40 Catholic Customs and Their Biblical Roots*. Image, 2009.

Heschmeyer, Joe. *The Eucharist Is Really Jesus*. Catholic Answers Press, 2023.

Ivanic, Suzanna. *Catholica: The Visual Culture of Catholicism*. Thames & Hudson, 2022.

Jungmann, Joseph A. *The Mass of the Roman Rite*. Ave Maria Press, 2012.

O'Brien, John. *A History of the Mass and Its Ceremonies in the Eastern and Western Church*. The Catholic Publication Society, 1880.

O'Neil, John. *The Fisherman's Tomb*. Our Sunday Visitor, 2018.

Selmys, Melinda. "Before Sin: Creation, Adam and Eve, and the Garden of Eden." *Catholic Culture,* May 2011. https://www.catholicculture.org/culture/library/view.cfm?recnum=9753.

Sri, Edward. *A Biblical Walk Through the Mass*. Ascension Press, 2011.

Francis de Sales, St. *Introduction to the Devout Life, 400th Anniversary Edition*. Eremitical Press, 2009.

Taylor, Lyrica. "Righteousness of the Heart." In *The Visual Commentary on Scripture*. Edited by Ben Quash. The Visual Commentary on Scripture Foundation, 2018. https://thevcs.org/sermon-mount#righteousness-heart.

Vonier, Abbot. *A Key to the Doctrine of the Eucharist*. Zaccheus Press, 1924.

Weigel, George. *Roman Pilgrimage*. Basic Books, 2013.

Image Credits

Supper at Emmaus by Caravaggio, National Gallery, London, Public Domain / Commons.wikimedia.org; *Winter* by Jean Antonine Houdon, Metropolitan Museum of Art, New York, MET / commons.wikimedia.org; *The Garden of Earthly Delights* by Hiermonymus Bosch, Museo del Prado, Madrid, Public Domain / Commons.wikimedia.org; *The Preaching of the Antichrist* by Luca Signorelli, S. Brizio Chapel, Orvieto, Public Domain / Commons.wikimedia.org; *The Good Shepherd*, Catacomb of Domitilla, Rome, Public Domain / Commons.wikimedia.org; *The Repentant Magdalen* by Georges de La Tour, National Gallery of Art, Washington D.C. Public Domain / Commons.wikimedia.org; *The Penitent Magdalen* by Georges de La Tour, Metropolitan Museum of Art, New York, Public Domain / Commons.wikimedia.org; *The Wedding at Cana* by Paolo Veronese, Louvre Museum, Paris, Public Domain / Commons.wikimedia.org; *Christ Crucified* by Diego Velazquez, Museo del Prado, Madrid, Public Domain / Commons.wikimedia.org; Facade (Orvieto Cathedral), Orvieto, Italy, (69182698) (c) JFL Photography / Stock.adobe.com; *The Crucifixion Medallion*, Abbey of Conque, Metropolitan Museum of Art, New York Public Domain / Commons.wikimedia.org; *St. Jerome in the Desert* by Bernadino Pinturicchio, Walters Museum of Art, Baltimore, Public Domain / Commons.wikimedia.org; *St. Jerome Praying in the Wilderness* by Leonardo da Vinci, Vatican Museums, Rome, Public Domain / Commons.wikimedia.org; *Musician Angel* by Melozzo da Forli, Vatican Museums, Rome, Public Domain / Commons.wikimedia.org; *Crucifix at Santa Croce* by Giovanni Ciambue, Chiesa di Santa Croce, Florence, Public Domain / Commons.wikimedia.org; *Pentecost by El Greco*, Museo del Prado, Madrid, Public Domain / Commons.wikimedia.org; *Penitent Magdalen* by Donatello, Museo dell'Opera del Duomo. Florence, CC3 Sailko / Commons.wikimedia.org; *The Return of the Prodigal Son* by Michel-Martin Drolling, *Return of the Prodigal Son*, Museo dell'Opera del duomo, Strasbourg, Ji-Elle / commons.wikimedia.org; *The Return of the Prodigal Son* by Rembrandt, Hermitage Museum, St. Petersburg, Public Domain / Commons.wikimedia.org; *St. Ignatius Being Received into Heaven* by Andrea Pozzo, Chiesa di Sant'Ignazio, Rome, Public Domain / Commons.wikimedia.org; *The Annunciation* by Sassetta, The Metropolitan Museum of Art, New York, Public Domain / Commons.wikimedia.org; *St. Matthew and the Angel* by Guido Reni, Vatican Museums, Rome, Public Domain / Commons.wikimedia.org; *Expulsion from the Garden of Eden* by Massacio, Branacci Chapel, Church of Santa Maria del Carmine, Florence, Public Domain / Commons.wikimedia.org; *The Flood by Michelangelo*, Sistine Chapel, St. Peter's Basilica, Rome, Public Domain / Commons.wikimedia.org; *The Drunkeness of Noah* by Michelangelo, Sistine Chapel, St. Peter's Basilica, Rome, Public Domain / Commons.wikimedia.org; *David* by Michelangelo, Galleria dell'Accademia, Florence, Public Domain / Commons.wikimedia.org; *The Good Shepherd*, Catacomb of Domitilla, Rome, Public Domain / Commons.wikimedia.org; *Bathsheba at Her Bath* by Rembrandt, Louvre, Paris, Public Domain / Commons.wikimedia.org; *The Toilet of Bathsheba* by Rembrandt, Metropolitan Museum of Art, New York, Public Domain (MET) / commons.wikimedia.org; *Conversion on the Way to Damascus* by Caravaggio, Cersi Chapel, Basilica of Santa Maria del Popolo, Rome, Public Domain / Commons.wikimedia.org; *Charity* by Guido Reni, Metropolitan Museum of Art, New York, MET / commons.wikimedia.org; *Charity* by Anthony Van Dyck, National Gallery, London, Public Domain / Commons.wikimedia.org; *Angels by Melozzo da Forlì*, Basillica dei Santi Apostoli, Rome, (c) Alvesgaspar / commons.wikimedia.org; *Saint Dominic Adoring the Cross* by Fra Angelico, Convent of San Marco, Florence, Public Domain / Commons.wikimedia.org; *Saint Dominic Adoring the Cross* by Fra Angelico, Convent of San Marco, Florence, Public Domain / Commons.wikimedia.org; *Saint Dominic Adoring the Cross* by Fra Angelico, Convent of San Marco, Florence, Public Domain / Commons.wikimedia.org; *The Calling of St. Matthew* by Caravaggio, Chiesa Franchesi, Rome, Public Domain / Commons.wikimedia.org; *Sermon on the Mount* by Jan Brueghel the Elder, Getty Museum, Los Angeles, Public Domain / Commons.wikimedia.org; *The Good Samaritan* by Vincent van Gogh, Kroller-Muller Museum, Netherlands Public Domain / Commons.wikimedia.org; *Dogmatic*

Sarcophagas, Vatican Museums, Rome, (c) Sailko / commons.wikimedia.org; *Multiplication of the Loaves*, Catacombs of Callistus, Rome, (MW23G9) (c) The Picture Art Collection / Alamy.com; *Christ Healing the Paralytic at the Pool of Bethesda* by Bartolome Esteban Murillo, National Gallery, London, Public Domain / Commons.wikimedia.org; *The Storm of the Sea of Galilee* by Rembrandt, Isabella Stewart Gardner Museum, Boston, Public Domain / Commons.wikimedia.org; *The Agony in the Garden* by Andrea Mantegna, National Gallery, London, Public Domain / Commons.wikimedia.org; *The Road to Emmaus* by Robert Zund, Kuntsmuseum, St. Gallen, Public Domain, uploaded by Adrian Michael / commons.wikimedia.org; Facade (Orvieto Cathedral), Orvieto, Italy, (c) Justinawind / commons.wikimedia.com; *Creation of Adam and Eve* (first pier), Orvieto Cathedral, (315397252) (c) barbamauro / Stock.adobe.com; *The Life of Jesus* (third pier), Orvieto Cathedral, (543736187) (c) ClaraNila / Stock.adobe.com; *Resurrection of Jesus* (third pier), Orvieto Cathedral (543736187) (c) ClaraNila / Stock.adobe.com; *Last Judgment* (fourth pier), Orvieto Cathedral, (188376596) (c) Claudio Colombo / Stock.adobe.com; *Annunciation and Baptism of Christ* from the facade of the Orvieto Cathedral, (502192881) (c) SNAB / Stock.adobe.com; *Old Testaments Prophets* (second pier), Orvieto Cathedral, (38855214) (c) Claudio Colombo / Stock.adobe.com; Rose Window surrounded by Apostles, from the Facade of Orvieto Cathedral, (145461676) (c) francis92 / Stock.adobe.com; Baptismal Font, Orvieto Cathedral, (695715999) (c) makasana photo / Stock.adobe.com; *The Resurrection of the Flesh* by Luca Signorelli, Orvieto Cathedral, Public Domain / Commons.wikimedia.org; *The Elect* by Luca Signorelli, Orvieto Cathedral, Public Domain / Commons.wikimedia.org; *Pentecost: the Birth of the Church*, Dony MacManus, (c) All rights reserved.; *Musician Angel* by Melozzo da Forlì, Vatican Museums, Rome, (2RTMHDC) (c) Carlo Bollo / Alamy.com; *Death and the Miser* by Hieronymus Bosch, National Gallery, Washington, D.C., Public Domain / Commons.wikimedia.org; *The Adoration of the Magi* by Lorenzo Monaco, Uffizi Gallery, Florence, Public Domain / Commons.wikimedia.org; *The Baptism of Christ* by Andrea del Verrocchio, Uffizi Gallery, Florence Public Domain / Commons.wikimedia.org; *The Annunciation* by Leonardo da Vinci, Uffizi Gallery, Florence, Public Domain / Commons.wikimedia.org; *School of Athens* by Raphael, Vatican Museums, Rome, Public Domain / Commons.wikimedia.org; *Disputation of the Holy Sacrament* by Raffaello Sanzio da Urbino Raphael, Vatican Museums, Rome, Public Domain / Commons.wikimedia.org; *The Adoration of the Shepherds* by El Greco, Museo del Prado, Madrid, Public Domain, commons.wikimedia.org; *Disputation of the Holy Sacrament* by Raffaello Sanzio da Urbino Raphael, Vatican Museums, Rome, Public Domain / Commons.wikimedia.org; *The Supper at Emmaus* by Caravaggio, National Gallery, London, Public Domain / Commons.wikimedia.org; *The Last Supper* by Juan de Juanes, Museo del Prado, Madrid, Public Domain / Commons.wikimedia.org; *The Last Supper* by Leonardo Da Vinci, Convent of Santa Maria delle Grazie, Milan, Public Domain / Commons.wikimedia.org; *The Mond Crucifixion* by Raffaello Sanzio da Urbino (Raphael), National Gallery, London, Public Domain / Commons.wikimedia.org; *The Crucifixion* by Pietro Lorenzetti, Metropolitan Museum of Art, New York, Public Domain / Commons.wikimedia.org; *The Resurrection of Christ* by Peter Paul Rubens, Cathedral of our Lady of Antwerp, Public Domain / Commons.wikimedia.org; *The Last Judgement* by Michelangelo, Sistine Chapel, Rome, Public Domain / Commons.wikimedia.org; *Le Penseur* (*The Thinker*) by Auguste Rodin, The Musee Rodin, (c) CrisNYCa / commons.wikimedia.org; *Pietà* by Michelangelo, St. Peter's Basilica, Rome, (c) Stanislav Traykov / commons.wikimedia.org; *The Deposition from the Cross* by Jacopo Pontormo, Chiesa Santa Felicita, Florence, Public Domain / Commons.wikimedia.org; *Pieta* by Vincent van Gogh, Van Gogh Museum, Amsterdam, Public Domain / Commons.wikimedia.org; Sainte-Chapelle, Paris, (363957647) (c) sforzza / Stock.adobe.com; *Apse with the Tree of Life*, Basilica of San Clemente, Rome, Public Domain / Commons.wikimedia.org; *Musician Angel* by Rosso Fiorentino, Uffizi Gallery, Florence, (c) Web Gallery of Art / commons.wikimedia.org; *Creation of Adam* by Michelangelo, Sistine Chapel, Rome, Public Domain / Commons.wikimedia.org; *The Incredulity of Thomas* by Giovanni Barbieri Guercino, Vatican Museums, Rome St. Bavo's Cathedral, Ghent, Public Domain / Commons.wikimedia.org; *The Adoration of the Mystic Lamb* by Hubert and Jan Van Eyck, National Gallery, London, (c) Web Gallery of Art / commons.wikimedia.org; *The Adoration of the Mystic Lamb* by Hubert and Jan Van Eyck, National Gallery, London, Public Domain / Commons.wikimedia.org; *The Adoration of the Mystic Lamb* by Hubert and Jan Van Eyck, National Gallery, London, Public Domain / Commons.wikimedia.com *The Last Supper and the Tree of Life* by Taddeo

Gaddi, Chiesa di Santa Croce, Florence, (c) Web Gallery of Art / commons.wikimedia.org; *Mary Magdalen Anointing the Feet of Jesus* (detail of *Tree of Life*) by Taddeo Gaddi, Chiesa di Santa Croce, Florence, (c) Sailko / commons.wikimedia.org; *Singing Angels* (from Ghent Altarpiece) by Hubert and Jan Van Eyck, St. Bavo's Cathedral, Ghent, (c) Web Gallery of Art / commons.wikimedia.org; *Angel Playing the Organ* (from Ghent Altarpiece) by Hubert and Jan Van Eyck, St. Bavo's Cathedral, Ghent, (c) Web Gallery of Art / commons.wikimedia.org; Santa Maria sopra Minerva, Rome, (40782749) (c) Renáta Sedmáková / stock.adobe.com; *Communion of the Apostles* by Federico Barocci, Santa Maria sopra Minerva, Rome, CC4 Accurimbono / Commons.wikimedia.org; *School of Athens* by Raphael, Vatican Museums, Rome, (c) The Yorck Project / commons.wikimedia.org; *The Annunciation* by Fra Angelico, Convent of San Marco, Florence, (HKTP42) (c) ART Collection / Alamy.com; *The Crucifixion* by Guido Reni, Chiesa di San Lorenzo, Rome, (102693182) (c) Renata Sedmakova / Stock.adobe.com; *Angel Playing the Organ* by Hubert and Jan Van Eyck, St. Bavo's Cathedral, Ghent, (c) Web Gallery of Art / commons.wikimedia.org; *First Holy Communion* by Picasso, Picasso Museum, Barcelona, (2WYRBGN) (c) Album / Alamy.com; *Saints Anthony Abbot and Paul the Hermit* by Diego Velásquez, Museo del Prado, Madrid, Public Domain / Commons.wikimedia.org; *Ascension of St. John the Evangelist* by Giotto di Bondone, Santa Croce, Florence, Public Domain / Commons.wikimedia.org; *Saint Teresa in Ecstasy* by Bernini, Chiesa di Santa Maria de Victoria, Rome, CC4 Alvesgaspar / Commons.wikimedia.org; *Communion of the Apostles* by Fra Angelico, Convent of San Marco, Florence, Public Domain / Commons.wikimedia.org; *Madonna and Child* by Duccio Di Buoninsegna, Metropolitan Museum of Art, New York, Public Domain / Commons.wikimedia.org; *The Virgin Adoring the Eucharist* by Jean August Dominique Ingres, Metropolitan Museum of Art, New York, Public Domain / Commons.wikimedia.org; *Adoration of the Child* by Gerrit van Honthorst, Uffizi Gallery, Florence, (407634165) (c) Oleksii Sergieiev / stock.adobe.com; *The Risen Christ Appearing to Saint Mary Magdalen* by Andrea del Sarto, Uffizi Gallery, Florence, Public Domain / commons.wikimedia.com; *The Trinity* by Agnolo Gaddi, Metropolitan Museum of Art, New York, (2W9J2FN) (c) ARTGEN / Alamy.com; *Domine, Quo Vadis?* by Annibale Carracci, National Gallery, London, Public Domain / Commons.wikimedia.org; *The Fall of the Rebel Angels* by Luca Giordano, Kunsthistorisches Museum, Vienna, Public Domain / Commons.wikimedia.org; *Christ of Saint John of the Cross* by Salvador Dali, Kelingrove Art Gallery and Museum, Glasgow, (2RGHJ7D) (c) Gina Rodgers / Alamy.com;

About the Authors

Stephen Auth is a Catholic businessman with a long career on Wall Street, first with Prudential Investments in the 1980s and 1990s and, since 2000, with Federated Hermes, where he serves as Executive Vice President and a Chief Investment Officer of Federated Global Equities, overseeing the firm's equity and multi-asset investment activities worldwide. He is a frequent guest on Fox Business News, CNBC, and Bloomberg TV. He earned his undergraduate degree at Princeton University, where he graduated summa cum laude, and earned his graduate degree at Harvard Business School, where he was a Baker Scholar. He has twice been profiled in *Barron's*.

Steve is also an author and active Catholic evangelist, and he speaks at Catholic spiritual venues around the world. He is a member of the Regnum Christi movement and a founding member and leader of the Lumen Institute, a faith-formation and outreach program for Catholic business leaders. With his wife, Evelyn, he has led the New York City street evangelization mission for more than fifteen years, and he and his team have helped bring thousands of fallen-away Catholics back to the Faith. His book *The Missionary of Wall Street* (Sophia Institute Press, 2019) tells the story of that mission. His book *Pilgrimage to the Museum: Man's Search for God through Art and Time* (Sophia Institute Press, 2022) is based on a spiritual tour of the Metropolitan Museum of Art that he and his wife give on occasional Friday evenings; *Pilgrimage* became a number-one bestseller in its category on Amazon Books for several weeks, as well as the basis for a miniseries on EWTN. Steve and

Evelyn were honored in 2024 to present *Pilgrimage* to the staff and docents of the Vatican Museums. Steve also serves on the board of the National Office of the Pontifical Mission Societies in the United States, to which all his royalties from *Visions of the Divine* are directed.

Evelyn Moreno Auth has been Steve's lifelong partner in marriage and, with him, raised their two wonderful sons, Richard and Michael. She has also been a leader in the Regnum Christi Movement since 2002. She is Steve's partner and inspiration in all his evangelical activities in New York City and co-authored with him *Pilgrimage to the Museum*. Evelyn also serves on the boards of Catholic World Mission and, previously, Divine Mercy University. She earned her undergraduate degree from University of the East, Philippines.

Msgr. Roger J. Landry, a priest of the Diocese of Fall River, Massachusetts, is National Director of the Pontifical Mission Societies in the United States. He has served as Catholic Chaplain to Columbia University in New York City and to the Thomas Merton Institute for Catholic Life. He is also Ecclesiastical Assistant to Aid to the Church in Need USA, a Papal Missionary of Mercy, Chaplain to the New York Chapter of the Leonine Forum, a Member of the Board of the Shrine of Our Lady of the Martyrs in Auriesville, New York, and a National Eucharistic Preacher for the USCCB's National Eucharistic Revival. He helped lead the Seton Route of the National Eucharistic Pilgrimage from New Haven, Connecticut, to Indianapolis from May through July 2024 in preparation for the Tenth National Eucharistic Congress.

A graduate of Harvard College (1992) and the Pontifical North American College in Rome (1999), Msgr. Landry served as Attaché to the Holy See's Permanent Observer Mission to the United Nations in New York (2015–2022) and has been a pastor, a newspaper editor, and a high school chaplain in the Diocese of Fall River. He writes for many publications, appears regularly on television and radio, and is the author of *Plan of Life: Habits to Help You Grow Closer to God* (Pauline Books and Media, 2018). His homilies, articles, retreats, conferences, educational videos, and other offerings are available free at catholicpreaching.com.

Endnotes

1 Stephen Auth, *The Missionary of Wall Street* (Sophia Institute Press, 2019), 31.

2 It's unclear that Marie Antoinette used this exact phrase, though it has been suggested that it characterized her attitude towards the crisis (Britannica).

3 Not all scholars agree the person in the garden is Jesus, but, from a Catholic perspective, most viewers would have instantly recognized Him as such. Immediately after the Council of Nicaea, where Jesus' "consubstantiality" with the Father was definitively proclaimed, some artists began picturing Jesus at the Father's side in the Creation story. An image of Him in this role is seen in the *Dogmatic Sarcophagus* (see page 130). Still, Bosch's fifteenth-century portrayal here was unusual.

4 Dr. Asa Simon Mittman, "Spotlight — Hieronymus Bosch, The Garden of Earthly Delights." *Smart History: The Center for Public Art History*, retrieved March 5, 2024. https://smarthistory.org/garden-bosch/.

5 For an alternative interpretation of the left panel, that it is itself an already fully corrupted world, see Margaret Sullivan, "The Timely Art of Hieronymus Bosch: The Left Panel of 'The Garden of Earthly Delights,'" *Oud Holland* 127, no. 4 (2014): 165–94, http://www.jstor.org/stable/24766228.

6 The dozens of symbols Bosch painted into *The Garden of Earthly Delights,* referencing all seven of the deadly sins, have kept scholars busy ever since. To probe more, see Peter Glum, "Divine Judgment in Bosch's Garden of Earthly Delights," *The Art Bulletin* 58, no. 1 (1976): 45–54, https://doi.org/10.2307/3049463.Judgment.

7 Walter S. Gibson, "The Garden of Earthly Delights by Hieronymus Bosch: The Iconography of the Central Panel," *Nederlands Kunsthistorisch Jaarboek (NKJ) / Netherlands Yearbook for History of Art* 24 (1973): 1–26, http://www.jstor.org/stable/24706821.

8 "Sr. Francesca" is a pseudonym for a devout nun living in Rome who has asked not to be named in *Visions.*

9 Janet Huskinson, "Some Pagan Mythological Figures and Their Significance in Early Christian Art," *Papers of the British School at Rome* 42 (1974): 68–97, http://www.jstor.org/stable/40310729.

10 Per Sr. Francesca, the symbol of the fish means "Jesus Christ, Son of God, Savior" because the word fish — *ICHTHUS* in Greek — recalls this expression. Therefore, the early Christian symbol of the fish stands for Jesus Christ. During the persecutions of the first four centuries A.D., it was also the sign of the Christians.

11 See John O'Neill, *The Fisherman's Tomb* (*Our Sunday Visitor*, 2018), for the incredible story of early Christian iconography and the tomb of St. Peter; see also Ralph Wilson, "Early Christian Symbols of the Ancient Church from the Catacombs," *Jesus Walk Bible Study Series,* accessed August 15, 2024, https://www.jesuswalk.com/christian-symbols/.

12 The missionaries referred to here are the street evangelists from the Regnum Christi mission around St. Patrick's Old Cathedral, whom Evelyn and I have led for the last fifteen years. Over that time our group has encountered nearly three million people on the streets and has brought ten to fifteen thousand back to Confession. Our story is told in my book, *The Missionary of Wall Street* (Sophia Institute Press, 2019).

13 The Gospel accounts are ambiguous about Mary's background before meeting Jesus, other than that He had driven "seven demons" out of her. (Luke 8:2) In de La Tour's time, however, most people thought of her as a prostitute, conflating her with the woman in Simon the Pharisee's House who washed Jesus' hair with her tears and dried them with her hair, who loved much because she had been forgiven much (see Luke 7:36–50), or even with the woman caught in adultery (see John 8:1–11).

14 Friedman, Samantha, *Georgia O'Keefe: To See Takes Time* (Museum of Modern Art, 2023).

15 Armand de Mallery, *Ego Eimi — It Is I: Falling in Eucharistic Love* (Sophia Institute Press, 2018), 16.

16 Scott Hahn uses this quotation from Revelation to open his moving reflection on the Catholic Mass, *The Lamb's Supper,* which has guided us often in the journey to come (Image, 2009).

17 The Miracle of Bolsena occurred in 1263, when a priest who'd begun to lose faith in the true presence was celebrating Mass. The Host began to bleed right after the Consecration, staining the corporal (the linen cloth placed atop of the altar cloth, beneath the chalice and paten, during Mass). It was that linen that was moved to Orvieto Cathedral, just twenty miles away, on its completion in the next century. See *The Catholic Travel Guide,* accessed September 16, 2024. https://thecatholictravelguide.com/destinations/italy/orvieto-italy-eucharistic-miracle-bolsena-cathedral-orvieto/.

18 Auth, *Pilgrimage to the Museum,* 53–59.

19 Auth, *Pilgrimage to the Museum,* 53–59. The stained-glass window featuring St. Vincent of Saragossa that is described in *Pilgrimage* is actually only half of the two-unit panel; the other half, which completes the mysterious story, is kept at the Walters Museum of Art in Baltimore.

20 "I Heard the Voice of Jesus Say," by Horatius Bonar (1808–1889), is in public domain.

21 For more on the restoration, see Isaac Messina, "A New Approach to the Restoration of Cimabue's Santa Croce Crucifix." *Renée Crown University Honors Thesis Projects* (2014). https://surface.syr.edu/honors_capstone/747/.

22 Messina, "A new Approach to the Restoration of Cimabue's Santa Croce Crucifix."

23 Auth, *Pilgrimage to the Museum,* 64–68.

24 If you plan on going to Strasbourg to view *The Return of the Prodigal Son,* be sure to call in advance. The painting is not always on view in the Museum of Fine Arts' relatively limited gallery space.

25 John O'Brien, *A History of the Mass and Its Ceremonies in the Eastern and Western Church* (The Catholic Publication Society, 1880), 205.

26 AnnaMaria Cardinalli, *Music and Meaning in the Mass* (Sophia Institute Press, 2020), 103.

27 O'Brien, *A History of the Mass,* 236.

28 The full altarpiece, long since cut into individual panels, may have been the so-called *Borgo San Sepolcro Altarpiece.* See James R. Banker, "The Program for the Sassetta Altarpiece in the Church of S. Francesco in Borgo S. Sepolcro," *I Tatti Studies in the Italian Renaissance* 4 (1991): 11–58, https://doi.org/10.2307/4603669.

29 I use the term "iconic apple" here as in the actual Genesis story. "The fruit of the tree of knowledge of good and evil" (Gen. 1:3–6) is never actually identified as an apple; the apple's role in the story developed sometime during the Middle Ages, perhaps due to confusion around the Hebrew term for "fruit" (Wikipedia).

30 Although some writers carry on the tradition that Michelangelo painted the ceiling on his back, Sr. Francesca insists that he did it standing up, with his neck turned skyward — "there's even a sketch." Either way, it was probably not easy.

31 According to the United States Conference of Catholic Bishops (USCCB), the psalm is meant to be sung, which is how the psalms were used in temple worship. However, particularly in weekday Masses where a choir might not be present, the psalm is often read.

32 Well, not exactly. Room Q10 was closed to visitors some time ago due to a cave-in on the route there. At the time of this printing, it was unclear if or when this room housing one of the first images of the Good Shepherd will be reopened.

33 Auth, *Pilgrimage to the Museum*, 48–50.

34 Ibid., 131.

35 Ibid.

36 Although Judas Iscariot, the twelfth apostle, committed suicide during Jesus' Passion, the remaining eleven replaced him with Matthias just prior to the Pentecost event (Acts 1:23–26).

37 The Psalm is actually the second reading of Sacred Scripture, though it is normally sung, not read.

38 Scott Hahn, *The Lamb's Supper: The Mass as Heaven on Earth* (Image, 2009).

39 Although Luke's account does not mention Saul's horse, it was commonly assumed at this time that Saul rode by horse to Damascus, and most paintings of Saul's conversion on the road included the horse.

40 The other two are "Amen" and "Hosanna."

41 It is used to begin several of the psalms of praise, especially Psalms 113 to 118 and 136. Edward Sri, *A Biblical Walk Through the Mass* (Ascension Press, 2011), 65.

42 William Hood, "Saint Dominic's Manners of Praying: Gestures in Fra Angelico's Cell Frescoes at S. Marco," *The Art Bulletin* 68, no. 2 (1986): 195–206, https://doi.org/10.2307/3050930.

43 See Matt. 4:18–22; Mark 1:16–20; Luke 5:4–11; John 1:35–51.

44 See Matt. 9:9–13; Mark 2:13–17; Luke 5:27–32.

45 The four days that the calling of St. Matthew from Matthew's Gospel are read are the First Saturday and Thirteenth Friday in Ordinary Time, the Saturday after Ash Wednesday, and on the Feast of St. Matthew on September 21.

46 Elizabeth Lev, *How Catholic Art Saved the Faith* (Sophia Institute Press, 2018), 156.

47 Ibid., 156.

48 Auth, *Pilgrimage to the Museum*, 183.

49 It seems possible that the verse deleted by the originalists was added for a good reason. While in John's day, most Jewish readers would have known of the story of the angel and his stirring of the waters, once the Church had grown across the Empire, most readers would not have known about it. So likely the verse was added as an explanation.

50 Rene Dewil, "The Agony in the Garden," *The Art of Painting*, January 2007, https://www.theartofpainting.be/AOP-Agony_in_the_Garden.htm. Today's Florence has less of its medieval towers pictured by Mantegna, but

Dewil clarifies that the image painted was pretty close to the Florence of the painter's day.

51 O'Brien, *A History of the Mass*, 241.

52 Pope Francis, apostolic exhortation *Evangelii Gaudium* (November 24, 2013), section 135.

53 As an example, the words describing Christ as "begotten, not made, consubstantial with the Father" were added at this time because one famous heresy had declared the opposite.

54 A full explanation of the development of the Nicene Creed is provided in O'Brien, *A History of the Mass*, 249–256.

55 Fr. Shawn is my lifetime friend and spiritual guide, and coauthor with Evelyn and me of *Pilgrimage to the Museum*.

56 Which one is Peter? Perhaps the bearded man in the lower right whose arms seem to be embracing the entire group, even while the finger of his right hand points upward, to God.

57 "Be Thou My Vision," an eighth-century Gaelic hymn, translated by Mary Byrne (1905) and Eleanor Hull (1912), is in the public domain.

58 See Anne M. Morganstern, "The Pawns in Bosch's 'Death and the Miser,'" *Studies in the History of Art* 12 (1982): 33–41. http://www.jstor.org/stable/42617947. See also Linus Meldrum, "Inspired Through Art: Death and the Miser by Hieronymus Bosch, c. 1490," *Catechetical Review* 6.3 (September 2009), https://review.catechetics.com/inspired-through-art-death-and-miser-hieronymus-bosch-c-1490.

59 Larry Silver, "God in the Details: Bosch and Judgment(s)," *The Art Bulletin* 83, no. 4 (2001): 626–50, https://doi.org/10.2307/317726.

60 Sri, *A Biblical Walk through the Mass*, 91.

61 O'Brien, *A History of the Mass*, 280.

62 Ibid., 289.

63 The timeliness of this image is apparent when we recall that, only ten years later, Martin Luther would challenge the very concept of transubstantiation as part of the new, Protestant theology that he would post on the door of Wittenberg Cathedral.

64 Common Preface I, Prefaces from the Roman Missal (liturgies.net), https://www.liturgies.net/Liturgies/Catholic/roman_missal/prefaces.htm#common1.

65 Sri, *A Biblical Walk Through the Mass*, 75.

66 Ibid., 102.

67 Eucharistic Prayer II.

68 Eucharistic Prayer I.

69 Joseph A. Jungmann, S.J., *The Mass of the Roman Rite* (Ave Maria Press, 2012).

70 Eucharistic Prayer, Part 2.

71 Sri, *The Mass,* 110.

72 See the earlier discussion of Cimabue's *Crucifixion,* 51.

73 Eucharistic Prayer III.

74 Giorgio Vasari, *Lives of the Artists,* 406.

75 Eucharistic Prayer III.

76 Vincent van Gogh, "Letter to Theo von Gough, Cuesmes, July 1880," trans. Johanna van Gogh-Bonger, *WebExhibits,* https://www.webexhibits.org/vangogh/letter/8/133.htm.

77 See Cliff Edwards, *Van Gogh and God,* (Loyola Press, 1989), 28–37. Interestingly, Edwards argues that it was Rembrandt's *Supper at Emmaus,* which we visited in the prologue, that played a key role in van Gogh's transformation from Methodist minister to artist.

78 Eucharistic Prayer III.

79 *The Apse Mosaic* at San Clemente, guide of San Clemente.

80 Sri, *The Mass,* 120; see also USCCB, "The Mystery of the Eucharist in the Life of the Church," 12, https://www.usccb.org/resources/7-703%20The%20Mystery%20of%20Eucharist,%20for%20RE-UPLOAD,%20JANUARY%202022.pdf.

81 See Pope Benedict, "The Our Father and Aquinas," in *Aquinas's Shorter Summa,* trans. by Cyril Vollert, SJ (Sophia Institute Press, 2002), 337–366.

82 This chronology of the creation of the Sistine Ceiling is drawn primarily from Ross King's exciting account of Michelangelo, Raphael, and their patron, Pope Julius II, in *Michelangelo and the Pope's Ceiling* (Bloomsbury Press, 2003).

83 See Scott Hahn, *The Lamb's Supper.*

84 Sri, *A Biblical Walk Through the Mass,* 135.

85 The most detailed study and description we've found of the Ghent Altarpiece is by Danny Praet and Maximiliaan P.J. Martens, *The Ghent Altarpiece: Art, History, Science and Religion* (Hannibal Book, 2019). Its close-up photographs and descriptions of the incredible little details within the painting are beautiful.

86 Praet and Martens, *The Ghent Altarpiece,* 209–13.

87 Ibid., 203.

88 "*Panis Angelicus*" by St. Thomas Aquinas, is in public domain. English verse by Heidi Saxton, all rights reserved.

89 Lev, *How Catholic Art Saved the Faith,* 32–33.

90 See also Vinny Flynn, *Seven Secrets of the Eucharist* (Mercy Press, 1986), 65. "Christ's plan is not merely to live in us, but also to enable us to live in Him."

91 Msgr. Landry explains Mary's response to the angel — "How can this be?" — in theological terms. "She asked a question about how this would come about because she already somehow had consecrated herself in virginity to God. Otherwise she would never have asked, 'How can this be? For I know not man,' for she would well have known how she would have conceived a child. She was essentially asking how she could conceive without breaking such a commitment."

92 Thérèse of Lisieux, *The Story of a Soul: The Autobiography of St. Thérèse of Lisieux* (Tan, 2010).

93 Cardinalli, *Music and Meaning in the Mass,* 140.

94 "Thou, Who at Thy First Eucharist Didst Pray" by W.H. Turton (1881) is in the public domain.

95 Auth, *Pilgrimage to the Museum,*188–199.

96 Excluding Judas, who died by suicide after he betrayed Christ.

97 Hahn, *The Lamb's Supper.*

98 Lev, *How Catholic Art Saved the Faith,* 151.

99 *The Life of St. Teresa of Jesus,* 28:12

100 Ibid., 29:17. Emphasis added.

101 Auth, *Pilgrimage to the Museum.*

102 Or in Mary's case, "Mary!" (John 20:16).

103 USCCB website, "Concluding Rites of the Mass," https://www.usccb.org/prayer-and-worship/the-mass/order-of-mass/concluding-rites.

104 "How Can I Keep from Singing" by Robert Lowry (1826–1899) is in public domain.

105 Auth, *Pilgrimage to the Museum,* 213.

106 As Fr. Emmanuel Nnadozie notes in "A Reflection on Salvador Dali's *Christ of St. John of the Cross,*" Dali's decision to omit the nails in Christ's hands, which were so prominent in St. John of the Cross's original sketch of this vision, was clearly deliberate and an effort to underscore the self-willing nature of Christ's sacrifice.

Sophia Institute

Sophia Institute is a nonprofit institution that seeks to nurture the spiritual, moral, and cultural life of souls and to spread the gospel of Christ in conformity with the authentic teachings of the Roman Catholic Church.

Sophia Institute Press fulfills this mission by offering translations, reprints, and new publications that afford readers a rich source of the enduring wisdom of mankind.

Sophia Institute also operates the popular online resource CatholicExchange.com. *Catholic Exchange* provides world news from a Catholic perspective as well as daily devotionals and articles that will help readers to grow in holiness and live a life consistent with the teachings of the Church.

In 2013, Sophia Institute launched Sophia Institute for Teachers to renew and rebuild Catholic culture through service to Catholic education. With the goal of nurturing the spiritual, moral, and cultural life of souls, and an abiding respect for the role and work of teachers, we strive to provide materials and programs that are at once enlightening to the mind and ennobling to the heart; faithful and complete, as well as useful and practical.

Sophia Institute gratefully recognizes the Solidarity Association for preserving and encouraging the growth of our apostolate over the course of many years. Without their generous and timely support, this book would not be in your hands.

www.SophiaInstitute.com
www.CatholicExchange.com
www.SophiaTeachers.org

Sophia Institute Press is a registered trademark of Sophia Institute.
Sophia Institute is a tax-exempt institution as defined by the Internal Revenue Code, Section 501(c)(3). Tax ID 22-2548708.